Decoding the TOEFL® iBT

Actual Test

READING 1 Answers & Explanations

Actual Test 01

ANSWERS

PASSAGE 1

1 Ⓒ	2 Ⓓ	3 Ⓓ	4 Ⓒ	5 Ⓓ
6 Ⓑ	7 Ⓒ	8 Ⓐ	9 ❹	
10 ①, ④, ⑤				

PASSAGE 2

11 Ⓓ	12 Ⓐ	13 Ⓑ	14 Ⓓ	15 Ⓐ
16 Ⓒ	17 Ⓑ	18 Ⓒ	19 ❸	
20 ①, ②, ⑤				

PASSAGE 3

21 Ⓑ	22 Ⓐ	23 Ⓐ	24 Ⓐ	25 Ⓒ
26 Ⓑ	27 Ⓓ	28 Ⓐ	29 ❹	

30 Social Animals: ①, ②, ⑦ Solitary Animals: ④, ⑥

PASSAGE 1   p. 11

Answer Explanations

1 Inference Question

Ⓒ About comets, the author points out, "However, the vast majority of comets never approach anywhere near Earth but instead wander through two of the outer regions of the solar system called the Kuiper Belt and the Oort Cloud. Occasionally, comets change directions and head toward the inner solar system, where they begin orbiting the sun at regular intervals." It can therefore be inferred that there are fewer comets in the inner solar system than there are in the Oort Cloud.

2 Vocabulary Question

Ⓓ When there are traces of something, it means that there are small amounts of it. Another word for this is "hints." When there is a hint of something, there is a small amount of it.

3 Factual Information Question

Ⓓ The passage reads, "The radiation of the sun's solar wind pushes the dust in the coma away from the main body of the comet, whereupon it forms a tail consisting of that dust."

4 Rhetorical Purpose Question

Ⓒ About Halley's Comet, the author notes that it "is a well-known short-term comet that appears roughly every seventy-five years."

5 Negative Factual Information Question

Ⓓ The paragraph does not compare the sizes of long-period and short-period comets. So Ⓓ is the correct answer.

6 Factual Information Question

Ⓑ The author writes, "Astronomers are uncertain as to why comets enter the inner solar system. One theory is that collisions between comets send them in new directions."

7 Vocabulary Question

Ⓒ When Jupiter was bombarded by pieces of the comet, it was assaulted by them.

8 Inference Question

Ⓐ The final sentence of the passage notes, "The comet broke apart and bombarded Jupiter by impacting it several times, which caused astronomers to fear that a similar action might happen on the Earth someday." In writing that, the author implies that some comets might hit the Earth in the future.

9 Insert Text Question

❹ The sentence in front of the fourth square reads, "Some comets in the past had tails so long and bright that they could be observed from the Earth during the daytime." The sentence to be added starts with "this." In this case, "this" refers to the fact that some bright comets could be observed from the planet during the day. So the sentence to be added should come after the fourth square.

10 Prose Summary Question

①, ④, ⑤ The important ideas in the passage that are mentioned in the summary sentence are that comets sometimes visit the inner solar system and that they get tails when they are close to the sun. Answer choices ①, ④, and ⑤ all focus on these main points. Answer choices ② and ③ are both minor points, so they are incorrect. Answer choice ⑥ is not mentioned in the passage, so it is incorrect as well.

PASSAGE 2   p. 18

Answer Explanations

11 Factual Information Question

Ⓓ About the cites in colonial America, the author writes, "By the mid-eighteenth century, Boston,

among the largest cities in colonial America. They were founded alongside or near the coast and had access to fine harbors and trade routes leading to Europe and Africa."

12 Vocabulary Question

Ⓐ When the Atlantic seaboard was bereft of a single great metropolis, it means that the region was deprived of any large cities since there were no large urban areas there.

13 Negative Factual Information Question

Ⓑ Although New York was founded by the Dutch, it was named New Amsterdam by them. It became New York later. Therefore Ⓑ is not true, so it is the correct answer.

14 Sentence Simplification Question

Ⓓ The sentence points out that there was a lot of timber available in America, so shipbuilding was a common industry, and the Americans built many ships. These thoughts are best expressed by the sentence in answer choice Ⓓ.

15 Rhetorical Purpose Question

Ⓐ About Gloucester, the author points out that its people became wealthy from fishing.

16 Factual Information Question

Ⓒ The author notes, "Most trade was with England since the English had enacted laws directing their colonists to trade with England and to purchase goods manufactured in England."

17 Vocabulary Question

Ⓑ When people flocked to Pennsylvania to escape persecution in other places, it means that they gathered there.

18 Inference Question

Ⓒ The passage reads, "Penn planned Philadelphia with broad streets and room between houses in the hope that the distances would lessen the problems caused by fire, disease, and overcrowding that plagued European cities during his lifetime." Since Penn planned Philadelphia in a way that would avoid problems common in European cities, it can be inferred that Philadelphia did not resemble any major European cities in how it looked.

19 Insert Text Question

❸ The sentence before the third square reads, "New York City was a close third with 13,000 residents." The sentence to be added mentions "none of them," which refers to the cities Philadelphia, Boston, and New York. It makes a comparison between those

three places and London and France. Thus the two sentences go well together.

20 Prose Summary Question

1, 2, 5 The important ideas in the passage that are mentioned in the summary sentence are that the cities in colonial America that grew became centers of trade while having distinct characteristics of their own. Answer choices 1, 2, and 5 all focus on these main points. Answer choices 3, 4, and 6 are all minor points, so they are all incorrect.

PASSAGE 3 p. 26

Answer Explanations

21 Factual Information Question

Ⓑ The author writes, "Social animals live in either small or large groups."

22 Vocabulary Question

Ⓐ When animals forage for food, they search for it.

23 Rhetorical Purpose Question

Ⓐ The author notes that wildebeests and zebras "make long migrations in Africa while traveling to feeding grounds when the seasons change."

24 Negative Factual Information Question

Ⓐ There is no mention in the paragraph about why some animals desert their young after they give birth to them.

25 Factual Information Question

Ⓒ It is written, "As an example, after a female penguin lays an egg, the male and female take turns guarding it—and later the chick—while the other hunts for food."

26 Vocabulary Question

Ⓑ When female-offspring pairings are ephemeral, they are temporary, so they do not last for a long time.

27 Factual Information Question

Ⓓ The author points out, "The primary benefit to social animals is that they can cooperate to help survive."

28 Inference Question

Ⓐ The passage reads, "If injured, they have a lower chance of survival than wounded animals that have a support group to provide them with food and protection while they heal." Therefore it can be inferred that injured solitary animals may have

trouble getting food for themselves.

29 Insert Text Question

■4 The sentence before the fourth square reads, "Another characteristic of social animals is that there are leaders, which are usually alpha males, and followers, which comprise the majority of the animals, in each group." The sentence to be added describes alpha males when the author writes that "the strongest male in the herd becomes the head of the group." Since it describes alpha males, which are mentioned in the sentence in the passage, the sentence to be added should go right after it.

30 Fill in a Table Question

Social Animals: 1, 2, 7 Solitary Animals: 4, 6
About social animals, the author describes several ways in which they work together to protect their young much better than solitary animals can. (1) In addition, the author writes, "The division of labor in social groups varies as some members hunt or gather food while others defend their group's territory and look after the young animals," (2) and, "The main drawback to living in groups is that resources may be lacking if there are too many animals in one place. In lean times, some group members may die from starvation." (7) About solitary animals, the author notes, "The majority of solitary animals are predators." (4) The author also comments that solitary animals "have fewer food options." (6)

Actual Test 02

ANSWERS

PASSAGE 1

1 Ⓒ	2 Ⓑ	3 Ⓐ, Ⓒ		
4 Ⓐ	5 Ⓓ	6 Ⓓ	7 Ⓒ	8 Ⓑ
9 ▣2	10 1, 4, 5			

PASSAGE 2

11 Ⓒ	12 Ⓐ	13 Ⓓ	14 Ⓒ	15 Ⓒ
16 Ⓐ	17 Ⓒ	18 Ⓐ	19 ▣3	
20 *Iliad*: 1, 3, 4 *Odyssey*: 2, 5				

PASSAGE 3

21 Ⓑ	22 Ⓒ	23 Ⓓ	24 Ⓐ	25 Ⓒ
26 Ⓒ	27 Ⓓ	28 Ⓐ	29 ▣1	
30 2, 5, 6				

PASSAGE 1   p. 35

Answer Explanations

1 Sentence Simplification Question

Ⓒ The sentence points out that nobody knew anything about the Dorset people until the 1900s even though they had lived for more than 1,000 years. These thoughts are best expressed by the sentence in answer choice Ⓒ.

2 Factual Information Question

Ⓑ About the Dorset people, the author notes, "They thrived in that region from approximately 500 B.C. to 1000 A.D."

3 Factual Information Question

Ⓐ, Ⓒ The passage reads, "The Dorset people survived since they managed to adapt to the frigid weather by developing tools and methods to hunt on ice."

4 Negative Factual Information Question

Ⓐ There is no mention about which animals the Dorset people were hunting when they stayed out on the ice.

5 Vocabulary Question

Ⓓ When the Dorset people used turf to make their homes, they were using grass.

6 Factual Information Question

Ⓓ The passage notes, "The biggest settlements were located near waters where sea mammals still thrive today."

7 Rhetorical Purpose Question

Ⓒ The author focuses on how the Thule people succeeded the Dorset people in writing, "Simultaneously, the warming period allowed the ancestors of the modern-day Inuit, called the Thule people, to migrate from Alaska. They had dogs and large sleds and had learned to hunt large whales from boats on the ocean. Able to provide plenty of food for themselves, the Thule people's population expanded, and they engaged in direct competition with the Dorset people. The combination of the warm weather and the Thule people caused the Dorset people to go into terminal decline."

8 Vocabulary Question

Ⓑ When the Dorset people went into terminal decline, they went extinct. They completely disappeared as a culture and all died.

9 Insert Text Question

② The sentence before the second square reads, "Occasionally, the Dorset people remained on the ice to hunt and collect meat for long periods of time, so, to survive, they developed the snow house, which is commonly known as the igloo, and burned animal blubber from whales and other animals to keep warm." The sentence to be added mentions that "it" was able to keep people safe even though it was made of snow and ice. The "it" in the sentence refers to the snow house, or igloo. Thus the two sentences go well together.

10 Prose Summary Question

①, ④, ⑤ The important idea in the passage that is mentioned in the summary sentence is that the Dorset people succeeded in adapting to the cold weather in the Arctic, so that is how they survived as a culture. Answer choices ①, ④, and ⑤ all focus on these main points. Answer choices ②, ③, and ⑥ are all minor points, so they are incorrect answers.

PASSAGE 2

p. 43

Answer Explanations

11 Inference Question

Ⓒ The author remarks, "Nobody knows if the poems are based on factual events, and whether Homer was real or not is another long-debated matter. Despite questions about their veracity and authorship, the *Iliad* and the *Odyssey* rank among the greatest works in the Western canon." Therefore it can be inferred that Homer might not actually have written either the *Iliad* or the *Odyssey*.

12 Rhetorical Purpose Question

Ⓐ The author writes, "The impetus for the war happened when the Trojan prince Paris—with assistance from the goddess Aphrodite—abducted Helen, the world's most beautiful woman and the wife of the Greek Menelaus. Enraged, the greatest Greek warriors joined an army led by Agamemnon, Menelaus's brother, and sailed to Troy to avenge the insult Paris had given them." Thus the author mentions Paris to explain the role that he played in causing the Trojan War to take place.

13 Vocabulary Question

Ⓓ When Achilles becomes livid, he is furious at Agamemnon.

14 Reference Question

Ⓒ The "he" that believed he had defeated Achilles was Hector.

15 Factual Information Question

Ⓒ The author notes, "Achilles relents and lends Patroclus his distinctive armor, but Patroclus is killed by Hector, Troy's greatest warrior and the older brother of Paris, who initially believes he has defeated Achilles. Saddened and further enraged, Achilles challenges Hector to single combat, slays him beneath the walls of Troy, and proceeds to drag Hector's corpse behind his chariot as he circles the city."

16 Vocabulary Question

Ⓐ Odysseus, the craftiest of the Greeks, was considered to be the sneakiest of every Greek in the army.

17 Negative Factual Information Question

Ⓒ There is no mention in the passage of how Odysseus and his men escaped from the Cyclops and Circe with their lives.

18 Factual Information Question

Ⓐ The author writes, "Telemachus sails off in search of his father."

19 Insert Text Question

③ The sentence before the third square reads, "As they try in vain to get home, Odysseus and his men have numerous encounters with monsters such

as Cyclops and the witch Circe." This sentence
mentions some of the hardships that Odysseus and
his men faced. The sentence to be added describes
some more of the difficulties that they had to deal
with, so both sentences cover the same topic and
therefore go together.

20 Fill in a Table Question

Iliad: ☐1, ☐3, ☐4   *Odyssey*: ☐2, ☐5
About the *Iliad*, the author writes that the *Iliad*
primarily concerned the ten-year conflict that the
Greeks fought. (☐1) In addition, it features the death
of Patroclus and covers much of what happens to
Achilles. (☐3, ☐4) As for the *Odyssey*, both Helios
and Poseidon feature in it since they both curse
Odysseus and his men on their way home. (☐2)
It also focuses on some of the events—namely
actions connected to Odysseus—that happened
after the Trojan War ended. (☐5)

PASSAGE 3

Answer Explanations

21 Vocabulary Question

Ⓑ When a set period of time has elapsed, the time
has passed.

22 Factual Information Question

Ⓒ It is written, "Most workers in cottage industries
belonged to farming families."

23 Negative Factual Information Question

Ⓓ In the paragraph, the author mentions nothing
about the amount of time that people in cottage
industries took to complete the tasks that they were
working on.

24 Rhetorical Purpose Question

Ⓐ The passage reads, "For example, in England,
the large herds of sheep in the West Country,
Yorkshire, and Norwich led to those places
dominating the wool-based textile industry for
centuries." These places are mentioned to point out
that they were dominant regions in the English textile
industry.

25 Sentence Simplification Question

Ⓒ The sentence points out that despite the fact
that children worked in cottage industries, they
had working conditions better than those of factory
workers in the Industrial Revolution. These thoughts
are best expressed in sentence Ⓒ.

26 Factual Information Question

Ⓒ The author notes, "Families usually had to pay
upfront for raw materials, which caused them to go
into debt."

27 Vocabulary Question

Ⓓ When something is induced to perish, it is
prompted to die or disappear.

28 Factual Information Question

Ⓐ The author mentions, "Since that time, most
products have been made in factories, yet there are
still places today where cottage industries exist. They
are primarily located in parts of the non-industrialized
world."

29 Insert Text Question

☐1 The sentence before the first square reads, "To
meet the schedules of the merchants, many people
were obligated to work seven days a week." The
sentence to be added mentions people taking time
off, which goes well with the previous sentence as it
points out that "many people were obligated to work
seven days a week." Thus the two sentences go well
together.

30 Prose Summary Question

☐2, ☐5, ☐6 The important ideas in the passage that are
mentioned in the summary sentence are that cottage
industries were the primary way people made goods
until the Industrial Revolution, when they mostly
disappeared. Answer choices ☐2, ☐5, and ☐6 all focus
on these main points. Answer choices ☐1, ☐3, and ☐4
are all minor points, so they are incorrect answers.

Actual Test 03

ANSWERS

PASSAGE 1

1 Ⓐ	2 Ⓐ	3 Ⓑ	4 Ⓑ	5 Ⓓ
6 Ⓐ	7 Ⓓ	8 Ⓒ	9 **1**	

10 1, 4, 6

PASSAGE 2

11 Ⓒ	12 Ⓓ	13 Ⓒ	14 Ⓓ	15 Ⓒ
16 Ⓒ	17 Ⓑ	18 Ⓐ	19 **4**	

20 1, 3, 5

PASSAGE 3

21 Ⓐ	22 Ⓒ	23 Ⓒ	24 Ⓑ	25 Ⓐ
26 Ⓓ	27 Ⓑ	28 Ⓐ	29 **4**	

30 Ganymede: 2, 5, 7   Callisto: 1, 4

PASSAGE 1

Answer Explanations

1   Negative Factual Information Question

Ⓐ According to paragraph 1, "Lions are native to Africa, where they primarily reside in the southeast part of the continent in regions with grassy plains upon which numerous large herds of prey animals roam." Therefore answer choice Ⓐ is not true.

2   Sentence Simplification Question

Ⓐ The sentence notes that fighting lions may have cuts that get infected, so they normally engage in displays of strength that are intended to scare off other animals. These thoughts are best explained in answer choice Ⓐ.

3   Vocabulary Question

Ⓑ When lions live on the fringes of controlled territories, they live on the outskirts of areas that are claimed by other lions.

4   Rhetorical Purpose Question

Ⓑ About zoologists, the author writes, "Zoologists believe the extreme amount of copulation is necessary because the females have difficulty getting pregnant." Thus the author focuses on a theory on the reproductive habits of lions that some zoologists have come up with.

5   Vocabulary Question

Ⓓ When young male lions are too boisterous, they are behaving in an energetic manner.

6   Factual Information Question

Ⓐ It is written, "Since lions do not mate with their siblings, these males must depart to find mates of their own."

7   Inference Question

Ⓓ About male lions, the author notes, "The males, which are brothers or cousins, leave the pride together, form a coalition, and live near the territories of other lions while hunting and surviving to the best of their ability." Then, the author writes, "The new male lions, unwilling to wait that long to pass on their genes to a new generation, therefore kill every cub in the pride they have taken over. Soon afterward, every female goes into heat, and the new males then have a chance to father their own cubs." It can therefore be inferred that all of the male lions in a pride are related to one another.

8   Factual Information Question

Ⓒ The passage points out, "The new male lions, unwilling to wait that long to pass on their genes to a new generation, therefore kill every cub in the pride they have taken over. Soon afterward, every female goes into heat, and the new males then have a chance to father their own cubs and to assert their position as the leaders of their pride."

9   Insert Text Question

1 The sentence before the first square reads, "Lions are native to Africa, where they primarily reside in the southeast part of the continent in regions with grassy plains upon which numerous large herds of prey animals roam." The sentence to be added provides the name of a specific place in Africa where many lions live. Thus this sentence belongs after the first square.

10   Prose Summary Question

1, 4, 6 The important ideas in the passage that are mentioned in the summary sentence are that the male and female lions in a pride have specific roles to do. Answer choices 1, 4, and 6 all focus on these main points. Answer choices 2 and 5 are minor points, so they are incorrect answers. Answer choice 3 is not mentioned in the passage, so it is an incorrect answer as well.

p. 67

11 Inference Question

ⓒ The author writes, "Only the residents and their invited guests are permitted entry into these gated communities, as they are called." Therefore the author implies that only a limited number of people may gain access to gated communities.

12 Vocabulary Question

ⓓ When criminals are deterred from entering gated communities, they are discouraged from going into them.

13 Negative Factual Information Question

ⓒ There is nothing mentioned in the passage about where children in gated communities play with their friends.

14 Inference Question

ⓓ The author mentions, "There is also the bothersome task of having to use an access card or key code to open and close the gates to enter and depart the community." In writing this, the author implies that some people are annoyed by having to use key codes to get into gated communities.

15 Factual Information Question

ⓒ The author points out, "A study carried out in the American state of Florida in 2005 showed that even though there were fewer traffic violations and accidents in gated communities."

16 Rhetorical Purpose Question

ⓒ The author claims that delivery personnel know how to get into gated communities by writing, "Lastly, delivery personnel from the post office, restaurants, and other places almost always know the proper codes to gain access."

17 Vocabulary Question

ⓑ When crime in rampant in an area, it is widespread.

18 Factual Information Question

ⓐ The passage reads, "In other nations, there are wide gaps between the rich and the poor, and crime is rampant, so gated communities are frequently the only bastions of safety for worried citizens. In Brazil, gated communities are popular on the peripheries of the crime-ridden urban areas of Rio de Janeiro and São Paulo."

19 Insert Text Question

❹ The sentence before the fourth square reads, "Any renovations and landscaping changes must usually be approved by a committee of community representatives." The sentence to be added mentions that bad feelings can arise when requests are rejected by the group, which refers to the "committee of community representatives" in the previous sentence. Thus the two sentences go well together.

20 Prose Summary Question

①, ③, ⑤ The important ideas in the passage that are mentioned in the summary sentence are that gated communities are getting more popular in recent years even though they have disadvantages in addition to their advantages. Answer choices ①, ③, and ⑤ all focus on these main points. The information in answer choice ② is not mentioned in the passage, so it is incorrect. And answer choices ④ and ⑥ are minor points, so they are both incorrect.

p. 74

21 Rhetorical Purpose Question

ⓐ The author writes, "The four largest moons of the planet Jupiter are called the Galilean moons because they were discovered by Italian astronomer Galileo Galilei in 1601."

22 Vocabulary Question

ⓒ When two moons have profound differences, then there are stark differences between them.

23 Reference Question

ⓒ The "it" that is mainly composed of carbon dioxide is "a thin atmosphere."

24 Inference Question

ⓑ In paragraph 2, the passage reads, "Ganymede is extremely old, having formed around 4.5 billion years ago, which was roughly when Jupiter itself came into being." In paragraph 3, it is written, "At 4,820 kilometers in diameter, Callisto is smaller than Ganymede, but the two are the same age." It can therefore be inferred that Callisto formed around 4.5 billion years ago.

25 Negative Factual Information Question

ⓐ There is no mention in the paragraph about how long it takes for Callisto to orbit Jupiter.

26 Vocabulary Question

Ⓓ When oceans are stacked between layers of ice, they are layered.

27 Factual Information Question

Ⓑ The passage notes, "Another characteristic both moons share is that it is likely that at least one internal ocean exists on each of them."

28 Factual Information Question

Ⓐ The author notes, "Ganymede was also caught in this bombardment of celestial objects, yet it orbits closer to Jupiter, so as the giant planet's gravity pulled many meteorites toward it, an even larger number managed to strike Ganymede. These impacts forced the icy surface to melt and pushed rocks deep into its core. The impacts drove heat into the core. This heat is still creating internal tectonic forces on Ganymede, which, in turn, cause its surface to change and many craters to disappear over time."

29 Insert Text Question

4 The sentence before the fourth square reads, "Some astronomers speculate that each moon may contain alien life in its subsurface waters." This sentence is about a theory some astronomers have. The sentence to be added is about the way in which the theory can possibly be proven. Thus the two sentences go together.

30 Fill in a Table Question

Ganymede: ②, ⑤, ⑦ Callisto: ①, ④
About Ganymede, the passage reads, "These dark regions comprise about forty percent of the moon's surface and have many impact craters whereas the lighter regions have fewer craters despite being the majority of the moon's surface." (②) The author also notes, "With a diameter of 5,268 kilometers, Ganymede is the largest moon in the solar system and is bigger than Mercury," (⑤) and, "This heat is still creating internal tectonic forces on Ganymede, which, in turn, cause its surface to change and many craters to disappear over time." (⑦) As for Callisto, the author notes, "There is evidence suggesting that Callisto may have an internal ocean of unfrozen salt water between fifty and 200 kilometers beneath its surface," (①) and, "Callisto's surface is much darker than Ganymede's and reflects little light." (④)

Actual Test 04

ANSWERS

PASSAGE 1

1 Ⓑ	2 Ⓒ	3 Ⓐ	4 Ⓐ	5 Ⓓ
6 Ⓒ	7 Ⓒ	8 Ⓑ	9 **1**	

10 Greece: ③, ⑤, ⑥ Rome: ①, ④

PASSAGE 2

11 Ⓓ	12 Ⓐ	13 Ⓐ	14 Ⓓ	15 Ⓒ
16 Ⓐ	17 Ⓓ	18 Ⓓ	19 **2**	

27 ②, ③, ④

PASSAGE 3

21 Ⓐ	22 Ⓑ	23 Ⓓ	24 Ⓑ	25 Ⓑ
26 Ⓒ	27 Ⓓ	28 Ⓐ	29 **3**	

30 ②, ④, ⑥

PASSAGE 1

p. 83

Answer Explanations

1 Vocabulary Question

Ⓑ When a group's influence is boosted, it is enhanced, or strengthened.

2 Negative Factual Information Question

Ⓒ There is no mention in the paragraph of the Romans giving captured Greeks direct roles in their government.

3 Inference Question

Ⓐ The passage reads, "At that time, there existed a tremendous gap between the two cultures. Most Romans were hardworking farmers wary of the literate, artistic, and intellectual Greeks, who took pleasure in the decadent aspects of life." It can therefore be inferred that the lives of the Romans were quite different from those of the Greeks.

4 Vocabulary Question

Ⓐ When the Romans were enamored of Greek art, they were captivated by it.

5 Rhetorical Purpose Question

Ⓓ About the dome and the arch, the author points out that they were "two architectural achievements never employed by the Greeks."

6 Factual Information Question

Ⓒ The passage reads, "Greek sculptures concentrated more on beauty and form."

7 Factual Information Question

Ⓒ The author writes, "Arguably the greatest influence the Greeks had upon the Romans came in the field of education. Among the slaves taken to Rome after the conquest of Greece were numerous teachers, who became the tutors of the children of the Roman elites. In time, these children, who had learned the Greek language as well as Greek history and literature, joined the leadership of the republic."

8 Sentence Simplification Question

Ⓑ The sentence points out that while the Romans had myths of their own, they adopted some gods from the Greek pantheon as well. These thoughts are best expressed by the sentence in answer choice Ⓑ.

9 Insert Text Question

❶ The sentence before the first square reads, "Romans in the early years of the republic were enamored of Greek art, and by the third century B.C., they were importing Greek sculptures and paintings." The sentence to be added mentions art dealers and states that they "found a ready market for these items," which refers to the "Greek sculptures and statues" in the previous sentence. Thus the two sentences go well together.

10 Fill in a Table Question

Greece: ③, ⑤, ⑥ Rome: ①, ④

About Greece, the author notes, "The Greek language became the language of education in the Roman Republic and later in the empire." (③) The author further writes, "Greek sculptures concentrated more on beauty and form,"(⑤) and, "The Romans may have conquered the Greeks in battle, but, ultimately, the Greeks dramatically influenced their Roman masters." (⑥) Concerning the Romans, the author points out, "The early Romans were a highly superstitious people whose beliefs originated from the historical founding of Rome as well as the Etruscans, who had previously dominated the region around Rome." (①) In addition, it is written, "The Romans conquered Greece in the second century B.C." (④)

Answer Explanations

11 Inference Question

Ⓓ The author writes, "Due to the fact that they are designed to kill or limit the activity of certain organisms, pesticides constitute a danger to all living things, including large animals and humans." It can therefore be inferred that pesticides may unintentionally harm animals that are not pests.

12 Vocabulary Question

Ⓐ A justification for a high cost is a rationalization for a great expense.

13 Sentence Simplification Question

Ⓐ The sentence points out that without pesticides, fewer crops would grow, and many people would not get enough to eat. These thoughts are best expressed by the sentence in answer choice Ⓐ.

14 Rhetorical Purpose Question

Ⓓ The author focuses on the effect of pesticides on the construction of the Panama Canal by writing, "During the construction of the Panama Canal, for instance, thousands of workers were sickened and killed by mosquito-borne illnesses. Pesticides later managed to reduce the mosquito population and enabled the canal to be built while saving countless lives."

15 Factual Information Question

Ⓒ The author notes, "But by the late 1960s, accusations that DDT harmed the environment led to its banning in nearly every nation worldwide."

16 Rhetorical Purpose Question

Ⓐ It is written, "Some typical side effects of those exposed to pesticides include irritated eyes, skin rashes, and respiratory problems."

17 Factual Information Question

Ⓓ The passage reads, "The majority of those harmed by pesticides are the workers who apply them."

18 Vocabulary Question

Ⓓ A tradeoff between advantages and disadvantages is a compromise.

19 Insert Text Question

❷ The sentence before the second square reads, "Pesticides later managed to reduce the mosquito population and enabled the canal to be built while saving countless lives." The sentence to be added

starts with "Without their usage." In this sentence, "their" refers to pesticides. The sentence in the passage further points out that the canal was built thanks to pesticides. The sentence to be added implies that without pesticides, the canal almost certainly would not have been built. Thus the two sentences go together.

20 **Prose Summary Question**

2, 3, 4 The important ideas in the passage that are mentioned in the summary sentence are that pesticides have advantages but can harm humans, animals, and the environment. Answer choices 2, 3, and 4 all focus on these main points. Answer choices 1 and 5 are minor points, so they are incorrect. Answer choice 6 is not mentioned in the passage, so it is incorrect as well.

PASSAGE 3   p. 97

21 **Vocabulary Question**

(A) When predators have correspondingly evolved with prey animals, they have similarly changed over time.

22 **Inference Question**

(B) The passage reads, "The great amount of rainfall and the high temperatures in these regions resulted in the appearing of massive rainforests that provide homes for large, diverse populations of animals." In noting that rainforests have "large and diverse populations of animals," the author implies that a large number of species of animals live within them.

23 **Rhetorical Purpose Question**

(D) The author focuses on how the green-eyed tree frog hides itself from other in writing, "The green-eyed tree frog takes camouflage one step further. It has greenish skin, which is the same as the mossy background in which it lives, and it additionally has a body shape broken up by a fringe of skin all around the frog. This helps break up the visual outline of the frog so that it blends in more easily with its background."

24 **Factual Information Question**

(B) The author points out, "many animals living within them have evolved to blend into these backgrounds. They generally do this in two ways: by having similar-colored skin, fur, or feathers and by imitating something else."

25 **Vocabulary Question**

(B) When prey animals look fearsome, they appear to be formidable animals.

26 **Negative Factual Information Question**

(C) There is no mention in the passage of a chameleon that has the shape of a dead tree branch.

27 **Factual Information Question**

(D) In discussing snakes, the author writes, "Many species of snakes have sensitive tongues that can pick up scents in the air and transmit them to their brains. Furthermore, they can detect heat from animals' bodies at night, so camouflage is useless against snakes hunting after sundown."

28 **Rhetorical Purpose Question**

(A) About tigers, the passage reads, "Large predators may also use camouflage while stalking their prey. Tigers have alternating colored stripes, so they can blend into the background and surprise potential prey."

29 **Insert Text Question**

3 The sentence before the third square reads, "Tigers have alternating colored stripes, so they can blend into the background and surprise potential prey." The sentence to be added mentions "another big cat," which refers to the tigers mentioned in the previous sentence. Thus the two sentences go well together.

30 **Prose Summary Question**

2, 4, 6 The important idea in the passage that is mentioned in the summary sentence is that both prey animals and predators hide from other animals by using a variety of methods of camouflage. Answer choices 2, 4, and 6 all focus on this main point. Answer choices 1, 3, and 5 are all minor points, so they are incorrect answers.

Actual Test 05

ANSWERS

PASSAGE 1

1 Ⓒ	2 Ⓑ	3 Ⓐ	4 Ⓓ	5 Ⓐ
6 Ⓑ	7 Ⓑ	8 Ⓒ	9 **4**	

10 ①, ②, ⑤

PASSAGE 2

11 Ⓓ	12 Ⓒ	13 Ⓑ	14 Ⓑ	15 Ⓑ
16 Ⓓ	17 Ⓑ	18 Ⓐ	19 **3**	

20 ①, ②, ③

PASSAGE 3

21 Ⓐ	22 Ⓓ	23 Ⓒ	24 Ⓐ	25 Ⓑ
26 Ⓐ	27 Ⓑ	28 Ⓐ	29 **2**	

30 ①, ③, ⑥

PASSAGE 1
p. 107

Answer Explanations

1 Factual Information Question

Ⓒ The author notes, "According to one estimate, nearly half of all natives of the two continents died because of European diseases."

2 Rhetorical Purpose Question

Ⓑ The author writes, "One unlucky tribe—the Taino—who lived on several Caribbean islands, including Hispaniola, suffered a 100% mortality rate from smallpox." So the author mentions the Taino to point out that imported diseases killed all of them.

3 Inference Question

Ⓐ It is written, "In the late fifteenth century, smallpox was well known in Europe and had a mortality rate of roughly thirty percent." It can therefore be inferred that, with a mortality rate of around thirty percent, smallpox killed fewer than half of the Europeans it infected.

4 Vocabulary Question

Ⓓ When sick people and villages need to be quarantined, they need to be isolated so that no one comes into contact with them.

5 Factual Information Question

Ⓐ The author remarks, "By not understanding that sick people and even entire villages needed to be quarantined, the natives enabled the diseases to spread further. Travelers carried these illnesses along trade routes, especially up and down the great river systems that served as highways for the natives in North and South America."

6 Negative Factual Information Question

Ⓑ There is no mention in the paragraph of the size of the land being controlled by many tribes being reduced.

7 Vocabulary Question

Ⓑ When the Native American populations were marginalized by the Europeans, the Native Americans lost power to the Europeans.

8 Factual Information Question

Ⓒ The author writes, "Nonetheless, while the tribes did not vanish entirely, they never recovered their empires and native lands. European incursions continued unabated, and those invaders established colonies and states of their own."

9 Insert Text Question

4 The sentence before the fourth square is "Rather small Spanish armies handily defeated both empires and made the lands the natives had once ruled colonies of Spain." This sentence points out that the natives were defeated and became colonies. The sentence to be added describes what happened to them next. Note the presence of the sequence word "then" in the sentence to be added. It helps connect the two sentences.

10 Prose Summary Question

①, ②, ⑤ The important ideas in the passage that are mentioned in the summary sentence are that the Europeans who went to the Americas after 1492 brought diseases with them that wound up killing millions of native Americans. Answer choices ①, ②, and ⑤ all focus on these main points. Answer choices ③, ④, and ⑥ are all minor points, so they are incorrect answers.

PASSAGE 2
p. 115

Answer Explanations

11 Negative Factual Information Question

Ⓓ There is no mention in the paragraph about whether or not the majority of musical pieces in modern times are homophonic or polyphonic.

12 Vocabulary Question

© A dominant type of music is the prevailing type of music in a certain time or place.

13 Rhetorical Purpose Question

Ⓑ While describing monophonic music, the author writes, "This form of music texture was the dominant type of church music in Europe for centuries subsequent to the fall of Rome. Its basic method was called plainchant."

14 Factual Information Question

Ⓑ The passage reads, "That first singing voice, in addition to music produced by someone whistling or humming a tune, has monophonic texture."

15 Reference Question

Ⓑ The "whose" that had Scott Joplin as its most famous composer was ragtime music.

16 Factual Information Question

Ⓓ The passage notes, "Homophonic music evolved during the Baroque Period, which lasted from around 1600-1750. During it, keyboard instruments such as the harpsichord, organ, and piano became prominent in music composition."

17 Factual Information Question

Ⓑ About polyphonic music, the author writes, "At that time, the Church disapproved of it. People found it too jarring when singers began experimenting with different voices in various layers, especially since they were used to the monophonic chanting popular then."

18 Vocabulary Question

Ⓐ Embellishments to music are additions to it.

19 Insert Text Question

❸ The sentence before the third square reads, "That first singing voice, in addition to music produced by someone whistling or humming a tune, has monophonic texture." It provides some examples of monophonic music. The sentence to be added begins with "Furthermore," which is a key sequence word, and then it provides some other examples of monophonic music. In this way, the two sentences go together.

20 Prose Summary Question

1, 2, 3 The summary sentence notes that there are four types of music texture that comprise the majority of all musical compositions. This thought is best described in answer choices 1, 2, and 3. Answer choices 4, 5, and 6 are all minor points, so they are incorrect answers.

Answer Explanations

21 Factual Information Question

Ⓐ The passage reads, "Yet Japanese architecture did not develop in a vacuum but was instead influenced by several outside factors, among them being the spread of Buddhism, the fighting of a civil war, and the Western world once contact with it was established."

22 Vocabulary Question

Ⓓ When Japanese structures were reconfigured, they were rearranged thanks to the interior walls that could move.

23 Inference Question

Ⓒ The author writes, "For instance, wood was the dominant building material in every period thanks to the ease with which it was attained." It can therefore be assumed that Japan has a large number of forested areas since so many people used wood to make homes with.

24 Negative Factual Information Question

Ⓐ There is no mention in the paragraph about Japanese homes being flat on their tops.

25 Factual Information Question

Ⓑ It is written, "These were wooden dwellings with two or three floors and peaked roofs with steep slopes extending practically to the ground. The steep roofs were necessary to prevent the accumulation of rain or snow during periods of heavy precipitation."

26 Vocabulary Question

Ⓐ When the building of castles was prompted, it was encouraged due to the social conditions in Japan at the time.

27 Rhetorical Purpose Question

Ⓑ The entire paragraph focuses on the changes that happened during the Tokugawa Shogunate period.

28 Inference Question

Ⓐ The author notes, "When widespread contact with the West began in the 1860s, the Japanese were exposed to Western notions of architecture. As a result, in spite of fears of damage from earthquakes, builders began widely utilizing brick and stone, and Japan's architectural style transformed again." Therefore it can be inferred that Western notions of architecture helped influence the Japanese to use brick and stone to construct various buildings.

29 Insert Text Question

2 The sentence before the second square reads, "Villagers additionally erected wooden watchtowers and wooden fences as defensive measures." The sentence to be added begins by noting "both." It refers to "wooden watchtowers and wooden fences." Therefore the two sentences go together.

30 Prose Summary Question

1, 3, 6 The important idea in the passage that is mentioned in the summary sentence is that Japanese architecture has remained steady in some aspects but has also changed greatly in others over time. Answer choices 1, 3, and 6 all focus on these main points. Answer choices 2, 4, and 5 are all minor points, so they are incorrect answers.

Actual Test 06

ANSWERS

PASSAGE 1

1 B	2 C	3 A	4 C	5 C
6 B	7 C	8 B	9 **2**	
10 2, 5, 6				

PASSAGE 2

11 D	12 B	13 C	14 D	15 A
16 B, C		17 D	18 C	19 **3**
20 2, 3, 4				

PASSAGE 3

21 D	22 D	23 C	24 B	25 A
26 A	27 C	28 D	29 **2**	
30 Shy: 2, 5, 6 Outgoing: 1, 4				

PASSAGE 1

p. 133

Answer Explanations

1 Vocabulary Question

B When laws are passed prohibiting people from engaging in a certain type of activity, the laws are forbidding people to act in a certain way.

2 Factual Information Question

C The passage reads, "Upon joining, they agreed to certain professional standards, including their pay rates and the quality of their work."

3 Sentence Simplification Question

A The sentence points out that an apprentice had to do everything the master told him or her to do and that the master gave the apprentice food, a home, and knowledge. These thoughts are best expressed by the sentence in answer choice A.

4 Negative Factual Information Question

C There is no mention in the paragraph about when apprentices were permitted to do more complicated tasks.

5 Reference Question

C The "it" that was judged and approved by the master craftsmen was "a great work."

6 Factual Information Question

B The author writes, "Once a person became a

journeyman, this individual was considered skilled enough at his or her trade to be a paid worker but was not talented enough to be called a master. A journeyman was permitted to make money by practicing his or her trade but was not allowed to employ others or to open a shop."

7 Factual Information Question

Ⓒ The passage notes, "Unfortunately for journeymen, skill was not the only factor the masters took into consideration. They frequently failed journeymen simply to prevent there from being too many masters in a region."

8 Vocabulary Question

Ⓑ When guild members jealously guarded their prerogatives, they were looking after the privileges that they gained from being members of a guild.

9 Insert Text Question

❷ The sentence before the second square reads, "Guilds also came to dominate many aspects of economic activity in medieval times, and their members jealously guarded their prerogatives and were suspicious of innovation." The sentence to be added notes how the behavior of guild members resulted in there being few inventions in trades that had guilds for a long period of time. The cause-effect relationship between the two sentences makes them go together.

10 Prose Summary Question

❷, ❺, ❻ The important idea in the passage that is mentioned in the summary sentence is that there was a long, hard process involved for a person to become a guild master. Answer choices ❷, ❺, and ❻ all focus on this main point. Answer choices ❶, ❸, and ❹ are all minor points, so they are incorrect.

PASSAGE 2
p. 141

Answer Explanations

11 Vocabulary Question

Ⓓ When a plant or animal occupies an environmental niche, it has a certain slot into which it fits.

12 Negative Factual Information Question

Ⓑ While the importance of water is noted, the author does not mention that it is the "most crucial element they need when they move to a new environment."

13 Inference Question

Ⓒ The passage reads, "Deserts with high temperatures and few water sources, as well as the frigid Arctic and Antarctic, are unforgiving to species that fail to adapt quickly." In noting that deserts, the Arctic, and the Antarctic are "unforgiving to species that fail to adapt quickly," the author is implying that most of the plants and animals that move to those regions do not adapt but instead die.

14 Rhetorical Purpose Question

Ⓓ About the Australian koala, the author points out, "The Australian koala almost exclusively eats the leaves of the eucalyptus tree and would not survive in any ecosystem lacking them." Therefore the author mentions the koala to point out how its fussy eating habits limit where it can live.

15 Vocabulary Question

Ⓐ When dead zones hinder the movement of plants and animals, they impede, or stop, the organisms from moving to other places.

16 Factual Information Question

Ⓑ, Ⓒ The author writes, "Humans, by building new population centers and highways across known migration routes, can limit species to specific areas" The author further notes, "Human polluting of the oceans is another problem since there are now dead zones, which have limited amounts of oxygen, in the oceans, and many coral reefs, which are home to myriad species of animals, have been damaged or destroyed, too."

17 Factual Information Question

Ⓓ It is mentioned, "Not all human distribution of plants and animals has been beneficial though as some invasive species have caused a great amount of damage both to the land and the native flora and fauna."

18 Rhetorical Purpose Question

Ⓒ In the previous paragraph, the author points out how humans are causing plants and animals to have limited distributions. In paragraph 5, the author mentions how humans have been responsible for spreading certain plant and animals.

19 Insert Text Question

❸ The sentence before the third square reads, "The Australian koala almost exclusively eats the leaves of the eucalyptus tree and would not survive in any ecosystem lacking them." The sentence to be added starts with "Likewise." Then, the sentence describes how the panda relies mostly on a diet of bamboo.

The word "Likewise" therefore provides a link between the two sentences, both of which are about animals that are fussy eaters.

20 Prose Summary Question

2, 3, 4 The important ideas in the passage that are mentioned in the summary sentence are that the distribution of plants and animals around the world is limited for many reasons. Answer choices 2, 3, and 4 all focus on these main points. Answer choices 1, 5, and 6 are all minor points, so they are incorrect answers.

PASSAGE 3   p. 149

Answer Explanations

21 Vocabulary Question

D A person with an innate sense of shyness has a shyness that is instinctive in nature.

22 Factual Information Question

D The passage reads, "The second is that children become shy due to the way they are brought up and the environment around them."

23 Negative Factual Information Question

C There is no mention in the paragraph of which groups of psychologists conducted the experiments in babies that are discussed.

24 Rhetorical Purpose Question

B The author comments, "Scientists have learned that people who are shy have a very sensitive nervous system, which is affected by a chemical in the brain called monoamine oxidase. It acts as an inhibitor on impulsive actions and causes people with high levels of it to be shyer and more introverted and people with lower levels to be more outgoing and extroverted."

25 Factual Information Question

A It is written, "Another region in the brain that affects shyness is the amygdala, which plays a role in causing fear."

26 Sentence Simplification Question

A The sentence points out that there are records of some children becoming shy and afraid because of traumatic events that happened in their lives. These thoughts are best expressed by the sentence in answer choice A.

27 Vocabulary Question

C Societies that are gregarious in nature have many extroverted people.

28 Inference Question

D The author writes, "In many cultures, there is a stigma attached to shy children in that they are regarded as having some sort of problem while outgoing children are considered normal. This has led to an emphasis in society on transforming shy children into more outgoing ones." Therefore it can be inferred that many cultures prefer outgoing children to shy children.

29 Insert Text Question

2 The sentence before the second square reads, "Some outgoing children additionally become adults who are constantly seeking new thrills to such a point that they harm both themselves and others." The sentence to be added mentions that either physical or mental problems can be caused by these individuals. Thus the two sentences go well together.

30 Fill in a Table Question

Shy: 2, 5, 6   Outgoing: 1, 4
About shy children the author notes, "Children who live in strict societies in which expressing themselves in an outgoing manner is frowned upon are nearly always shyer than children raised in more gregarious societies." (2) In addition, the author writes, "In contrast, between fifteen and twenty percent had extreme reactions in which they waved their arms, thrashed about, screamed, cried, or engaged in some combination of those actions. The studies revealed that the sedate babies grew up to be quite outgoing whereas the babies that reacted in extreme manners became shyer as they grew older." (5) Finally, the author points out, "Another region in the brain that affects shyness is the amygdala, which plays a role in causing fear. People with an overly active amygdala tend to inflate their fears and are therefore shyer in nature." (6) As for outgoing children, the passage reads, "The studies revealed that the sedate babies grew up to be quite outgoing," (1) and, "Very outgoing children may exhibit behavioral problems associated with attention deficit hyperactivity disorder, also known as ADHD." (4)

Actual Test 07

ANSWERS

PASSAGE 1
1 (D)   2 (A)   3 (B)   4 (C)   5 (A)
6 (A)   7 (B)   8 (C)   9 [1]
10 [1], [2], [3]

PASSAGE 2
11 (B)   12 (D)   13 (A)   14 (A)   15 (B)
16 (D)   17 (A)   18 (A)   19 [1]
20 Inner Core: [5], [7] Outer Core: [1], [6]
   Mantle: [2], [3], [9]

PASSAGE 3
21 (D)   22 (B)   23 (D)   24 (A)   25 (C)
26 (D)   27 (A)   28 (B)   29 [1]
30 [2], [5], [6]

PASSAGE 1
p. 159

Answer Explanations

1 Vocabulary Question

(D) Marauding tribes are ones that engage in raiding and other similar behavior.

2 Negative Factual Information Question

(A) There is no mention in the paragraph of a wide variety of grains growing well in the fertile soil of the Nile River Valley.

3 Factual Information Question

(B) The passage reads, "Eventually, the nomads learned how to farm, so they established permanent settlements in the region around 5500 B.C."

4 Sentence Simplification Question

(C) The sentence points out that when the course of the Nile River changed, some of the old areas that in flowed through were higher than others. This thought is best expressed by the sentence in answer choice (C).

5 Rhetorical Purpose Question

(A) About bricks, the author writes, "Many years later, they realized that the mud left behind by the annual floods could be combined with straw to make bricks."

6 Vocabulary Question

(A) Rudimentary dwellings are ones that are very simple in their construction.

7 Inference Question

(B) The author comments, "Their homes were well built, but those of poorer individuals crumbled after a few years and had to undergo major repairs or be entirely rebuilt." Therefore it can be inferred that the low quality of the homes of poor individuals resulted in them not lasting a long time.

8 Factual Information Question

(C) The author notes, "Furniture was rare in Egyptian homes as most Egyptians had mats for sleeping and sitting on."

9 Insert Text Question

[1] The sentence before the first square reads, "Most domiciles that were built had two floors; the bottom one was used to store grain, and the top one was the family's living space." The sentence to be added mentions "this arrangement," which refers to the fact that families had their living space on the second floor. This allowed them to avoid encounters with dangerous animals. Thus the two sentences go well together.

10 Prose Summary Question

[1], [2], [3] The important ideas in the passage that are mentioned in the summary sentence are that the ancient Egyptians built their homes in the Nile River Valley in different places and that the homes varied in their quality. Answer choices [1], [2], and [3] all focus on these main points. Answer choices [4], [5], and [6] are all minor points, so they are incorrect answers.

PASSAGE 2
p. 167

Answer Explanations

11 Sentence Simplification Question

(B) The sentence points out that scientists have used many ways to learn about the inner planet despite not having been able to go there physically. These points are simplified the best in answer choice (B).

12 Negative Factual Information Question

(D) In paragraph 1, there is no mention about how the Earth's layers compare to one another in terms of their size.

13 Inference Question

(A) The author writes, "It consists of a solid ball of iron that also contains the elements nickel and sulfur." Then, the author adds, "While the Earth cooled, the heavier elements sank to the center of the Earth while the lighter elements—mostly silicates—remained closer to the surface." Thus it can be inferred that iron is one of the heavier elements.

14 Vocabulary Question

(A) When there are substantial amounts of nickel and sulfur, there are considerable amounts of them.

15 Factual Information Question

(B) It is written, "The lower mantle has temperatures around 4,000 degrees Celsius whereas the temperature in the upper mantle ranges between 500 and 900 degrees Celsius."

16 Vocabulary Question

(D) When the movement of the plates instigates geological activity, it causes earthquakes and volcanic eruptions.

17 Factual Information Question

(A) The author notes, "It is thought that the large tectonic plates comprising the Earth's crust float on the asthenosphere. Temperature changes within the asthenosphere cause convection currents in this layer. These make the molten rock in the asthenosphere move, which, in turn, causes the tectonic plates to move."

18 Rhetorical Purpose Question

(A) About the Moho Discontinuity, the author writes, "By studying seismic activity, geologists have been able to determine where the crust ends and the mantle begins. The boundary between the two is known as the Moho Discontinuity."

19 Insert Text Question

[1] The sentence before the first square reads, "Surrounding the inner core is the 2,300-kilometer-thick outer core, which is composed mostly of liquid iron but, like the inner core, contains substantial amounts of nickel and sulfur." The sentence to be added mentions two other elements—silicon and oxygen—that are thought to be located in the outer core. Thus the two sentences go well together.

20 Fill in a Table Question

Inner Core: [5], [7]   Outer Core: [1], [6]
Mantle: [2], [3], [9]
At 2,400 kilometers in diameter, the inner core is the

second largest of the Earth's layers. ([5]) In addition, the author points out, "Despite this intense heat, the core does not melt due to the enormous amount of pressure being exerted on it." ([7]) As for the outer core, "The Earth's magnetic field is created by the outer core," ([1]) and it "contains substantial amounts of nickel and sulfur" in their liquid forms. ([6]) Concerning the mantle, the author writes, "This liquid rock rises and falls within the mantle as it cools and then becomes hotter." ([2]) In addition, "It consists of molten rock, mainly silicates high in concentrations of magnesium and iron," ([3]) and "At the topmost part of the upper mantle is a region known as the asthenosphere, which is roughly eighty to 200 kilometers beneath the surface of the Earth. It is thought that the large tectonic plates comprising the Earth's crust float on the asthenosphere."([9])

PASSAGE 3

Answer Explanations

21 Factual Information Question

(D) About the Hanseatic League, the author writes, "Its members agreed to established rules and regulations governing trade."

22 Sentence Simplification Question

(B) The sentence points out that because merchants controlled a lot of the cities on the North Sea and Baltic Sea in the 1100s, it was natural that they would seek alliances based on trade. This thought is best expressed by the sentence in answer choice (B).

23 Factual Information Question

(D) It is written, "The motivation to form a merchant league arose from the lack of security most merchants experienced in the Middle Ages, a time before nation-states and permanent armies and navies were the norm. On land and sea, merchants and their wares were subject to numerous risks from brigands. In the Middle Ages, Germanic merchants started forming guilds, called *hansa*, and armed men to protect their cities and trade routes."

24 Rhetorical Purpose Question

(A) In paragraph 3, the author stresses the importance of the role that the city of Lubeck played in the founding of the Hanseatic League.

25 Vocabulary Question

(C) When Lubeck reaped many benefits, it secured them to its advantage.

26 **Vocabulary Question**

(D) When noblemen and kings began lashing out at the Hanseatic League, they were assailing, or attacking, it.

27 **Inference Question**

(A) The passage reads, "The merchant guilds and their cities became so rich and powerful that the league and its member cities actually went to war with Denmark over trade rights in the 1360s." Since the league went to war with Denmark, it can be inferred that it had armed soldiers that it employed.

28 **Negative Factual Information Question**

(B) There is no mention in the paragraph about either Sweden or Denmark gaining power in the Baltic Sea and thereby causing the Hanseatic League to lose power.

29 **Insert Text Question**

[1] The sentence in front of the first square reads, "Soon afterward, other cities realized the benefits of establishing protected trade routes." The sentence to be added then explains how the cities could benefit by establishing protected routes: Fewer merchants would be robbed, so the citizens of the cities would become more prosperous. Therefore the two sentences go together with one another.

30 **Prose Summary Question**

[2], [5], [6] The important ideas in the passage that are mentioned in the summary sentence are that until a few factors caused the Hanseatic League to go into decline, it economically dominated the area around the Baltic and North seas. Answer choices [2], [5], and [6] all focus on these main points. Choices [1], [3], and [4] are all minor points, so they are incorrect answers.

Actual Test 08

ANSWERS

PASSAGE 1

1 (B) 2 (C) 3 (A) 4 (A) 5 (B)
6 (D) 7 (B) 8 (D) 9 [3]
10 Binocular: [1], [2], [7] Monocular: [3], [5]

PASSAGE 2

11 (D) 12 (C) 13 (A) 14 (D) 15 (C)
16 (B) 17 (C), (D) 18 (C) 19 [2]
20 [2], [3], [4]

PASSAGE 3

21 (D) 22 (A) 23 (A) 24 (D) 25 (A)
26 (A) 27 (B) 28 (D) 29 [4]
30 [2], [4], [6]

PASSAGE 1

p. 185

Answer Explanations

1 **Reference Question**

(B) The "them" that are provided with specialized eyes are some animals.

2 **Vocabulary Question**

(C) When an animal can judge depth, it can determine how close or far away something is.

3 **Factual Information Question**

(A) The passage reads, "The manner in which the brain interprets the images seen by each eye in a slightly different position allows for depth perception. Many predators with binocular vision are ambush hunters that typically wait in silence until the prey animal they are targeting is close enough to attack. For them, a sense of depth is vital to ensure a successful attack."

4 **Vocabulary Question**

(A) Animals that are susceptible to another predator are open to attack by it.

5 **Rhetorical Purpose Question**

(B) The author shows how some animals detect unsafe situations in writing, "Most animals with binocular vision cannot see an area covering more than 180 degrees. This leaves them susceptible to

another predator that may be tracking them from behind. As a result, many predators have developed heightened senses of smell and hearing to permit them to know when danger is approaching."

6   Inference Question

Ⓓ In writing, "The advantage of this eye positioning is that animals are provided with a wide field of vision—nearly 360 degrees for some species," the author implies that some animals can see nearly everything in front of and behind them at the same time.

7   Factual Information Question

Ⓑ The author writes, "Having eyes on the sides of the head reduces an animal's ability to perceive depth, yet creatures with monocular vision can attain a slight degree of depth perception by comparing a moving object with more distant stationary background objects."

8   Factual Information Question

Ⓓ It is written, "With predators able to spot prey from far distances and then focus on them, prey animals had to evolve eyes that could detect danger before it was too late. In turn, as prey animals developed methods of avoiding attacks, predators came up with different styles of hunting. Some evolved into ambush hunters whereas others, such as lions, learned to use natural cover such as tall grasses to get near grazing prey animals in a stealthy manner."

9   Insert Text Question

■3 The sentence before the fourth square reads, "While grazing in open fields, the eyes of these prey animals shift positions so that when their heads dip as they feed on plant matter, their pupils remain in a horizontal position." The sentence to be added refers to the positions of the animals' pupils and points out that the animals can still see even though it may seem that they cannot. Thus the two sentences go well together.

10   Fill in a Table Question

Binocular: ①, ②, ⑦   Monocular: ③, ⑤
Regarding binocular vision, the author writes, "An animal with binocular vision has its eyes placed close together on the front of its head," (①) and, "Many predators with binocular vision are ambush hunters that typically wait in silence until the prey animal they are targeting is close enough to attack." (②) The author then adds, "There are disadvantages to binocular vision though, the primary one of which is the lack of a wide field of vision. Most animals with

binocular vision cannot see an area covering more than 180 degrees. This leaves them susceptible to another predator that may be tracking them from behind." (⑦) As for monocular vision, the author notes, "As for animals with monocular vision, they tend to be those that are hunted and include deer, rabbits, warthogs, and numerous other herbivores," (③) and, "Having eyes on the sides of the head reduces an animal's ability to perceive depth, yet creatures with monocular vision can attain a slight degree of depth perception by comparing a moving object with more distant stationary background objects." (⑤)

PASSAGE 2   p. 192

Answer Explanations

11   Negative Factual Information Question

Ⓓ It is not true that the Chinese first began to make ceramic bases during the Ming Dynasty as the author writes, "Prior to the advent of the Ming Dynasty, the Chinese had been making pottery for centuries."

12   Vocabulary Question

Ⓒ Something made for utilitarian purposes is made for practical usage.

13   Inference Question

Ⓐ In writing, "Later, the Chinese discovered deposits of fine white clay, called kaolin, near the city of Jingdezhen in southeastern China. This led to the creation of porcelain ceramics," the author implies that porcelain can be made when it contains kaolin.

14   Factual Information Question

Ⓓ The author writes, "At first, the Chinese had difficulty with the color blue because the mineral cobalt, which was used to make blue dyes, tended to bleed when fired in kilns; however, by adding manganese to the cobalt dyes, this problem was overcome."

15   Vocabulary Question

Ⓒ When the glazes were more translucent, they were more radiant in appearance.

16   Rhetorical Purpose Question

Ⓑ In writing about Emperor Xuande, the author notes, "Ming rulers began ordering vast quantities of ceramics for their own use and for commercial purposes. One record shows that during the reign of Emperor Xuande in 1433, he ordered more than 400,000 pieces from imperial ceramic makers."

17 Factual Information Question

ⓒ, ⓓ About Ming vase makers, the author points out, "This style for vases was not novel to China when the Ming Dynasty was established, but by the early fifteenth century, Ming vase makers had attained new heights of skill and design. New recipes for mixing kaolin enabled them to create thinner yet stronger vases. New glazes were more translucent, permitting a glossier finish."

18 Inference Question

ⓒ In writing, "Most of the cobalt used in Chinese ceramics came from Iran," the author implies that Chinese ceramics relied upon materials imported from other lands.

19 Insert Text Question

❷ The sentence before the second square reads, "However, to complicate matters, for many centuries after the dynasty ended, Chinese artists marked their ceramics with the names of Ming emperors to bestow honor upon them." The "this" in the sentence to be added refers to the usage of design marks on ceramics made after the Ming Dynasty ended. That action is what makes it almost impossible for regular people to determine the authenticity of vases that are claimed to be from the Ming Dynasty. Thus the two sentences go well together.

20 Prose Summary Question

②, ③, ④ The summary sentence points out that Ming Dynasty ceramics were well made and are valued by people today. This thought is best described in answer choices ②, ③, and ④. Answer choices ① and ⑤ are minor points, so they are incorrect. And answer choice ⑥ is not mentioned in the passage, so it is not a correct answer either.

PASSAGE 3
p. 199

Answer Explanations

21 Sentence Simplification Question

ⓓ The sentence points out that animals need to weigh little and to have strong, large wings that they can flap in order to fly. This thought is best expressed by the sentence in answer choice ⓓ.

22 Vocabulary Question

ⓐ Prototypes for wings are models of them.

23 Negative Factual Information Question

ⓐ While the author writes, "Many insects lived in water and had gills which they utilized to breathe

underwater. Movable gill plates may have acted as early prototypes for wings," it is not true that insects first arose as underwater creatures with gills and then moved to land millions of years ago.

24 Factual Information Question

ⓓ About protobirds, it is written, "Early protobirds began their lives on the ground but gradually moved higher to acquire food and to avoid predators. Perhaps they moved upward to avoid predators at first and then returned to the ground each day when the time of danger had passed."

25 Rhetorical Purpose Question

ⓐ Regarding the dodo bird, the author focusing on what is likely to happen to birds that cannot fly in writing, "A classic example of what can happen to birds that never evolved to fly is the dodo bird of Mauritius Island, which lived in isolation with no natural predators, never became capable of flight, and built nests on the ground. When humans arrived on the island and brought various predatory animals, the dodo became easy prey and rapidly went extinct."

26 Factual Information Question

ⓐ The author writes, "However, their opponents argue that modern birds required millions of years to evolve to this stage and that early birds could not achieve ground takeoff. To do so, early birds would have required the ability to overcome the force of gravity by using all their strength to run and to flap their wings."

27 Vocabulary Question

ⓑ When there are cardinal rules of animal survival, the rules are fundamental ones that are essential to the survival of animals.

28 Negative Factual Information Question

ⓓ There is no mention in the passage about how long the force of gravity prevented early birds from taking off from the ground.

29 Insert Text Question

❹ The sentence before the fourth square reads, "When humans arrived on the island and brought various predatory animals, the dodo became easy prey and rapidly went extinct." The sentence to be added mentions the moa and how it "met a similar fate," which implies that it went extinct like the dodo. Thus the two sentences go well together.

30 Prose Summary Question

2, 4, 6 The summary sentence notes that there are many questions about how animals learned to fly, including when it first happened and from where it occurred. This thought is best described in answer choices 2, 4, and 6. Answer choices 1 and 5 are minor points, so they are incorrect answers. And answer choice 3 is merely implied in the passage, so it is also wrong.

Actual Test 09

ANSWERS

PASSAGE 1

1 Ⓐ	2 Ⓓ	3 Ⓒ	4 Ⓑ	5 Ⓒ
6 Ⓑ	7 Ⓑ	8 Ⓑ	9 4	
10 1, 2, 5				

PASSAGE 2

11 Ⓓ	12 Ⓐ	13 Ⓒ	14 Ⓓ	15 Ⓑ
16 Ⓓ	17 Ⓑ	18 Ⓓ	19 2	
20 2, 3, 5				

PASSAGE 3

21 Ⓑ	22 Ⓒ	23 Ⓐ	24 Ⓓ	25 Ⓑ
26 Ⓑ	27 Ⓒ	28 Ⓐ	29 2	
30 2, 5, 6				

PASSAGE 1

p. 209

Answer Explanations

1 Factual Information Question

Ⓐ About the seismometers, the author writes, "They were in operation between 1969 and 1977, and during that time, scientists received data from approximately 12,000 lunar seismic events."

2 Reference Question

Ⓓ The "That" which is strong enough to cause earthbound buildings to shake and objects to fall and break but is unlikely to cause widespread death and destruction is a rating higher than 5.5.

3 Vocabulary Question

Ⓒ When there is intermittent shaking for several hours, there was irregular shaking going on.

4 Vocabulary Question

Ⓑ When water puts a damper on seismic activity, it reduces the lengths of the earthquakes that are taking place.

5 Inference Question

Ⓒ In paragraph 4, the author writes, "The second type is called a thermal moonquake and happens because of the great differences in the moon's surface's temperature when it passes in and out of direct sunlight. When the surface begins reheating, it expands, causing ripples of movement in the upper crust. These can be intense enough to qualify as seismic activity, but they are relatively mild moonquakes low in intensity." Then, in paragraph 5, it is written, "The third type of moonquake occurs far underneath the surface roughly 800 to 1,200 kilometers deep. These moonquakes are mild, rarely reaching above two on the Richter scale." It can therefore be inferred that the thermal moonquakes recorded have had low ratings on the Richter scale.

6 Rhetorical Purpose Question

Ⓑ In writing, "The pull of the moon's gravity causes the tides on the Earth, so it is possible that the Earth's gravity also influences the moon. Nevertheless, exactly how tidal forces cause these moonquakes is uncertain. It is known that the gravitational pull of the Earth causes some small-scale distortion of the moon as it approaches the Earth and then moves away from it. However, this has not been verified as being the direct cause of deep moonquakes," the author discusses a theory that some people have thought about.

7 Negative Factual Information Question

Ⓑ There is no mention in the passage of precisely which part of the moon the moonquakes occurring far underneath the moon's surface most commonly occurred.

8 Factual Information Question

Ⓑ About the seismometers, the author writes, "The first three types of moonquakes produce mild seismic activity in comparison with the last, shallow moonquakes, which normally occur twenty to thirty kilometers beneath the moon's surface. Between 1969 and 1977, the seismometers detected twenty-eight shallow moonquakes, seven of which had intensity ratings above five on the Richter scale."

9 Insert Text Question

4 The sentence before the fourth square reads, "The strongest earthquakes normally occur where these plates meet in places called fault lines on account of the enormous amount of stress built up in those regions." The "many of them" in the sentence to be added refers to "where these places meet." The sentence to be added notes that many powerful earthquakes have happened along fault lines. Thus the two sentences go well together.

10 Prose Summary Question

1, **2**, **5** The summary sentence notes that there are several types of moonquakes, and they are different from earthquakes. This thought is best described in answer choices **1**, **2**, and **5**. Answer choices **3** and **4** are minor points, so they are incorrect answers. And answer choice **6** contains incorrect information, so it is also wrong.

PASSAGE 2   p. 217

Answer Explanations

11 Vocabulary Question

D When an impetus to industrialize is stifled, it is suppressed, so industrialization does not happen.

12 Vocabulary Question

A When the French restricted the powers of guilds, they lessened them, so the guilds had less power than they had before.

13 Inference Question

C In writing, "The French promptly instituted reforms related to land ownership and restricted the powers of guilds, thereby opening the way for more interest in industrial enterprises. These helped the Germans industrialize after the final French defeat in 1815 with assistance from several other factors," the author implies that guilds actively sought to prevent the German states from developing new industries.

14 Rhetorical Purpose Question

D The author uses the Zollverein to explain how the taxation of goods in German became more simplified in writing, "More significantly, the web of various laws and taxes on trade between states was simplified by a trade union formed in 1834. This Zollverein, or German Customs Union, abolished the multitude of taxes imposed on goods moving across the numerous borders of the German states and replaced them with a single tax on goods no matter

where they went."

15 Sentence Simplification Question

B The sentence points out that while some leaders of small states opposed the Zollverein since they wanted tax revenues, Prussia persuaded many German states to join it. This thought is best expressed by the sentence in answer choice **B**.

16 Factual Information Question

D It is written, "Chief among them was the swift development of a large internal railway system. The first railway lines opened in 1836. By 1845, Germany had more than 2,000 kilometers of railways, and by the 1850s, the German states served as a central hub of the growing European railway network."

17 Factual Information Question

B The author notes, "These railways opened new regions to development, especially the Ruhr River region of western Germany. The Ruhr had extensive deposits of coal, which fueled the developing iron and steel industries. Much of the early Ruhr development can be credited to the Krupp family of Essen, which started by making metal household goods in the eighteenth century and eventually became a global leader in iron, steel, and armament production."

18 Negative Factual Information Question

D It is not true Germany looked to the United States and Britain for help with social welfare programs. About them, the author writes, "Still, after German unification, Chancellor Otto von Bismarck introduced a series of welfare reforms to aid workers. Some were hospital insurance, accident insurance, a national pension plan, and a child labor act restricting the use of children in industry. These reforms protected workers and provided further stimulus for industrial growth. Ultimately, by the onset of the twentieth century, Germany was an industrial powerhouse behind only Britain and the United States."

19 Insert Text Question

2 The sentence before the second square reads, "The same was true of the German iron industry and coal mining." The sentence to be added points out that those two industries were smaller than those of "two European Great Powers." This refers to Britain and France, which are mentioned earlier in the paragraph. Thus the two sentences go well together.

20 Prose Summary Question

2, **3**, **5** The summary sentence notes that Germany

began the nineteenth century by industrializing slowly but then increased the pace of development for various reasons. This thought is best described in answer choices [2], [3], and [5]. Answer choices [4] and [6] are minor points, so they are incorrect answers. And answer choice [1] contains information not mentioned in the passage, so it is also incorrect.

PASSAGE 3

p. 224

Answer Explanations

21 Negative Factual Information Question

Ⓑ There is no mention in the passage of which provinces in the Roman Empire provided most of the items that were traded.

22 Vocabulary Question

Ⓒ When people circumvent social and legal restrictions, they get around these restrictions.

23 Rhetorical Purpose Question

Ⓐ Regarding agents, the author explains what types of work they did in writing, "To circumvent these social and legal restrictions, those wishing to engage in trade employed agents to do so. Some agents negotiated trade deals, others served as accountants, and others sold goods directly in open-air markets. As the Roman Republic and, later, the Roman Empire increased in size and power, these agents traveled far and wide to make new contracts and to develop new trade routes."

24 Factual Information Question

Ⓓ It is written, "The wealthy families of Rome depended on land ownership and local sales of surplus farm produce for the majority of their wealth, so for many families, investing in international trade was a needless venture. There was an element of snobbery involved as wealthy landowning families considered trade beneath their status, too."

25 Vocabulary Question

Ⓑ When people toiled on farms and in industries, they worked on them. Another word for work is "labor."

26 Factual Information Question

Ⓑ First, the author writes, "The principal Roman trade routes were to Gaul and Spain in the west, North Africa, especially Egypt, to the south." Next, the author notes, "North Africa was the breadbasket of Rome as huge amounts of grain were shipped from there across the Mediterranean Sea to Rome's main port of Ostia."

27 Sentence Simplification Question

Ⓒ The sentence points out that while transportation by road cost more than sea transportation, but moving goods by sea involved various problems. This thought is best expressed by the sentence in answer choice Ⓒ.

28 Factual Information Question

Ⓐ The passage points out, "While the Roman Republic had embraced a free-market system, the Roman Empire gradually asserted state control over trade. It developed a state-controlled merchant fleet as opposed to depending on private shipowners for its transportation needs to ensure the constant supply of necessary goods, particularly food. Greater state control allowed more taxation on trade, bringing much-needed wealth to Rome's coffers while simultaneously improving the quality of goods and reducing fraud."

29 Insert Text Question

[2] The sentence before the second square reads, "Most items were desired to maintain the lavish lifestyles wealthy Romans enjoyed." The sentence to be added mentions that some items were "not purchased by the rich." This matches the sentence before the second square, which mentions items being desired by "wealthy Romans." Thus the two sentences go well together.

30 Prose Summary Question

[2], [5], [6] The summary sentence notes that international trade was important to Rome for various reasons. This thought is best described in answer choices [2], [5], and [6]. Answer choices [1] and [3] are minor points, so they are incorrect answers. And answer choice [4] is not mentioned in the passage, so it is also wrong.

Decoding the TOEFL® iBT

Actual Test

READING 1

INTRODUCTION

For many learners of English, the TOEFL® iBT will be the most important standardized test they ever take. Unfortunately for a large number of these individuals, the material covered on the TOEFL® iBT remains a mystery to them, so they are unable to do well on the test. We hope that by using the *Decoding the TOEFL® iBT* series, individuals who take the TOEFL® iBT will be able to excel on the test and, in the process of using the book, may unravel the mysteries of the test and therefore make the material covered on the TOEFL® iBT more familiar to themselves.

The TOEFL® iBT covers the four main skills that a person must learn when studying any foreign language: reading, listening, speaking, and writing. The *Decoding the TOEFL® iBT* series contains books that cover all four of these skills. The *Decoding the TOEFL® iBT* series contains books with three separate levels for all four of the topics, and it also contains *Decoding the TOEFL® iBT Actual Test* books. These books contain several actual tests that learners can utilize to help them become better prepared to take the TOEFL® iBT. This book, *Decoding the TOEFL® iBT Actual Test Reading 1*, covers the reading aspect of the test and includes reading passages that are arranged in the same format as the TOEFL® iBT. Finally, the TOEFL® iBT underwent a number of changes in August 2019. This book—and the others in the series—takes those changes into account and incorporates them in the texts and questions, so readers of this second edition can be assured that they have up-to-date knowledge of the test.

Decoding the TOEFL® iBT Actual Test Reading 1 can be used by learners who are taking classes and also by individuals who are studying by themselves. It contains a total of nine full-length reading actual tests. Each actual test contains three reading passages. All of the passages are the same length and have the same difficulty levels as those found on the TOEFL® iBT. In addition, the passages contain the same numbers and types of questions that appear on the actual TOEFL® iBT, and the questions also have the same difficulty levels as those found on the TOEFL® iBT. Individuals who use *Decoding the TOEFL® iBT Actual Test Reading 1* will therefore be able to prepare themselves not only to take the TOEFL® iBT but also to perform well on the test.

We hope that everyone who uses *Decoding the TOEFL® iBT Actual Test Reading 1* will be able to become more familiar with the TOEFL® iBT and will additionally improve his or her score on the test. As the title of the book implies, we hope that learners can use it to crack the code on the TOEFL® iBT, to make the test itself less mysterious and confusing, and to get the highest score possible. Finally, we hope that both learners and instructors can use this book to its full potential. We wish all of you the best of luck as you study English and prepare for the TOEFL® iBT, and we hope that *Decoding the TOEFL® iBT Actual Test Reading 1* can provide you with assistance during the course of your studies.

Michael A. Putlack
Stephen Poirier
Allen C. Jacobs

TABLE
OF
CONTENTS

ABOUT THE TOEFL® iBT READING SECTION

Changes in the Reading Section

TOEFL® underwent many changes in August of 2019. The following is an explanation of the changes that have been made to the Reading section.

Format

The number of passages that appear in the Reading section is either 3 or 4. The time given for the Reading section is either 54 (3 passages) or 72 (4 passages) minutes.

Passages

The length of each passage has been slightly shortened. A typical Reading passage is between 690 and 710 words. However, there are some passages with as few as 670 words.

In addition, there is a heavier emphasis on science topics. This includes topics such as biology, zoology, and astronomy.

There are sometimes pictures accompanying the text. They are used to provide visual evidence of various objects discussed in the passage. On occasion, there are also pictures used for glossary words.

The glossary typically defines 0-2 words or phrases.

Questions

There are only 10 questions per Reading passage now. This is a decrease from the 12-14 questions that were asked on previous tests.

Question Types

TYPE 1 Vocabulary Questions

Vocabulary questions require the test taker to understand specific words and phrases that are used in the passage. Each of these questions asks the test taker to select another word or phrase that is the most similar in meaning to a word or phrase that is highlighted. The vocabulary words that are highlighted are often important words, so knowing what these words mean can be critical for understanding the entire passage. The highlighted words typically have several different meanings, so test takers need to be careful to avoid selecting an answer choice simply because it is the most common meaning of the word or phrase.

- There are 1-3 Vocabulary questions per passage.
- Passages typically have 2 Vocabulary questions.

TYPE 2 Reference Questions

Reference questions require the test taker to understand the relationships between words and their referents in the passage. These questions most frequently ask the test taker to identify the antecedent of a pronoun. In many instances, the pronouns are words such as *he, she,* or *they* or *its, his, hers,* or *theirs.* However, in other instances, relative pronouns such as which or demonstrative pronouns such as *this* or *that* may be asked about instead.

- There are 0-1 Reference questions per passage. However, these questions rarely appear anymore.

TYPE 3 Factual Information Questions

Factual Information questions require the test taker to understand and be able to recognize facts that are mentioned in the passage. These questions may be about any facts or information that is explicitly covered in the passage. They may appear in the form of details, definitions, explanations, or other kinds of data. The facts which the questions ask about are typically found only in one part of the passage—often just in a sentence or two in one paragraph—and do not require a comprehensive understanding of the passage as a whole.

- There are 1-3 Factual Information questions per passage. There is an average of 2 of these questions per passage.
- Some Factual Information questions require test takers to understand the entire paragraph, not just one part of it, to find the correct answer.

TYPE 4 Negative Factual Information Questions

Negative Factual Information questions require the test taker to understand and be able to recognize facts that are mentioned in the passage. These questions may be about any facts or information that is explicitly covered in the passage. However, these questions ask the test taker to identify the incorrect information in the answer choices. Three of the four answer choices therefore contain correct information that is found in the passage. The answer the test taker must choose therefore either has incorrect information or information that is not mentioned in the passage.

- There are 0-2 Negative Factual Information questions per passage.

TYPE 5 Sentence Simplification Questions

Sentence Simplification questions require the test taker to select a sentence that best restates one that has been highlighted in the passage. These questions ask the test taker to recognize the main points in the sentence and to make sure that they are mentioned in the rewritten sentence. These rewritten sentences use words, phrases, and grammar that are different from the highlighted sentence. Sentence Simplification questions do not always appear in a passage. When they are asked, there is only one Sentence Simplification question per passage.

- There are 0-1 Sentence Simplification questions per passage.
- The answer choices for these questions are approximately half the length of the sentences being asked about.

TYPE 6 Inference Questions

Inference questions require the test taker to understand the argument that the passage is attempting to make. These questions ask the test taker to consider the information that is presented and then to come to a logical conclusion about it. The answers to these questions are never explicitly stated in the passage. Instead, the test taker must infer what the author means. These questions often deal with cause and effect or comparisons between two different things, ideas, events, or people.

- There are 0-2 Inference questions per passage. Most passages have at least 1 Inference question though.
- The difficulty level of these questions has increased. In some cases, test takers must be able to understand an entire paragraph rather than only a part of it.

TYPE 7 Rhetorical Purpose Questions

Rhetorical Purpose questions require the test taker to understand why the author mentioned or wrote about something in the passage. These questions ask the test taker to consider the reasoning behind the information being presented in the passage. For these questions, the function—not the meaning—of the material is the most important aspect for the test taker to be aware of. The questions often focus on the relationship between the information mentioned or covered either in paragraphs or individual sentences in the passage and the purpose or intention of the information that is given.

- There are 1-2 Rhetorical Purpose questions per passage.
- There is a special emphasis on these questions. Some questions ask about entire sentences, not just words or phrases.

TYPE 8 Insert Text Questions

Insert Text questions require the test taker to determine where in the passage another sentence should be placed. These questions ask the test taker to consider various aspects, including grammar, logic, connecting words, and flow, when deciding where the new sentence best belongs. Insert Text questions do not always appear in a passage. When they are asked, there is only one Insert Text question per passage. This question always appears right before the last question.

- There are 0-1 Insert Text questions per passage.
- There is a special emphasis on these questions. Almost every passage now has 1 Insert Text question.

TYPE 9 Prose Summary Questions

Prose Summary questions require the test taker to understand the main point of the passage and then to select sentences which emphasize the main point. These questions present a sentence which is essentially a thesis statement for the entire passage. The sentence synthesizes the main points of the passage. The test taker must then choose three out of six sentences that most closely describe points mentioned in the introductory sentence. As for the other three choices, they describe minor points, have incorrect information, or contain information that does not appear in the passage, so they are all therefore incorrect. This is always the last question asked about a Reading passage, but it does not always appear. Instead, a Fill in a Table question may appear in its place.

- There are 0-1 Prose Summary questions per passage.
- There is a special emphasis on these questions. Almost every passage now has 1 Prose Summary question.

TYPE 10 Fill in a Table Questions

Fill in a Table questions require the test taker to have a comprehensive understanding of the entire passage. These questions typically break the passage down into two—or sometimes three—main points or themes. The test taker must then read a number of sentences or phrases and determine which of the points or themes the sentences or phrases refer to. These questions may ask the test taker to consider cause and effect, to compare and contrast, or to understand various theories or ideas covered. This is always the last question asked about a Reading passage, but it does not always appear. Instead, a Prose Summary question may appear in its place.

- There are 0-1 Fill in a Table questions per passage.
- These questions rarely appear anymore. Prose Summary questions are much more common than Fill in a Table questions.

Actual Test

01

Reading Section Directions

This section measures your ability to understand academic passages in English. You will have **54 minutes** to read and answer questions about **3 passages**. A clock at the top of the screen will show you how much time is remaining.

Most questions are worth 1 point but the last question for each passage is worth more than 1 point. The directions for the last question indicate how many points you may receive.

Some passages include a word or phrase that is underlined in blue. Click on the word or phrase to see a definition or an explanation.

When you want to move to the next question, click on **NEXT**. You may skip questions and go back to them later. If you want to return to previous questions, click on **BACK**. You can click on **REVIEW** at any time, and the review screen will show you which questions you have answered and which you have not answered. From this review screen, you may go directly to any question you have already seen in the Reading section.

Click on **CONTINUE** to go on.

Comets

Halley's Comet in 1986

Among the most beautiful of all heavenly bodies are comets, which glow brightly as they streak across the sky. However, the vast majority of comets never approach anywhere near Earth but instead wander through two of the outer regions of the solar system called the Kuiper Belt and the Oort Cloud. Occasionally, comets change directions and head toward the inner solar system, where they begin orbiting the sun at regular intervals. Depending upon how much time elapses between sightings, their orbits may be termed either short period or long period. Eventually, most comets that enter the inner solar system are destroyed by the heat of the sun.

The primary reason that the sun's heat tears comets apart is that they are relatively small and are composed mostly of ice, rock, and dust. Astronomers believe comets may have inner cores comprised of solid rock while their outer layers contain ice and dust coated with various organic substances. The ice is mostly frozen water, but it may contain traces of methane, ammonia, carbon dioxide, and carbon monoxide as well. When the comets are in the extensive cold regions of the outer solar system, they remain frozen balls, yet as they venture closer to the sun, they start warming up. Their outer layers melt and become gaseous in form, giving the comets the cloudy atmosphere that astronomers call a coma.

The radiation of the sun's solar wind pushes the dust in the coma away from the main body of the comet, whereupon it forms a tail consisting of that dust. Meanwhile, the radiation converts some of the comet's gases into ions, which form an additional tail. Due to the action of the solar wind pushing the comet, the dust tail and gas tail always point away from the sun. Additionally, the two do not combine but instead appear as separate tails streaming away from the comet in different directions. While astronomers believe the cores of most comets are fewer than sixteen kilometers wide, their tails can be immensely longer. Small tails may be around one million kilometers in length, and longer tails can be up to one

hundred million kilometers long. A comet with a long tail is more easily observable because, as it passes near the sun, its tail may glow since it is reflecting sunlight. Some comets in the past had tails so long and bright that they could be observed from the Earth during the daytime.

All known comets are classified as either short-period or long-period comets. The former make regular appearances in the inner solar system at intervals of fewer than two hundred years, yet they are most commonly found in the Kuiper Belt, a cold region which is located past Neptune and is between thirty and fifty-five astronomical units (AU) from the sun. Halley's Comet, named after the astronomer who predicted the period of its orbit, is a well-known short-term comet that appears roughly every seventy-five years. Long-period comets, however, arrive in the inner solar system at intervals of more than two centuries. Astronomers think they mostly reside in the Oort Cloud, a region in the solar system between at least 2,000 and 50,000 AU from the sun. Comet McNaught, which appeared in 2007, is a long-period comet with an orbit of the sun estimated to take more than 92,000 years.

Astronomers are uncertain as to why comets enter the inner solar system. One theory is that collisions between comets send them in new directions, and another is that the gravitational pull of the outer planets—or even passing stars—may pull or push comets toward the sun. Almost all comets that move through the inner solar system eventually die as, over thousands of years of continuously orbiting the sun, their ice and rocky substance melts away until they become small lumps of rock that can no longer produce comas or tails. Other comets are destroyed when they collide with the sun or planets. A spectacular example of the latter happened when Comet Shoemaker-Levy 9 collided with Jupiter in July 1994. The comet broke apart and bombarded Jupiter by impacting it several times, which caused astronomers to fear that a similar action might happen on the Earth someday.

*Glossary

inner solar system: the part of the solar system that contains the planets Mercury, Venus, Earth, and Mars
astronomical unit: the average distance between Earth and the sun

1 Which of the following can be inferred from paragraph 1 about comets?

  Ⓐ It can take them thousands of years to reach the inner solar system.

  Ⓑ The sun's gravity causes some of them to change their orbits.

  Ⓒ There are fewer of them in the inner solar system than there are in the Oort Cloud.

  Ⓓ They have been known to collide with planets in the inner solar system.

  Paragraph 1 is marked with an arrow (➡).

2 The word "traces" in the passage is closest in meaning to

  Ⓐ varieties

  Ⓑ deposits

  Ⓒ profusions

  Ⓓ hints

Comets

➡ Among the most beautiful of all heavenly bodies are comets, which glow brightly as they streak across the sky. However, the vast majority of comets never approach anywhere near Earth but instead wander through two of the outer regions of the solar system called the Kuiper Belt and the Oort Cloud. Occasionally, comets change directions and head toward the inner solar system, where they begin orbiting the sun at regular intervals. Depending upon how much time elapses between sightings, their orbits may be termed either short period or long period. Eventually, most comets that enter the inner solar system are destroyed by the heat of the sun.

The primary reason that the sun's heat tears comets apart is that they are relatively small and are composed mostly of ice, rock, and dust. Astronomers believe comets may have inner cores comprised of solid rock while their outer layers contain ice and dust coated with various organic substances. The ice is mostly frozen water, but it may contain traces of methane, ammonia, carbon dioxide, and carbon monoxide as well. When the comets are in the extensive cold regions of the outer solar system, they remain frozen balls, yet as they venture closer to the sun, they start warming up. Their outer layers melt and become gaseous in form, giving the comets the cloudy atmosphere that astronomers call a coma.

*Glossary

inner solar system: the part of the solar system that contains the planets Mercury, Venus, Earth, and Mars

3 According to paragraph 3, which of the following is true about the tails of comets?

   (A) Both of them are formed due to the effects of ions.

   (B) They often combine with one another to create a single tail.

   (C) They can grow to be as long as one astronomical unit.

   (D) The action of solar wind on dust can cause one of them to form.

Paragraph 3 is marked with an arrow (➡).

4 In paragraph 4, the author uses "Halley's Comet" as an example of

   (A) one of the few comets that many people have heard of

   (B) the only comet that has been seen for thousands of years

   (C) a comet that orbits the sun in a short-term period

   (D) the first comet to be named after an astronomer

Paragraph 4 is marked with an arrow (⇨).

5 According to paragraph 4, which of the following is NOT true about long-period comets?

   (A) They are more commonly found in the Oort Cloud than in the Kuiper Belt.

   (B) They take more than two centuries to return to the inner solar system.

   (C) They are often more than 2,000 AU away from the sun during their orbits.

   (D) They are larger in size than comets that orbit the sun more quickly.

Paragraph 4 is marked with an arrow (⇨).

➡ The radiation of the sun's solar wind pushes the dust in the coma away from the main body of the comet, whereupon it forms a tail consisting of that dust. Meanwhile, the radiation converts some of the comet's gases into ions, which form an additional tail. Due to the action of the solar wind pushing the comet, the dust tail and gas tail always point away from the sun. Additionally, the two do not combine but instead appear as separate tails streaming away from the comet in different directions. While astronomers believe the cores of most comets are fewer than sixteen kilometers wide, their tails can be immensely longer. Small tails may be around one million kilometers in length, and longer tails can be up to one hundred million kilometers long. A comet with a long tail is more easily observable because, as it passes near the sun, its tail may glow since it is reflecting sunlight. Some comets in the past had tails so long and bright that they could be observed from the Earth during the daytime.

⇨ All known comets are classified as either short-period or long-period comets. The former make regular appearances in the inner solar system at intervals of fewer than two hundred years, yet they are most commonly found in the Kuiper Belt, a cold region which is located past Neptune and is between thirty and fifty-five astronomical units (AU) from the sun. Halley's Comet, named after the astronomer who predicted the period of its orbit, is a well-known short-term comet that appears roughly every seventy-five years. Long-period comets, however, arrive in the inner solar system at intervals of more than two centuries. Astronomers believe they mostly reside in the Oort Cloud, a region in the solar system between at least 2,000 and 50,000 AU from the sun. Comet McNaught, which appeared in 2007, is a long-period comet with an orbit of the sun estimated to take more than 92,000 years.

*Glossary

astronomical unit: the average distance between Earth and the sun

6   According to paragraph 5, comets may enter the inner solar system because

   Ⓐ planets in the inner solar system exert gravitational pull on them

   Ⓑ they may hit other comets and therefore change the course of their orbits

   Ⓒ the sun's gravitational force causes them to move closer to it

   Ⓓ nearby stars that have just formed can make them change their orbits

Paragraph 5 is marked with an arrow (➡).

7   The word "bombarded" in the passage is closest in meaning to

   Ⓐ invaded

   Ⓑ transformed

   Ⓒ assaulted

   Ⓓ damaged

8   In paragraph 5, the author implies that comets

   Ⓐ could possibly collide with the Earth sometime in the future

   Ⓑ seldom enter the inner solar system due to Jupiter's powerful gravity

   Ⓒ strike the sun more often than they hit any of the planets

   Ⓓ may sometimes stop orbiting the sun and start orbiting a planet

Paragraph 5 is marked with an arrow (➡).

➡ Astronomers are uncertain as to why comets enter the inner solar system. One theory is that collisions between comets send them in new directions, and another is that the gravitational pull of the outer planets—or even passing stars—may pull or push comets toward the sun. Almost all comets that move through the inner solar system eventually die as, over thousands of years of continuously orbiting the sun, their ice and rocky substance melts away until they become small lumps of rock that can no longer produce comas or tails. Other comets are destroyed when they collide with the sun or planets. A spectacular example of the latter happened when Comet Shoemaker-Levy 9 collided with Jupiter in July 1994. The comet broke apart and bombarded Jupiter by impacting it several times, which caused astronomers to fear that a similar action might happen on the Earth someday.

9 Look at the four squares [■] that indicate where the following sentence could be added to the passage.

This, however, is a rare occurrence, and most people live their entire lives without even seeing a comet at night, let alone during the daylight hours.

Where would the sentence best fit?

Click on a square [■] to add the sentence to the passage.

The radiation of the sun's solar wind pushes the dust in the coma away from the main body of the comet, whereupon it forms a tail consisting of that dust. Meanwhile, the radiation converts some of the comet's gases into ions, which form an additional tail. Due to the action of the solar wind pushing the comet, the dust tail and gas tail always point away from the sun. Additionally, the two do not combine but instead appear as separate tails streaming away from the comet in different directions. While astronomers believe the cores of most comets are fewer than sixteen kilometers wide, their tails can be immensely longer. **1** Small tails may be around one million kilometers in length, and longer tails can be up to one hundred million kilometers long. **2** A comet with a long tail is more easily observable because, as it passes near the sun, its tail may glow since it is reflecting sunlight. **3** Some comets in the past had tails so long and bright that they could be observed from the Earth during the daytime. **4**

10 **Directions:** An introductory sentence for a brief summary of the passage is provided below. Complete the summary by selecting the THREE answer choices that express the most important ideas of the passage. Some sentences do not belong because they express ideas that are not presented in the passage or are minor ideas in the passage. **This question is worth 2 points.**

Drag your answer choices to the spaces where they belong. To remove an answer choice, click on it. To review the passage, click on **VIEW TEXT**.

Comets are heavenly bodies that sometimes visit the inner solar system and develop tails when they get near the sun.

-

-

-

ANSWER CHOICES

1. Short-period comets move near Earth every two centuries or sooner whereas long-period comets take longer to appear.

2. On rare occasions, the orbits of some comets cause them to run into the sun, the planets, or even asteroids.

3. Halley's Comet and Comet McNaught both have orbits that took them near Earth in recent times.

4. Comets that venture into the interior of the solar system may often be destroyed or may collide with a celestial body.

5. Solar wind can cause both dust tails and gas tails to manifest on comets in the inner solar system.

6. Some comets have tails which are so bright that they take up a large portion of the night sky.

The Development of Cities in Colonial America

When Europeans first arrived in the lands comprising the thirteen colonies that would become the United States, there were no cities of any kind. The initial years of European settlement were a period during which survival was emphasized as settlers lived inside or near small fortified outposts such as Jamestown, Virginia. Over time, those settlements would become villages, towns, and, eventually, cities. By the mid-eighteenth century, Boston, New York City, Philadelphia, and Charleston ranked among the largest cities in colonial America. They were founded alongside or near the coast and had access to fine harbors and trade routes leading to Europe and Africa. They became the business, political, military, religious, social, and intellectual centers of the colonies and, later, the United States after it attained independence.

Native Americans founded great cities in Mexico and South America, where the Spanish and Portuguese established their colonies, yet the Atlantic seaboard was bereft of even a single great metropolis when the Europeans arrived. The majority of Native Americans instead dwelled in large villages. At first, European colonization along the Atlantic Ocean was slow, so it was not until the early 1600s that permanent settlements were established by people other than the Spanish. In 1607, the first permanent English colony was founded at Jamestown, Virginia. Soon afterward, several other settlements arose in Virginia. In 1620, the Pilgrims founded Plymouth, Massachusetts, and the Puritans started nearby Boston in 1630. Dutch colonists established New Amsterdam, which eventually became New York City, in 1625. William Penn founded Philadelphia in 1682, and, despite its late start, it had become the largest colonial city by the 1750s. Further south, Charleston, South Carolina, was established by English settlers from Bermuda in 1670.

These towns immediately became centers of trade, and, as trade expanded, they increased in size and developed into cities. Most trade was with England since the English had enacted laws directing their colonists to trade with England and to purchase goods manufactured in England. The most common colonial industries were farming, furniture building, shipbuilding, fishing, and whaling. Surplus food—especially wheat—was traded overseas through port towns. Shipbuilding was a common industry up and down the coast as the colonists had access to vast supplies of timber in the untamed wilderness of the American interior, so skilled shipwrights were able to construct many sailing vessels. The offshore waters also had enormous stocks of cod, haddock, and other food fish. The men in New England towns such as Gloucester amassed a great amount of wealth from fishing and whaling.

As cities grew, so did their populations. By 1750, Philadelphia, with a population of approximately 25,000 people, was the largest city in colonial America. It overtook Boston, which had 16,000 inhabitants by the same year. New York City was a close third with 13,000 residents. One reason Philadelphia

attracted so many people was that William Penn had established a policy of religious tolerance upon founding the colony of Pennsylvania, so people flocked there to escape persecution. Each major American city had differences in the religious practices of the majority of its residents as well as divisions according to class. The wealthiest merchants stood at the top of society. They were followed by a middle class comprised of professionals, clergymen, educators, and skilled craftsmen and a lower class dominated by unskilled laborers, fishermen, and sailors.

As cities expanded, efforts at urban planning were made, but places still experienced haphazard growth. Most American cities used grid plans that had streets intersecting at right angles. Penn planned Philadelphia with broad streets and room between houses in the hope that the distances would lessen the problems caused by fire, disease, and overcrowding that plagued European cities during his lifetime. Boston, meanwhile, suffered from a lack of planning, so its streets were built in various directions. Along the streets of American cities were massive houses—some several stories high—which were built for the wealthy, and more modest dwellings for members of the middle and lower classes. Housing styles varied from region to region and depended primarily upon which countries' settlers had first moved there. As a result, American cities had their own characteristics, making them distinct from one another.

*Glossary

fortified: strengthened for the purpose of defending against physical attacks
grid: a network of horizontal and perpendicular lines

Beginning ▲

11 In paragraph 1, the author's description of cities in colonial America mentions which of the following?

  Ⓐ The average population of the largest cities in the American colonies

  Ⓑ The fortifications that were constructed to keep the cities safe from attack

  Ⓒ The colonies in which the most important of these cities were located

  Ⓓ The relative locations of the cities and the importance of their positions

Paragraph 1 is marked with an arrow (➡).

12 The phrase "bereft of" in the passage is closest in meaning to

  Ⓐ deprived of

  Ⓑ considered for

  Ⓒ located by

  Ⓓ sufficient for

13 According to paragraph 2, which of the following is NOT true about the American colonies?

  Ⓐ William Penn was the founder of one about the first American colonies.

  Ⓑ The Dutch established a colony of their own that they named New York.

  Ⓒ The first one that was permanent in nature was Jamestown, Virginia.

  Ⓓ Several were established by the Atlantic coast in the seventeenth century.

Paragraph 2 is marked with an arrow (⇨).

The Development of Cities in Colonial America

➡ When Europeans first arrived in the lands comprising the thirteen colonies that would become the United States, there were no cities of any kind. The initial years of European settlement were a period during which survival was emphasized as settlers lived inside or near small fortified outposts such as Jamestown, Virginia. Over time, those settlements would become villages, towns, and, eventually, cities. By the mid-eighteenth century, Boston, New York City, Philadelphia, and Charleston ranked among the largest cities in colonial America. They were founded alongside or near the coast and had access to fine harbors and trade routes leading to Europe and Africa. They became the business, political, military, religious, social, and intellectual centers of the colonies and, later, the United States after it attained independence.

⇨ Native Americans founded great cities in Mexico and South America, where the Spanish and Portuguese established their colonies, yet the Atlantic seaboard was bereft of even a single great metropolis when the Europeans arrived. The majority of Native Americans instead dwelled in large villages. At first, European colonization along the Atlantic Ocean was slow, so it was not until the early 1600s that permanent settlements were established by people other than the Spanish. In 1607, the first permanent English colony was founded at Jamestown, Virginia. Soon afterward, several other settlements arose in Virginia. In 1620, the Pilgrims founded Plymouth, Massachusetts, and the Puritans started nearby Boston in 1630. Dutch colonists established New Amsterdam, which eventually became New York City, in 1625. William Penn founded Philadelphia in 1682, and, despite its late start, it had become the largest colonial city by the 1750s. Further south, Charleston, South Carolina, was established by English settlers from Bermuda in 1670.

*Glossary

fortified: strengthened for the purpose of defending against physical attacks

▼

14 Which of the sentences below best expresses the essential information in the highlighted sentence in the passage? Incorrect answer choices change the meaning in important ways or leave out essential information.

Shipbuilding was a common industry up and down the coast as the colonists had access to vast supplies of timber in the untamed wilderness of the American interior, so skilled shipwrights were able to construct many sailing vessels.

(A) Many expert shipbuilders moved to America since they were able to have access to high-quality timber that could be found in the expansive forests in the American interior.

(B) The colonists frequently chopped down trees in the American interior and then transported them to the coast, where they were used to make all kinds of ships.

(C) The American shipbuilding industry became one of the world's largest thanks to the enormous supply of lumber as well as the numerous shipwrights living in the colonies.

(D) Thanks to the large amounts of wood that were readily available in America, many colonists worked in the shipbuilding industry and built a large number of ships.

15 In paragraph 3, the author uses "Gloucester" as an example of

(A) a city in New England that benefitted from the catching of fish

(B) the American city that is best remembered for whaling nowadays

(C) the New England city that was the leader of the fishing industry

(D) a colonial American city that survived thanks to its fishermen

Paragraph 3 is marked with an arrow (➡).

➡ These towns immediately became centers of trade, and, as trade expanded, they increased in size and developed into cities. Most trade was with England since the English had enacted laws directing their colonists to trade with England and to purchase goods manufactured in England. The most common colonial industries were farming, furniture building, shipbuilding, fishing, and whaling. Surplus food—especially wheat—was traded overseas through port towns. Shipbuilding was a common industry up and down the coast as the colonists had access to vast supplies of timber in the untamed wilderness of the American interior, so skilled shipwrights were able to construct many sailing vessels. The offshore waters also had enormous stocks of cod, haddock, and other food fish. The men in New England towns such as Gloucester amassed a great amount of wealth from fishing and whaling.

PASSAGE 2

REVIEW

HELP

BACK

NEXT

HIDE TIME 00:54:00

More Available

16 According to paragraph 3, the American colonists mostly traded with England because

Ⓐ they preferred to trade with the people living in their country of origin

Ⓑ the fact that they all spoke the same language made trading more convenient

Ⓒ they were required to do so by laws that had been passed by the English

Ⓓ it was faster to sail to England than to any other countries in Europe

Paragraph 3 is marked with an arrow (➡).

17 The word "flocked" in the passage is closest in meaning to

Ⓐ visited

Ⓑ gathered

Ⓒ toured

Ⓓ transferred

➡ These towns immediately became centers of trade, and, as trade expanded, they too increased in size and developed into cities. Most trade was with England since the English had enacted laws directing their colonists to trade with England and to purchase goods manufactured in England. The most common colonial industries were farming, furniture building, shipbuilding, fishing, and whaling. Surplus food—especially wheat—was traded overseas through port towns. Shipbuilding was a common industry up and down the coast as the colonists had access to vast supplies of timber in the untamed wilderness of the American interior, so skilled shipwrights were able to construct many sailing vessels. The offshore waters also had enormous stocks of cod, haddock, and other food fish. The men in New England towns such as Gloucester amassed a great amount of wealth from fishing and whaling.

As cities grew, so did their populations. By 1750, Philadelphia, with a population of approximately 25,000 people, was the largest city in colonial America. It overtook Boston, which had 16,000 inhabitants by the same year. New York City was a close third with 13,000 residents. One reason Philadelphia attracted so many people was that William Penn had established a policy of religious tolerance upon founding the colony of Pennsylvania, so people flocked there to escape persecution. Each major American city had differences in the religious practices of the majority of its residents as well as divisions according to class. The wealthiest merchants stood at the top of society. They were followed by a middle class comprised of professionals, clergymen, educators, and skilled craftsmen and a lower class dominated by unskilled laborers, fishermen, and sailors.

18 In paragraph 5, the author implies that Philadelphia

Ⓐ had been designed by William Penn while he was still living in England

Ⓑ quickly became larger than Boston thanks to the planning that went into building it

Ⓒ was planned in a way so that it did not resemble any major European cities

Ⓓ had a design that was imitated by the founders of several other American cities

Paragraph 5 is marked with an arrow (➡).

➡ As cities expanded, efforts at urban planning were made, but places still experienced haphazard growth. Most American cities used grid plans that had streets intersecting at right angles. Penn planned Philadelphia with broad streets and room between houses in the hope that the distances would lessen the problems caused by fire, disease, and overcrowding that plagued European cities during his lifetime. Boston, meanwhile, suffered from a lack of planning, so its streets were built in various directions. Along the streets of American cities were massive houses—some several stories high—which were built for the wealthy, and more modest dwellings for members of the middle and lower classes. Housing styles varied from region to region and depended primarily upon which countries' settlers had first moved there. As a result, American cities had their own characteristics, making them distinct from one another.

*Glossary

grid: a network of horizontal and perpendicular lines

More Available

19 Look at the four squares [■] that indicate where the following sentence could be added to the passage.

None of them was comparable in size to European urban centers such as London and Paris, yet they were still highly influential in the American colonies.

Where would the sentence best fit?

Click on a square [■] to add the sentence to the passage.

As cities grew, so did their populations. By 1750, Philadelphia, with a population of approximately 25,000 people, was the largest city in colonial America. ■ It overtook Boston, which had 16,000 inhabitants by the same year. ■ New York City was a close third with 13,000 residents. ■ One reason Philadelphia attracted so many people was that William Penn had established a policy of religious tolerance upon founding the colony of Pennsylvania, so people flocked there to escape persecution. ■ Each major American city had differences in the religious practices of the majority of its residents as well as divisions according to class. The wealthiest merchants stood at the top of society. They were followed by a middle class comprised of professionals, clergymen, educators, and skilled craftsmen and a lower class dominated by unskilled laborers, fishermen, and sailors.

20 **Directions:** An introductory sentence for a brief summary of the passage is provided below. Complete the summary by selecting the THREE answer choices that express the most important ideas of the passage. Some sentences do not belong because they express ideas that are not presented in the passage or are minor ideas in the passage. **This question is worth 2 points.**

Drag your answer choices to the spaces where they belong. To remove an answer choice, click on it. To review the passage, click on **VIEW TEXT**.

As cities in colonial America grew in size, they became centers of trade and also developed their own unique characteristics.

-

-

-

ANSWER CHOICES

1 Cities in the American colonies were the religious, intellectual, and economic centers of the colonies in which they were located.

2 While many American cities were established with grid plans, they each had characteristics that made them unique.

3 William Penn founded Philadelphia, which became the largest city in the American colonies by 1750.

4 Most of the people living in colonial American cities belonged to the lower class, but there were also people in the upper and middle classes.

5 When American towns started trading with England, several of them saw their populations increase so that they became cities.

6 The majority of the settlements founded in America in the 1600s were small fortified areas that provided protection to the colonists.

Social and Solitary Animals

A mother penguin and her chick

Animals are either social or solitary in nature. Social animals live in either small or large groups while solitary animals live alone and typically only join others of their species to mate and to produce offspring. Most social animals are prey whereas the majority of solitary animals are predators, but there are exceptions. All mammals, fish, birds, reptiles, and amphibians engage in one of these lifestyles. The reasons animals live with others or alone differ from species to species, but both kinds of behavior have some common advantages and disadvantages.

The two main types of social animal groups consist of families that remain together as a single unit and animals that have instinctual needs to form herds. Typical family groups consist of a small number of animals of the same species. Lions, wolves, and many primates are well-known examples of animals that form family groups. Males, females, and offspring live together and share a territory in which they hunt or forage for food. Meanwhile, herd animals gather in larger numbers and typically consist of unrelated animals. The animals in these groups act in concert with one another in many ways, including feeding, defending their young, and making long journeys together. For instance, herds comprising hundreds of thousands of wildebeests and zebras make long migrations in Africa while traveling to feeding grounds when the seasons change. Other animals, such as caribou in North America and countless species of birds, whales, and fish, make extensive annual migrations to their traditional breeding and birthing grounds.

In a social animal group, there are different degrees of cooperation among members. How animals care for their offspring varies. Animals such as lions, wolves, and elephants care for their young for several years whereas others look after them for shorter periods, and still others abandon their young either after giving birth or laying their eggs. Care for offspring may be shared by adults even if the young animals are

not theirs. Additionally, the division of labor in social groups varies as some members hunt or gather food while others defend their group's territory and look after the young animals. As an example, after a female penguin lays an egg, the male and female take turns guarding it—and later the chick—while the other hunts for food. Another characteristic of social animals is that there are leaders, which are usually alpha males, and followers, which comprise the majority of the animals, in each group. Finally, in some social animal groups, different generations of adults remain together for many years.

Conversely, solitary animals are the complete opposites of social animals. Predators, including tigers, leopards, hawks, eagles, and great white sharks, are commonly solitary animals. When they join others of their species, they do so to mate. Some may choose the same mate for many years despite not forming long-term family groups. Sometimes the males help raise their offspring for a short time, but most of them leave the females to take care of the newborn animals by themselves. Even female-offspring pairings are ephemeral since the offspring generally leave their mothers after reaching adulthood.

There are advantages and disadvantages to social and solitary lifestyles. The primary benefit to social animals is that they can cooperate to help survive. Lions and wolves hunt in packs, permitting them to bring down bigger prey and therefore get more food. They can also defend their territory better as a group. Musk oxen and water buffalo form tight groups to protect their young from predatory animals. The main drawback to living in groups is that resources may be lacking if there are too many animals in one place. In lean times, some group members may die from starvation. Solitary animals have the opposite advantages and disadvantages of social animals. While they may not starve during times of drought or famine, they have fewer food options. A single leopard, for instance, cannot normally kill a herd animal such as a buffalo whereas lions working together can. Solitary animals are also vulnerable to attacks by others. If injured, they have a lower chance of survival than wounded animals that have a support group to provide them with food and protection while they heal.

*Glossary

pack: a group of animals that run and hunt together
famine: a period in which there is a lack of food, often due to conditions caused by the weather

Social and Solitary Animals

➡ Animals are either social or solitary in nature. Social animals live in either small or large groups while solitary animals live alone and typically only join others of their species to mate and to produce offspring. Most social animals are prey whereas the majority of solitary animals are predators, but there are exceptions. All mammals, fish, birds, reptiles, and amphibians engage in one of these lifestyles. The reasons animals live with others or alone differ from species to species, but both kinds of behavior have some common advantages and disadvantages.

⇨ The two main types of social animal groups consist of families that remain together as a single unit and animals that have instinctual needs to form herds. Typical family groups consist of a small number of animals of the same species. Lions, wolves, and many primates are well-known examples of animals that form family groups. Males, females, and offspring live together and share a territory in which they hunt or forage for food. Meanwhile, herd animals gather in larger numbers and typically consist of unrelated animals. The animals in these groups act in concert with one another in many ways, including feeding, defending their young, and making long journeys together. For instance, herds comprising hundreds of thousands of wildebeests and zebras make long migrations in Africa while traveling to feeding grounds when the seasons change. Other animals, such as caribou in North America and countless species of birds, whales, and fish, make extensive annual migrations to their traditional breeding and birthing grounds.

21 According to paragraph 1, which of the following is true about social animals?

Ⓐ Birds, mammals, and fish are the most common types of social animals.

Ⓑ The sizes of the groups in which they live may be either big or small.

Ⓒ They live together with others in order to mate and to reproduce.

Ⓓ The only social animals are those which are commonly hunted as prey.

Paragraph 1 is marked with an arrow (➡).

22 The word "forage" in the passage is closest in meaning to

Ⓐ search

Ⓑ farm

Ⓒ dig

Ⓓ steal

23 In paragraph 2, the author uses "wildebeests and zebras" as examples of

Ⓐ social animals that make long migratory trips with one another

Ⓑ the animals that are found in the greatest number in Africa

Ⓒ herd animals that gather together for the purpose of protecting their young

Ⓓ two species of animals that are social in behavior to avoid African predators

Paragraph 2 is marked with an arrow (⇨).

24 In paragraph 3, the author's description of how social animals cooperate with one another mentions all of the following EXCEPT:

- (A) the reason that some animals desert their young after they give birth
- (B) the amount of time that certain animals spend caring for their young
- (C) the manner in which some animals divide the labor that they do
- (D) the breakdown of some groups into alpha males and followers

Paragraph 3 is marked with an arrow (➡).

25 According to paragraph 3, penguins divide labor by

- (A) having the female guard the egg or chick while the male searches for food
- (B) having large groups guard the eggs and chicks while other penguins search for food
- (C) having a male or female guard the egg or chick while the other searches for food
- (D) having chicks guard the eggs while both male and female adults search for food

Paragraph 3 is marked with an arrow (➡).

26 The word "ephemeral" in the passage is closest in meaning to

- (A) conditional
- (B) temporary
- (C) inadequate
- (D) reversible

➡ In a social animal group, there are different degrees of cooperation among members. How animals care for their offspring varies. Animals such as lions, wolves, and elephants care for their young for several years whereas others look after them for shorter periods, and still others abandon their young either after giving birth or laying their eggs. Care for offspring may be shared by adults even if the young animals are not theirs. Additionally, the division of labor in social groups varies as some members hunt or gather food while others defend their group's territory and look after the young animals. As an example, after a female penguin lays an egg, the male and female take turns guarding it—and later the chick—while the other hunts for food. Another characteristic of social animals is that there are leaders, which are usually alpha males, and followers, which comprise the majority of the animals, in each group. Finally, in some social animal groups, different generations of adults remain together for many years.

Conversely, solitary animals are the complete opposites of social animals. Predators, including tigers, leopards, hawks, eagles, and great white sharks, are commonly solitary animals. When they join others of their species, they do so to mate. Some may choose the same mate for many years despite not forming long-term family groups. Sometimes the males help raise their offspring for a short time, but most of them leave the females to take care of the newborn animals by themselves. Even female-offspring pairings are ephemeral since the offspring generally leave their mothers after reaching adulthood.

End

27 According to paragraph 5, social animals benefit from their behavior because

  Ⓐ their living together can ensure that the young generation is taken care of

  Ⓑ they can evolve more easily when there are large groups of them

  Ⓒ their large numbers can deter most predators from attacking them

  Ⓓ the fact that they work together makes it easier for all of them to survive

Paragraph 5 is marked with an arrow (➡).

28 In paragraph 5, the author implies that solitary animals

  Ⓐ have trouble getting food for themselves when they are injured

  Ⓑ usually exist in smaller numbers than social animals

  Ⓒ tend to bear only a few offspring when they reproduce

  Ⓓ are the first animals to starve whenever a region suffers from famine

Paragraph 5 is marked with an arrow (➡).

➡ There are advantages and disadvantages to social and solitary lifestyles. The primary benefit to social animals is that they can cooperate to help survive. Lions and wolves hunt in packs, permitting them to bring down bigger prey and therefore get more food. They can also defend their territory better as a group. Musk oxen and water buffalo form tight groups to protect their young from predatory animals. The main drawback to living in groups is that resources may be lacking if there are too many animals in one place. In lean times, some group members may die from starvation. Solitary animals have the opposite advantages and disadvantages of social animals. While they may not starve during times of drought or famine, they have fewer food options. A single leopard, for instance, cannot normally kill a herd animal such as a buffalo whereas lions working together can. Solitary animals are also vulnerable to attacks by others. If injured, they have a lower chance of survival than wounded animals that have a support group to provide them with food and protection while they heal.

*Glossary

pack: a group of animals that run and hunt together
famine: a period in which there is a lack of food, often due to conditions caused by the weather

29 Look at the four squares [■] that indicate
    where the following sentence could be added
    to the passage.

    **As a general rule, the strongest male in the
    herd becomes the head of the group while
    the others accept his leadership until he
    no longer has the strength to maintain his
    position.**

    Where would the sentence best fit?

    Click on a square [■] to add the sentence to the passage.

In a social animal group, there are different degrees of cooperation among the members. How animals care for their offspring may vary. Animals such as lions, wolves, and elephants care for their young for several years whereas other look after them for shorter periods, and still others abandon their young either after giving birth or laying their eggs. Care for the offspring may be shared by the adults even if the young animals are not theirs. **1** Additionally, the division of labor in social groups varies as some members hunt or gather food while others defend their group's territory and look after the young animals. **2** As an example, after a female penguin lays an egg, the male and female take turns guarding it—and later the chick—while the other hunts for food in the ocean. **3** Another characteristic of social animals is that there are leaders, which are usually alpha males, and followers, which comprise the majority of the animals, in each group. **4** Finally, in some social animal groups, different generations of adults remain together for many years.

30 Directions: Select the appropriate statements from the answer choices and match them to the type of animal to which they relate. TWO of the answer choices will NOT be used. **This question is worth 3 points.**

Drag your answer choices to the spaces where they belong. To remove an answer choice, click on it. To review the passage, click on **VIEW TEXT**.

ANSWER CHOICES

1. Are better able to protect their offspring from attacking animals

2. May divide the labor between one another whenever they are together

3. Are more susceptible to dying from diseases than members of the other group

4. Are more frequently predators than they are prey animals

5. Usually belong to either the amphibian or reptile families

6. Do not have as many options for food as the other type of animal

7. Are among the first to die when there is little food in an area

TYPE OF ANIMAL

Social Animals (Select 3)

-
-
-

Solitary Animals (Select 2)

-
-

Actual Test

02

CONTINUE

Reading Section Directions

This section measures your ability to understand academic passages in English. You will have **54 minutes** to read and answer questions about **3 passages**. A clock at the top of the screen will show you how much time is remaining.

Most questions are worth 1 point but the last question for each passage is worth more than 1 point. The directions for the last question indicate how many points you may receive.

Some passages include a word or phrase that is underlined in blue. Click on the word or phrase to see a definition or an explanation.

When you want to move to the next question, click on **NEXT**. You may skip questions and go back to them later. If you want to return to previous questions, click on **BACK**. You can click on **REVIEW** at any time, and the review screen will show you which questions you have answered and which you have not answered. From this review screen, you may go directly to any question you have already seen in the Reading section.

Click on **CONTINUE** to go on.

The Dorset Culture

Presently, the Arctic regions of Canada are inhabited by the Inuit people, but prior to their appearance, a different group of individuals, called the Dorset people, dominated the icy lands of the north. They thrived in that region from approximately 500 B.C. to 1000 A.D. but then gradually went into decline for several reasons. Although the Dorset people lived in the area for more than a millennium, the first evidence proving their existence was not uncovered until the early twentieth century. At an archaeological site at Cape Dorset on Baffin Island, numerous strange artifacts clearly from a group of people older than the Inuit were unearthed. In 1925, Canadian anthropologist Diamond Jenness named this newfound culture for the place where the artifacts had been discovered.

The Dorset people were descendants of a group of Arctic denizens known to contemporary archaeologists as Palaeo-Eskimo cultures. The individuals in these cultures lived during a time when the weather was much warmer than today, so they could hunt in the interior parts of the Arctic. Then, around 500 B.C., the Arctic climate changed and became much colder. The Dorset people survived since they managed to adapt to the frigid weather by developing tools and methods to hunt on ice. For instance, knowing that seals surfaced in holes in the ice to breathe oxygen, they would wait patiently by ice holes for their unwary prey to break the water's surface. They additionally made large harpoons they utilized to spear walruses living on the shore as well as small whales they attacked from the edge of the ice. Among the whale species they hunted from shore—there is no evidence they constructed boats to hunt whales from—were the beluga and narwhal.

Occasionally, the Dorset people remained on the ice to hunt and collect meat for long periods of time, so, to survive, they developed the snow house, which is commonly known as the igloo, and burned animal blubber from whales and other animals to keep warm. The blubber was burned in soapstone lamps that the Dorset people carved and which have the appearance of small bowls. To assist their movement on the ice, the Dorset people developed sled shoes made of bone and ivory that enabled them to slide along the ice like modern-day ice skaters, and they created what appear to be crampons made from the jawbones and teeth of animals they hunted.

Since they needed to be near their food supply, the Dorset people mainly resided near the shores of the Arctic Ocean on the modern-day Canadian mainland, but small groups of others lived on the many islands comprising the Arctic Archipelago. The biggest settlements were located near waters where sea mammals still thrive today. There is no evidence that the Dorset people ever made their homes in the interior of the Canadian Arctic. As for their permanent homes, they primarily constructed them with stones and turf. First, they dug a foundation about half a meter into the ground, and then they utilized dug-up turf and nearby large stones for the walls. The roof was a frame of driftwood or animal bones covered with

animal hides. While Dorset settlements were not large, different groups of them maintained contact with one another and traded items made from jade, copper, quartz, and iron from meteorites.

The Dorset people relied on the sea, winter ice, and mammals that lived near them for their survival. When the northern area experienced a warming period around 1000, the ice began forming later in autumn and breaking up earlier in spring and additionally failed to cover much of the ocean, which left long stretches of water the Dorset people could not cross to reach their traditional hunting areas. Simultaneously, the warming period allowed the ancestors of the modern-day Inuit, called the Thule people, to migrate from Alaska. They had dogs and large sleds and had learned to hunt large whales from boats on the ocean. Able to provide plenty of food for themselves, the Thule people's population expanded, and they engaged in direct competition with the Dorset people. The combination of the warm weather and the Thule people caused the Dorset people to go into terminal decline, and they vanished entirely sometime between 1200 and 1500.

*Glossary

crampon: a piece of metal designed to help a person climb or walk better in snowy or icy conditions

archipelago: a chain of islands

The Dorset Culture

→ Presently, the Arctic regions of Canada are inhabited by the Inuit people, but prior to their appearance, a different group of individuals, called the Dorset people, dominated the icy lands of the north. They thrived in that region from approximately 500 B.C. to 1000 A.D. but then gradually went into decline for several reasons. Although the Dorset people lived in the area for more than a millennium, the first evidence proving their existence was not uncovered until the early twentieth century. At an archaeological site at Cape Dorset on Baffin Island, numerous strange artifacts clearly from a group of people older than the Inuit were unearthed. In 1925, Canadian anthropologist Diamond Jenness named this newfound culture for the place where the artifacts had been discovered.

1 Which of the sentences below best expresses the essential information in the highlighted sentence in the passage? Incorrect answer choices change the meaning in important ways or leave out essential information.

Although the Dorset people lived in the area for more than a millennium, the first evidence proving their existence was not uncovered until the early twentieth century.

(A) The Dorset people managed to hide all evidence of their existence for more than 1,000 years after they vanished.

(B) It was not until the twentieth century, more than 1,000 years after the Dorset people lived, that Dorset artifacts were first found.

(C) Nothing was known of the Dorset people until the 1900s despite them having existed for more than 1,000 years.

(D) During the twentieth century, a large number of artifacts produced by the Dorset people were discovered.

2 According to paragraph 1, which of the following is true about the Dorset people?

(A) The land that they lived on was first occupied by the Inuit people.

(B) They disappeared as a culture after existing for around 1,500 years.

(C) There was one primary reason that caused them to die out.

(D) They were the first humans to live in the Arctic part of Canada.

Paragraph 1 is marked with an arrow (→).

3   Select the TWO answer choices from paragraph 2 that explain how the Dorset people managed to survive in very cold weather. *To receive credit, you must select TWO answers.*

- Ⓐ They came up with innovative hunting methods.
- Ⓑ They built small boats that they could sail on.
- Ⓒ They invented tools that helped them live better.
- Ⓓ They learned how to hunt all kinds of large mammals.

Paragraph 2 is marked with an arrow (➡).

4   In paragraph 3, the author's description of developments by the Dorset people mentions all of the following EXCEPT:

- Ⓐ the animals that they hunted while they remained out on the ice
- Ⓑ which body parts of some animals they used to make objects with
- Ⓒ some of the methods they used to keep themselves from getting too cold
- Ⓓ which invention let them move about more easily on the ice and snow

Paragraph 3 is marked with an arrow (⇨).

➡ The Dorset people were descendants of a group of Arctic denizens known to contemporary archaeologists as Palaeo-Eskimo cultures. The individuals in these cultures lived during a time when the weather was much warmer than today, so they could hunt in the interior parts of the Arctic. Then, around 500 B.C., the Arctic climate changed and became much colder. The Dorset people survived since they managed to adapt to the frigid weather by developing tools and methods to hunt on ice. For instance, knowing that seals surfaced in holes in the ice to breathe oxygen, they would wait patiently by ice holes for their unwary prey to break the water's surface. They additionally made large harpoons they utilized to spear walruses living on the shore as well as small whales they attacked from the edge of the ice. Among the whale species they hunted from shore—there is no evidence they constructed boats to hunt whales from—were the beluga and narwhal.

⇨ Occasionally, the Dorset people remained on the ice to hunt and collect meat for long periods of time, so, to survive, they developed the snow house, which is commonly known as the igloo, and burned animal blubber from whales and other animals to keep warm. The blubber was burned in soapstone lamps that the Dorset people carved and which have the appearance of small bowls. To assist their movement on the ice, the Dorset people developed sled shoes made of bone and ivory that enabled them to slide along the ice like modern-day ice skaters, and they created what appear to be crampons made from the jawbones and teeth of animals they hunted.

*Glossary

crampon: a piece of metal designed to help a person climb or walk better in snowy or icy conditions

5 The word "turf" in the passage is closest in meaning to

Ⓐ bark

Ⓑ moss

Ⓒ branches

Ⓓ grass

6 According to paragraph 4, the Dorset people stayed near the coast because

Ⓐ the weather there was milder than in the interior

Ⓑ it gave them access to an abundant water supply

Ⓒ the soil there was fertile enough for them to grow crops

Ⓓ they remained closer to where their food was

Paragraph 4 is marked with an arrow (➡).

➡ Since they needed to be near their food supply, the Dorset people mainly resided near the shores of the Arctic Ocean on the modern-day Canadian mainland, but small groups of others lived on the many islands comprising the Arctic Archipelago. The biggest settlements were located near waters where sea mammals still thrive today. There is no evidence that the Dorset people ever made their homes in the interior of the Canadian Arctic. As for their permanent homes, they primarily constructed them with stones and turf. First, they dug a foundation about half a meter into the ground, and then they utilized dug-up turf and nearby large stones for the walls. The roof was a frame of driftwood or animal bones covered with animal hides. While Dorset settlements were not large, different groups of them maintained contact with one another and traded items made from jade, copper, quartz, and iron from meteorites.

*Glossary

archipelago: a chain of islands

7   The author discusses "the Thule people" in paragraph 5 in order to

 Ⓐ focus on the land in which they had lived before they migrated elsewhere

 Ⓑ compare the hunting methods they used with those of the Dorset people

 Ⓒ explain how they became the successors to the Dorset people

 Ⓓ provide the years during which they were successful as a culture

Paragraph 5 is marked with an arrow (➡).

8   In stating that the Dorset people went into "terminal decline," the author means that the Dorset people

 Ⓐ moved elsewhere

 Ⓑ went extinct

 Ⓒ lost a war

 Ⓓ failed to adapt

➡ The Dorset people relied on the sea, winter ice, and mammals that lived near them for their survival. When the northern area experienced a warming period around 1000, the ice began forming later in autumn and breaking up earlier in spring and additionally failed to cover much of the ocean, which left long stretches of water the Dorset people could not cross to reach their traditional hunting areas. Simultaneously, the warming period allowed the ancestors of the modern-day Inuit, called the Thule people, to migrate from Alaska. They had dogs and large sleds and had learned to hunt large whales from boats on the ocean. Able to provide plenty of food for themselves, the Thule people's population expanded, and they engaged in direct competition with the Dorset people. The combination of the warm weather and the Thule people caused the Dorset people to go into terminal decline, and they vanished entirely sometime between 1200 and 1500.

9   Look at the four squares [■] that indicate
    where the following sentence could be added
    to the passage.

    **It was capable of keeping multiple people
    safe from the elements despite being made
    primarily of packed snow and ice.**

    Where would the sentence best fit?

    Click on a square [■] to add the sentence to the passage.

■ Occasionally, the Dorset people remained on the ice to hunt and collect meat for long periods of time, so, to survive, they developed the snow house, which is commonly known as the igloo, and burned animal blubber from whales and other animals to keep warm. ■ The blubber was burned in soapstone lamps that the Dorset people carved and which have the appearance of small bowls. ■ To assist their movement on the ice, the Dorset people developed sled shoes made of bone and ivory that enabled them to slide along the ice like modern-day ice skaters, and they created what appear to be crampons made from the jawbones and teeth of animals they hunted. ■

10 **Directions:** An introductory sentence for a brief summary of the passage is provided below. Complete the summary by selecting the THREE answer choices that express the most important ideas of the passage. Some sentences do not belong because they express ideas that are not presented in the passage or are minor ideas in the passage. **This question is worth 2 points.**

Drag your answer choices to the spaces where they belong. To remove an answer choice, click on it. To review the passage, click on **VIEW TEXT**.

The Dorset people survived as a culture in the Arctic region of Canada on account of their ability to adapt to the frigid weather.

-
-
-

ANSWER CHOICES

1. Thanks to a number of inventions, the Dorset people managed to adapt to the harsh weather in which they lived.

2. The Dorset people were one of many different groups, including the Inuit, that lived in the frozen areas of Canada.

3. The Thule people and the Dorset people simultaneously lived in the same region for a short period of time.

4. The Dorset people arose around 500 B.C. and dominated the land that they lived upon until around 1000 A.D.

5. The Dorset people utilized hunting methods that they devised in order to kill animals such as seals, walruses, and whales.

6. The first artifacts that belonged to the Dorset people were discovered during the twentieth century.

The *Iliad* and the *Odyssey*

A statue of Homer

Two of the earliest works of Western literature are the epic poems the *Iliad* and the *Odyssey*, which were composed by the Greek poet Homer. The poems focus primarily on the Trojan War and its aftermath as well as the relationships between mortal men and the Greek gods. Nobody knows if the poems are based on factual events, and whether Homer was real or not is another long-debated matter. Despite questions about their veracity and authorship, the *Iliad* and the *Odyssey* rank among the greatest works in the Western canon.

The Trojan War was a ten-year conflict between the invading Greeks and the defending Trojans. The impetus for the war happened when the Trojan prince Paris—with assistance from the goddess Aphrodite—abducted Helen, the world's most beautiful woman and the wife of the Greek Menelaus. Enraged, the greatest Greek warriors joined an army led by Agamemnon, Menelaus's brother, and sailed to Troy to avenge the insult Paris had given them. Homer's story, told in the *Iliad*, starts near the war's end. According to the *Iliad*, one of the gods has caused the Greek army to fall sick, and the only way to recover is by releasing one of their captives, the daughter of a priest of the god Apollo. The girl had been claimed by Agamemnon, who releases her, but he then takes one of the captives of Achilles, the greatest Greek warrior, as compensation. Achilles becomes livid when Agamemnon seizes the girl Briseis and refuses to battle the Trojans.

Agamemnon assaults the city, but this tactic fails without the presence of Achilles. The Greek leader offers apologies and gifts to Achilles—including returning Briseis—but, still not mollified, Achilles refuses. Achilles's cousin Patroclus begs to be allowed to join the fight. Achilles relents and lends Patroclus his distinctive armor, but Patroclus is killed by Hector, Troy's greatest warrior and the older brother of Paris, who initially believes he has defeated Achilles. Saddened and further enraged, Achilles challenges Hector

to single combat, slays him beneath the walls of Troy, and proceeds to drag Hector's corpse behind his chariot as he circles the city. Later that night, thanks to the assistance of the gods, King Priam of Troy enters the Greek camp, finds Achilles, and begs for his son's body to be returned for a proper funeral. Achilles, touched by the old man's pleas, permits Priam to depart with Hector's body.

At that point in the story, the *Iliad* comes to an end, and subsequent events are covered in the *Odyssey*. The *Odyssey* focuses on the ten-year journey home by Odysseus, the craftiest of the Greeks. He is the king of Ithaca and left behind his wife Penelope and young son Telemachus when he sailed off to war. While the *Odyssey* does not start with the end of the Trojan War, it eventually tells the tale of the death of Achilles, the success of the Trojan Horse, which was Odysseus's idea, and the sacking and burning of Troy. After the war, Odysseus and his men set sail for home but are cursed by the gods Poseidon and Helios, who prevent them from returning to Ithaca. As they try in vain to get home, Odysseus and his men have numerous encounters with monsters such as Cyclops and the witch Circe. Odysseus himself spends seven years on an island with Calypso, a nymph, where he is a virtual prisoner until she relents and permits his departure.

Meanwhile, in Ithaca, Odysseus is believed to have perished, so numerous suitors are competing for Penelope's hand in marriage. She puts them off in the hope that Odysseus will return home, and Telemachus sails off in search of his father. After ten years, Odysseus's men have all died, but he manages to return home at the same time as Telemachus. They decide to kill the suitors and warn Penelope of their plan. She declares that she will marry the person who is strong enough to bend Odysseus's great bow and to shoot an arrow with it. Every suitor fails, but Odysseus, who has disguised himself, successfully strings the bow. He promptly shoots a suitor, and then he, Telemachus, and some loyal followers slaughter the remaining interlopers.

*Glossary

canon: a collection of literary works representative of a particular field or place
Cyclops: a giant from Greek mythology that has a single eye in the middle of its head

Beginning

The *Iliad* and the *Odyssey*

➡ Two of the earliest works of Western literature are the epic poems the *Iliad* and the *Odyssey*, which were composed by the Greek poet Homer. The poems focus primarily on the Trojan War and its aftermath as well as the relationships between mortal men and the Greek gods. Nobody knows if the poems are based on factual events, and whether Homer was real or not is another long-debated matter. Despite questions about their veracity and authorship, the *Iliad* and the *Odyssey* rank among the greatest works in the Western canon.

⇨ The Trojan War was a ten-year conflict between the invading Greeks and the defending Trojans. The impetus for the war happened when the Trojan prince Paris—with assistance from the goddess Aphrodite—abducted Helen, the world's most beautiful woman and the wife of the Greek Menelaus. Enraged, the greatest Greek warriors joined an army led by Agamemnon, Menelaus's brother, and sailed to Troy to avenge the insult Paris had given them. Homer's story, told in the *Iliad*, starts near the war's end. According to the *Iliad*, one of the gods has caused the Greek army to fall sick, and the only way to recover is by releasing one of their captives, the daughter of a priest of the god Apollo. The girl had been claimed by Agamemnon, who releases her, but he then takes one of the captives of Achilles, the greatest Greek warrior, as compensation. Achilles becomes livid when Agamemnon seizes the girl Briseis and refuses to battle the Trojans.

11 In paragraph 1, the author implies that Homer

Ⓐ was the first person from ancient Greece to write epic poetry

Ⓑ intended for his poems to be spoken rather than read

Ⓒ may not be the name of the author of the *Iliad* and the *Odyssey*

Ⓓ is considered the greatest poet the ancient Greeks produced

Paragraph 1 is marked with an arrow (➡).

12 In paragraph 2, why does the author mention "the Trojan prince Paris"?

Ⓐ To explain his role in causing the Trojan War to take place

Ⓑ To describe the battle that he fought against the Greek Achilles

Ⓒ To argue that he was widely considered the greatest Trojan hero

Ⓓ To remark on his relationship with the Greek god Apollo

Paragraph 2 is marked with an arrow (⇨).

13 The word "livid" in the passage is closest in meaning to

Ⓐ apprehensive

Ⓑ depressed

Ⓒ outspoken

Ⓓ furious

*Glossary

canon: a collection of literary works representative of a particular field or place

PASSAGE 2

REVIEW

HELP

BACK

NEXT

HIDE TIME 00:54:00

More Available

14 The word "he" in the passage refers to

- (A) Achilles
- (B) Patroclus
- (C) Hector
- (D) Paris

15 According to paragraph 3, Achilles fights Hector in single combat because

- (A) Hector is encouraged to do so by his brother Paris
- (B) the two great warriors want to see who the better fighter is
- (C) Achilles is eager to avenge the death of his cousin
- (D) they agree to a duel to settle the outcome of the war

Paragraph 3 is marked with an arrow (➡).

➡ Agamemnon assaults the city, but this tactic fails without the presence of Achilles. The Greek leader offers apologies and gifts to Achilles—including returning Briseis—but, still not mollified, Achilles refuses. Achilles's cousin Patroclus begs to be allowed to join the fight. Achilles relents and lends Patroclus his distinctive armor, but Patroclus is killed by Hector, Troy's greatest warrior and the older brother of Paris, who initially believes he has defeated Achilles. Saddened and further enraged, Achilles challenges Hector to single combat, slays him beneath the walls of Troy, and proceeds to drag Hector's corpse behind his chariot as he circles the city. Later that night, thanks to the assistance of the gods, King Priam of Troy enters the Greek camp, finds Achilles, and begs for his son's body to be returned for a proper funeral. Achilles, touched by the old man's pleas, permits Priam to depart with Hector's body.

REVIEW

HELP

BACK

NEXT

HIDE TIME 00:54:00

End ▲

16 The word "craftiest" in the passage is closest in meaning to

   Ⓐ sneakiest

   Ⓑ wisest

   Ⓒ smartest

   Ⓓ subtlest

17 In paragraph 4, the author's description of the events in the *Odyssey* mentions all of the following EXCEPT:

   Ⓐ which tales covering the events of the Trojan War are included in it

   Ⓑ what Odysseus spends the majority of his time doing while trying to go home

   Ⓒ how Odysseus and his men manage to escape the Cyclops and Circe

   Ⓓ the reasons that Odysseus cannot get home for so many years

Paragraph 4 is marked with an arrow (➡).

18 According to paragraph 5, why does Telemachus depart Ithaca?

   Ⓐ He is on a quest to find Odysseus.

   Ⓑ He is sent away by Penelope.

   Ⓒ He is driven away by Penelope's suitors.

   Ⓓ He is searching for help to fight Penelope's suitors.

Paragraph 5 is marked with an arrow (⇨).

➡ At that point in the story, the *Iliad* comes to an end, and subsequent events are covered in the *Odyssey*. The *Odyssey* focuses on the ten-year journey home by Odysseus, the craftiest of the Greeks. He is the king of Ithaca and left behind his wife Penelope and young son Telemachus when he sailed off to war. While the *Odyssey* does not start with the end of the Trojan War, it eventually tells the tale of the death of Achilles, the success of the Trojan Horse, which was Odysseus's idea, and the sacking and burning of Troy. After the war, Odysseus and his men set sail for home but are cursed by the gods Poseidon and Helios, who prevent them from returning to Ithaca. As they try in vain to get home, Odysseus and his men have numerous encounters with monsters such as Cyclops and the witch Circe. Odysseus himself spends seven years on an island with Calypso, a nymph, where he is a virtual prisoner until she relents and permits his departure.

⇨ Meanwhile, in Ithaca, Odysseus is believed to have perished, so numerous suitors are competing for Penelope's hand in marriage. She puts them off in the hope that Odysseus will return home, and Telemachus sails off in search of his father. After ten years, Odysseus's men have all died, but he manages to return home at the same time as Telemachus. They decide to kill the suitors and warn Penelope of their plan. She declares that she will marry the person who is strong enough to bend Odysseus's great bow and to shoot an arrow with it. Every suitor fails, but Odysseus, who has disguised himself, successfully strings the bow. He promptly shoots a suitor, and then he, Telemachus, and some loyal followers slaughter the remaining interlopers.

*Glossary

Cyclops: a giant from Greek mythology that has a single eye in the middle of its head

Q
REVIEW

?
HELP

‹
BACK

›
NEXT

HIDE TIME 00:54:00

More Available ▲

19 Look at the four squares [■] that indicate where the following sentence could be added to the passage.

They also survive sailing past the island of the sirens and successfully escape the terrible monsters Scylla and Charybdis.

Where would the sentence best fit?

Click on a square [■] to add the sentence to the passage.

At that point in the story, the *Iliad* comes to an end, and subsequent events are covered in the *Odyssey*. The *Odyssey* focuses on the ten-year journey home by Odysseus, the craftiest of the Greeks. He is the king of Ithaca and left behind his wife Penelope and young son Telemachus when he sailed off to war. While the *Odyssey* does not start with the end of the Trojan War, it eventually tells the tale of the death of Achilles, the success of the Trojan Horse, which was Odysseus's idea, and the sacking and burning of Troy. **1** After the war, Odysseus and his men set sail for home but are cursed by the gods Poseidon and Helios, who prevent them from returning to Ithaca. **2** As they try in vain to get home, Odysseus and his men have numerous encounters with monsters such as Cyclops and the witch Circe. **3** Odysseus himself spends seven years on an island with Calypso, a nymph, where he is a virtual prisoner until she relents and permits his departure. **4**

*Glossary

Cyclops: a giant from Greek mythology that has a single eye in the middle of its head

20 **Directions:** Select the appropriate statements from the answer choices and match them to the Greek epic poem to which they relate. TWO of the answer choices will NOT be used. **This question is worth 3 points.**

> Drag your answer choices to the spaces where they belong. To remove an answer choice, click on it. To review the passage, click on **VIEW TEXT**.

ANSWER CHOICES

1 Mainly concerns a ten-year war that the Greeks fought

2 Includes events involving the gods Helios and Poseidon

3 Tells about the death of Patroclus and the results of it

4 Focuses on events concerning the warrior Achilles

5 Describes the events occurring at the conclusion of the Trojan War

6 Tells about some fights that took place between the Greek gods

7 Discusses what happened in Greece to cause the Trojan War

GREEK EPIC POEM

Iliad (Select 3)

-
-
-

Odyssey (Select 2)

-
-

Cottage Industries

Prior to the Industrial Revolution, which originated in the eighteenth century, people working inside their homes made the majority of the world's products. These cottage industries were responsible for the creation of numerous items, most of which were made by hand from raw materials. Oftentimes, merchants provided workers with raw materials and then collected finished products after a set period of time had elapsed. Most workers in cottage industries belonged to farming families and had time to work between the planting and harvesting seasons as well as during winter. Entire families—and sometimes villages and districts—worked to produce a single product, among them being textiles, lace, furniture, toys, and candles.

One of the primary advantages of cottage industries was the ability of workers to get to and from their workplaces quickly. In most cottage industries, people worked in their homes, in a building on their property such as a shed or barn, or in a place relatively close to their homes. This drastically reduced the workers' travel time, which, in an age when walking and riding on horses were the main means of land transportation, was a practical necessity. How useful it was to live and work in the same place became clear at the onset of the Industrial Revolution. Then, factory owners founded dormitories or erected housing near manufacturing centers so that the workers they employed could have short, easy commutes.

Another advantage provided by cottage industries was the centralization of the manufacturing of certain products. As a result, over time, various regions became renowned for having people skilled in specific industries. For example, in England, the large herds of sheep in the West Country, Yorkshire, and Norwich led to those places dominating the wool-based textile industry for centuries. This centralization additionally allowed for the easier transporting of raw materials and finished products to and from markets.

A third advantage of cottage industries was that the working conditions in them were frequently excellent. People could rest whenever they wanted, and they ate meals whenever they became hungry. Parents could also care for their young children while working in their homes. This was a marked contrast with the Industrial Revolution, which saw the working conditions of people employed at factories decrease so much that exhaustion and illness became enormous problems. While children—some as young as four years of age—often worked alongside their parents in cottage industries, they had far better conditions than the ones that workers toiled in at factories during the Industrial Revolution. Parents could additionally pass on their skills to their children, which provided them with the knowledge they needed to earn a living in adulthood.

Cottage industries had disadvantages though, particularly with regard to money. Families usually had to pay upfront for raw materials, which caused them to go into debt. In general, they paid off their

debts with their finished products, yet, if they could not manufacture enough products on time, their debt increased. To meet the schedules of the merchants, many people were obligated to work seven days a week. Despite people working as fast as they could, it took a long time to make certain products. In an age in which there was no competition, this was not a problem. However, once industrialization began and factories started turning out similar products at faster rates and in higher numbers, cottage industries simply could not compete with them.

The Industrial Revolution, which started in England and then moved to Europe, America, and other places, was what induced most cottage industries gradually to perish. Thanks to mass-production techniques made possible by the invention of various machines, factories could manufacture products faster and cheaper. People working in cottage industries therefore lost lots of business. Having lost their livelihoods, these people often sought work in the very factories that had taken their jobs. Since that time, most products have been made in factories, yet there are still places today where cottage industries exist. They are primarily located in parts of the non-industrialized world but may also be found in developed countries as some individuals create various handmade items—usually traditional arts and crafts—and sell them at markets or on the Internet.

*Glossary

textile: material that is made of cloth
mass-production: the large-scale manufacturing of products

PASSAGE 3

REVIEW

HELP

BACK

NEXT

HIDE TIME 00:54:00

Beginning

21 The word "elapsed" in the passage is closest in meaning to

(A) intervened

(B) passed

(C) taken

(D) reduced

22 According to paragraph 1, who were most of the people that worked in cottage industries?

(A) Merchants who later sold the materials

(B) All of the members of certain villages

(C) People who also engaged in farming

(D) Young women who had no other jobs

Paragraph 1 is marked with an arrow (➡).

23 In paragraph 2, all of the following questions are answered EXCEPT:

(A) Where did most of the people employed in cottage industries do their work?

(B) Why did the owners of factories in the Industrial Revolution build dormitories for their employees?

(C) What was the main benefit of cottage industries to the people who worked in them?

(D) How long did it take most people working in cottage industries to complete their tasks?

Paragraph 2 is marked with an arrow (⇨).

Cottage Industries

➡ Prior to the Industrial Revolution, which originated in the eighteenth century, people working inside their homes made the majority of the world's products. These cottage industries were responsible for the creation of numerous items, most of which were made by hand from raw materials. Oftentimes, merchants provided workers with raw materials and then collected finished products after a set period of time had elapsed. Most workers in cottage industries belonged to farming families and had time to work between the planting and harvesting seasons as well as during winter. Entire families—and sometimes villages and districts—worked to produce a single product, among them being textiles, lace, furniture, toys, and candles.

⇨ One of the primary advantages of cottage industries was the ability of workers to get to and from their workplaces quickly. In most cottage industries, people worked in their homes, in a building on their property such as a shed or barn, or in a place relatively close to their homes. This drastically reduced the workers' travel time, which, in an age when walking and riding on horses were the main means of land transportation, was a practical necessity. How useful it was to live and work in the same place became clear at the onset of the Industrial Revolution. Then, factory owners founded dormitories or erected housing near manufacturing centers so that the workers they employed could have short, easy commutes.

*Glossary

textile: material that is made of cloth

24 In paragraph 3, why does the author mention "the West Country, Yorkshire, and Norwich"?

(A) To name some of the dominant regions in the textile industry in England

(B) To emphasize how long these regions were important to sheep farming

(C) To explain the methods the people in those places used to spin wool

(D) To describe the quality of the goods made in cottage industries in those places

Paragraph 3 is marked with an arrow (➡).

25 Which of the sentences below best expresses the essential information in the highlighted sentence in the passage? *Incorrect* answer choices change the meaning in important ways or leave out essential information.

While children—some as young as four years of age—often worked alongside their parents in cottage industries, they had far better conditions than the ones that workers toiled in at factories during the Industrial Revolution.

(A) The Industrial Revolution was a time when people began working in factories, so one benefit was that young children no longer had to be employed in cottage industries.

(B) Cottage industries saw children as young as four years of age having to work, but children that young were not employed in factories in the Industrial Revolution.

(C) Even though young children worked in cottage industries, their working conditions were not as bad as those of factory workers during the Industrial Revolution.

(D) Parents and young children often worked together in cottage industries, so the children, unlike factory workers in the Industrial Revolution, learned valuable skills.

➡ Another advantage provided by cottage industries was the centralization of the manufacturing of certain products. As a result, over time, various regions became renowned for having people skilled in specific industries. For example, in England, the large herds of sheep in the West Country, Yorkshire, and Norwich led to those places dominating the wool-based textile industry for centuries. This centralization additionally allowed for the easier transporting of raw materials and finished products to and from markets.

A third advantage of cottage industries was that the working conditions in them were frequently excellent. People could rest whenever they wanted, and they ate meals whenever they became hungry. Parents could also care for their young children while working in their homes. This was a marked contrast with the Industrial Revolution, which saw the working conditions of people employed at factories decrease so much that exhaustion and illness became enormous problems. While children—some as young as four years of age—often worked alongside their parents in cottage industries, they had far better conditions than the ones that workers toiled in at factories during the Industrial Revolution. Parents could additionally pass on their skills to their children, which provided them with the knowledge they needed to earn a living in adulthood.

26 According to paragraph 5, what was a disadvantage of cottage industries?

Ⓐ Some merchants were unwilling to lend people money for raw materials.

Ⓑ Most workers disliked having to work every day of the week.

Ⓒ Families had to assume debt to get the raw materials that they needed.

Ⓓ The workers did not always turn out products of the highest quality.

Paragraph 5 is marked with an arrow (➡).

27 The word "induced" in the passage is closest in meaning to

Ⓐ inspired

Ⓑ requested

Ⓒ encouraged

Ⓓ prompted

28 According to paragraph 6, some people work in cottage industries today because

Ⓐ they live in countries that are undeveloped and have few industries

Ⓑ they prefer to make their living by selling goods from online stores

Ⓒ they feel that handmade goods are better than those made with machines

Ⓓ they prefer to create various goods whenever they have free time

Paragraph 6 is marked with an arrow (⇨).

➡ Cottage industries had disadvantages though, particularly with regard to money. Families usually had to pay upfront for raw materials, which caused them to go into debt. In general, they paid off their debts with their finished products, yet, if they could not manufacture enough products on time, their debt increased. To meet the schedules of the merchants, many people were obligated to work seven days a week. Despite people working as fast as they could, it took a long time to make certain products. In an age in which there was no competition, this was not a problem. However, once industrialization began and factories started turning out similar products at faster rates and in higher numbers, cottage industries simply could not compete with them.

⇨ The Industrial Revolution, which started in England and then moved to Europe, America, and other places, was what induced most cottage industries gradually to perish. Thanks to mass-production techniques made possible by the invention of various machines, factories could manufacture products faster and cheaper. People working in cottage industries therefore lost lots of business. Having lost their livelihoods, these people often sought work in the very factories that had taken their jobs. Since that time, most products have been made in factories, yet there are still places today where cottage industries exist. They are primarily located in parts of the non-industrialized world but may also be found in developed countries as some individuals create various handmade items—usually traditional arts and crafts—and sell them at markets or on the Internet.

*Glossary

mass-production: the large-scale manufacturing of products

29 Look at the four squares [■] that indicate where the following sentence could be added to the passage.

The only opportunities that had to take time off were on the various holidays or feast days that happened throughout the year.

Where would the sentence best fit?

Click on a square [■] to add the sentence to the passage.

Cottage industries had disadvantages though, particularly with regard to money. Families usually had to pay upfront for raw materials, which caused them to go into debt. In general, they paid off their debts with their finished products, yet, if they could not manufacture enough products on time, their debt increased. To meet the schedules of the merchants, many people were obligated to work seven days a week. **1** Despite people working as fast as they could, it took a long time to make certain products. **2** In an age in which there was no competition, this was not a problem. **3** However, once industrialization began and factories started turning out similar products at faster rates and in higher numbers, cottage industries simply could not compete with them. **4**

30 **Directions:** An introductory sentence for a brief summary of the passage is provided below. Complete the summary by selecting the THREE answer choices that express the most important ideas of the passage. Some sentences do not belong because they express ideas that are not presented in the passage or are minor ideas in the passage. **This question is worth 2 points.**

Drag your answer choices to the spaces where they belong. To remove an answer choice, click on it. To review the passage, click on **VIEW TEXT**.

Cottage industries were once the primary way that people made certain goods, but they mostly disappeared when the Industrial Revolution began.

-
-
-

ANSWER CHOICES

1. Cottage industries inspired many factory owners during the Industrial Revolution to provide housing for their employees.

2. The machines of the Industrial Revolution made products so quickly and cheaply that cottage industries were not competitive.

3. There are still some places where people work in cottage industries nowadays, but they are few in number.

4. Certain regions in England came to dominate the wool-based textile industry for hundreds of years.

5. Cottage industries benefitted people in many ways, especially with regard to their working conditions.

6. Families running cottage industries often had to borrow money, and they could not work fast enough to compete with machines.

Actual Test

03

Reading Section Directions

This section measures your ability to understand academic passages in English. You will have **54 minutes** to read and answer questions about **3 passages**. A clock at the top of the screen will show you how much time is remaining.

Most questions are worth 1 point but the last question for each passage is worth more than 1 point. The directions for the last question indicate how many points you may receive.

Some passages include a word or phrase that is underlined in blue. Click on the word or phrase to see a definition or an explanation.

When you want to move to the next question, click on **NEXT**. You may skip questions and go back to them later. If you want to return to previous questions, click on **BACK**. You can click on **REVIEW** at any time, and the review screen will show you which questions you have answered and which you have not answered. From this review screen, you may go directly to any question you have already seen in the Reading section.

Click on **CONTINUE** to go on.

Lion Prides

A lion pride

Lions are native to Africa, where they primarily reside in the southeast part of the continent in regions with grassy plains upon which numerous large herds of prey animals roam. Among the most social of all animals, lions live in groups called prides, which consist of two to four males, three or more females, and their offspring, called cubs. The pride controls the territory in which it hunts, and defending this region is essential to the survival of every member. Within a lion pride, there are special relationships between the males and females, the females and their cubs, and the cubs and the males. Additionally, each lion has a specific role it must play to guarantee that the pride thrives and is not overtaken by predators.

The male lions rule the pride and defend it and its territory from predators, including other lions, which they do by patrolling their claimed land and marking it with chemical scents their bodies produce. If other lions approach, the males will fight in defense of their territory and pride. However, this fight may simply be a show of strength intended to frighten off their opponents rather than an actual battle because, in a physical confrontation, the slightest injury could kill a lion if it suffers an infection from a cut. As they age, the males become less able to defend their pride, so, eventually, they are killed or driven off by younger, stronger lions. Old males that survive after being ousted from their prides typically live lonely lives by themselves on the fringes of controlled territories until they die.

The females in a pride are the most numerous and are related to one another as well. They do the majority of the hunting for the pride by running down and killing prey, and then the males and the cubs share the kill. While the males almost always claim the choicest morsels, they are not so greedy that they consume an entire kill by themselves. Anytime a female lion goes into estrus, or heat, she is able to become pregnant. When one female in the pride reaches this stage, the other females—except for those already pregnant or with young cubs to care for—do the same. The males sense when the females are in

heat and copulate with them several times over a period of a few days. Zoologists believe the extreme amount of copulation is necessary because the females have difficulty getting pregnant. Despite that hardship, several usually become pregnant and then give birth at roughly the same time, whereupon the young cubs are raised together and protected by all of the adult females.

As the cubs mature, they take their place in the pride. The female cubs eventually reach their offspring-bearing years and subsequently join their female relatives on hunts and become adult members of the pride. The male cubs, however, receive treatment of a different nature. When they are around three or four years of age, they become too big and boisterous to remain in the pride. Since lions do not mate with their siblings, these males must depart to find mates of their own. The males, which are brothers or cousins, leave the pride together, form a coalition, and live near the territories of other lions while hunting and surviving to the best of their ability.

Soon, these males will feel the urge to mate and will desire to form a pride of their own, but the only way to do this is to attack the males in an existing pride and to drive them off or to kill them. Once the coalition succeeds in taking over a pride, its members want the females to go into heat as soon as possible; however, a female with cubs cannot do that again until her cubs are nearly two years old. The new male lions, unwilling to wait that long to pass on their genes to a new generation, therefore kill every cub in the pride they have taken over. Soon afterward, every female goes into heat, and the new males then have a chance to father their own cubs and to assert their position as the leaders of their pride.

*Glossary

estrus: a period when a female is in heat and is capable of becoming pregnant
copulate: to engage in sexual activity

1 According to paragraph 1, which of the following is NOT true about lions?

(A) They are only found living on grassy plains in the northeastern region of Africa.

(B) They live together in groups that have males, females, and cubs.

(C) They all work together by doing specific tasks so that their pride can do well.

(D) They must protect the area that they consider their own in order to survive.

Paragraph 1 is marked with an arrow (➡).

Lion Prides

➡ Lions are native to Africa, where they primarily reside in the southeast part of the continent in regions with grassy plains upon which numerous large herds of prey animals roam. Among the most social of all animals, lions live in groups called prides, which consist of two to four males, three or more females, and their offspring, called cubs. The pride controls the territory in which it hunts, and defending this region is essential to the survival of every member. Within a lion pride, there are special relationships between the males and females, the females and their cubs, and the cubs and the males. Additionally, each lion has a specific role it must play to guarantee that the pride thrives and is not overtaken by predators.

More Available ▲

2   Which of the sentences below best expresses the essential information in the highlighted sentence in the passage? Incorrect answer choices change the meaning in important ways or leave out essential information.

However, this fight may simply be a show of strength intended to frighten off their opponents rather than an actual battle because, in a physical confrontation, the slightest injury could kill a lion if it suffers an infection from a cut.

(A) Since lions might die if they get a cut which then gets infected, they usually only engage in displays meant to scare away other animals instead of physically fighting with them.

(B) Lions often engage both in shows of strength as well as actual battles with other lions, but they sometimes die because they get infections in one of the cuts they obtain while fighting.

(C) More lions die from infections that happen when they get cut than from engaging in physical battles with other lions that are trying to take over their prides.

(D) When a show of strength against an opponent does not succeed in frightening it off, a lion may be forced to battle another one in a fight that involves physical violence.

3   The word "fringes" in the passage is closest in meaning to

(A) sidelines

(B) outskirts

(C) communities

(D) frontiers

➡ The male lions rule the pride and defend it and its territory from predators, including other lions, which they do by patrolling their claimed land and marking it with chemical scents their bodies produce. If other lions approach, the males will fight in defense of their territory and pride. However, this fight may simply be a show of strength intended to frighten off their opponents rather than an actual battle because, in a physical confrontation, the slightest injury could kill a lion if it suffers an infection from a cut. As they age, the males become less able to defend their pride, so, eventually, they are killed or driven off by younger, stronger lions. Old males that survive after being ousted from their prides typically live lonely lives by themselves on the fringes of controlled territories until they die.

4   In paragraph 3, why does the author mention "Zoologists"?

    (A) To describe their efforts to increase the population of wild lions

    (B) To discuss one of their theories on the reproductive habits of lions

    (C) To note one of their attempts at researching lions in their natural habitats

    (D) To explain their theory on why male and female lions act differently

Paragraph 3 is marked with an arrow (➡).

5   The word "boisterous" in the passage is closest in meaning to

    (A) violent

    (B) famished

    (C) inconsiderate

    (D) energetic

6   According to paragraph 4, why do young male lions leave their prides?

    (A) They are in search of unrelated female lions that they can mate with.

    (B) The older male lions force them to depart from the pride.

    (C) They feel an instinctual need to rule over a pride of their own.

    (D) The females refuse to hunt for them, so they leave in search of food.

Paragraph 4 is marked with an arrow (⇨).

➡ The females in a pride are the most numerous and are related to one another as well. They do the majority of the hunting for the pride by running down and killing prey, and then the males and the cubs share the kill. While the males almost always claim the choicest morsels, they are not so greedy that they consume an entire kill by themselves. Anytime a female lion goes into estrus, or heat, she is able to become pregnant. When one female in the pride reaches this stage, the other females—except for those already pregnant or with young cubs to care for—do the same. The males sense when the females are in heat and copulate with them several times over a period of a few days. Zoologists believe the extreme amount of copulation is necessary because the females have difficulty getting pregnant. Despite that hardship, several usually become pregnant and then give birth at roughly the same time, whereupon the young cubs are raised together and protected by all of the adult females.

⇨ As the cubs mature, they take their place in the pride. The female cubs eventually reach their offspring-bearing years and subsequently join their female relatives on hunts and become adult members of the pride. The male cubs, however, receive treatment of a different nature. When they are around three or four years of age, they become too big and boisterous to remain in the pride. Since lions do not mate with their siblings, these males must depart to find mates of their own. The males, which are brothers or cousins, leave the pride together, form a coalition, and live near the territories of other lions while they hunting and surviving to the best of their ability.

*Glossary

estrus: a period when a female is in heat and is capable of becoming pregnant

copulate: to engage in sexual activity

7   Which of the following can be inferred from paragraphs 4 and 5 about male lions?

Ⓐ A few of them prefer living by themselves, so they do not attempt to take over a pride.

Ⓑ They will fight with one another to determine which one is the alpha male of the group.

Ⓒ They consume up to twice as much food as female lions the same age as them.

Ⓓ All of the male lions that belong to the same pride are related to one another.

Paragraphs 4 and 5 are marked with arrows (➡) and (⇨).

8   According to paragraph 5, why do male lions that take over a pride kill all of the cubs?

Ⓐ To reduce the size of the pride to a more manageable level

Ⓑ To prevent the cubs from growing older and then attacking them

Ⓒ To force every female to go into estrus so that they can mate

Ⓓ To ensure that the adult lions get a sufficient amount of food to eat

Paragraph 5 is marked with an arrow (⇨).

➡ As the cubs mature, they take their place in the pride. The female cubs eventually reach their offspring-bearing years and subsequently join their female relatives on hunts and become adult members of the pride. The male cubs, however, receive treatment of a different nature. When they are around three or four years of age, they become too big and boisterous to remain in the pride. Since lions do not mate with their siblings, these males must depart to find mates of their own. The males, which are brothers or cousins, leave the pride together, form a coalition, and live near the territories of other lions while hunting and surviving to the best of their ability.

⇨ Soon, these males will feel the urge to mate and will desire to form a pride of their own, but the only way to do this is to attack the males in an existing pride and to drive them off or to kill them. Once the coalition succeeds in taking over a pride, its members want the females to go into heat as soon as possible; however, a female with cubs cannot do that again until her cubs are nearly two years old. The new male lions, unwilling to wait that long to pass on their genes to a new generation, therefore kill every cub in the pride they have taken over. Soon afterward, every female goes into heat, and the new males then have a chance to father their own cubs and to assert their position as the leaders of their pride.

REVIEW

HELP

BACK

NEXT

HIDE TIME 00:54:00

Beginning

9 Look at the four squares [■] that indicate where the following sentence could be added to the passage.

One place that lions may be found in Africa is the Serengeti, an extensive plain located in Tanzania and Kenya.

Where would the sentence best fit?

Click on a square [■] to add the sentence to the passage.

Lions are native to Africa, where they primarily reside in the southeast part of the continent in regions with grassy plains upon which numerous large herds of prey animals roam. **1** Among the most social of all animals, lions live in groups called prides, which consist of two to four males, three or more females, and their offspring, called cubs. **2** The pride controls the territory in which it hunts, and defending this region is essential to the survival of every member. **3** Within a lion pride, there are special relationships between the males and females, the females and their cubs, and the cubs and the males. **4** Additionally, each lion has a specific role it must play to guarantee that the pride thrives and is not overtaken by predators.

10 **Directions:** An introductory sentence for a brief summary of the passage is provided below. Complete the summary by selecting the THREE answer choices that express the most important ideas of the passage. Some sentences do not belong because they express ideas that are not presented in the passage or are minor ideas in the passage. **This question is worth 2 points.**

Drag your answer choices to the spaces where they belong. To remove an answer choice, click on it. To review the passage, click on **VIEW TEXT**.

The male and female members of a lion pride each have a variety of roles that they must do.

-

-

-

ANSWER CHOICES

1 Male lions protect the territory that they have claimed as their own from other lions.

2 There are many male lions that have no pride, so they wander the land in small groups of two to four.

3 The number of lions living in the wild is decreasing because of hunting by poachers.

4 The female lions in a pride take care of the cubs and also do a great deal of hunting.

5 All of the cubs in a pride are killed if a new group of males takes over the leadership.

6 Female lions go into estrus and later give birth to cubs soon after the old males in a pride are defeated.

Gated Communities

Around the world, there are areas in cities in which some residences are surrounded by walls accessed solely by gates in various locations. Only the residents and their invited guests are permitted entry into these gated communities, as they are called. The gates themselves are manned by security personnel, who also patrol the community. Most gated communities, which offer protection from crime, are enclaves for the wealthy or retirement villages for the elderly. Within them, there are normally amenities such as health clubs, swimming pools, tennis courts, golf courses, beaches, playgrounds, and even restaurants and stores. While gated communities have a great amount of appeal to many people, they have a few drawbacks as well.

The greatest advantage gated communities offer is that they increase the safety of the people living in them in numerous ways. With no through traffic, there are fewer traffic accidents, which provides parents with children more peace of mind when their young ones are playing outside or returning home from school. Gated communities further provide more protection from criminals. Thanks to their gates, walls, cameras, and security personnel, most criminals are deterred from entering gated communities, so their crime rates are lower than those in neighboring districts. The people who live in gated communities tend to be close to one another, too. One reason is that the communities sponsor frequent social events, so there are chances for families to meet one another and to become friends who look out for the welfare of their neighbors.

On the other hand, the homes in gated communities are typically much more expensive than others, so houses are often out of the price ranges of all but the wealthiest members of society. Furthermore, the cost of maintaining the gates, walls, and security is borne by the people living in the communities. There is also the bothersome task of having to use an access card or key code to open and close the gates to enter and depart the community. Finally, most gated communities have strict rules on what people can and cannot do with their property. Any renovations and landscaping changes must usually be approved by a committee of community representatives.

Gated communities are occasionally criticized for the fact that they may appear safer than they actually are. While they offer the perception of safety, some do not have lower crime rates than non-gated communities. A study carried out in the American state of Florida in 2005 showed that even though there were fewer traffic violations and accidents in gated communities, there were similar rates of car theft and burglary in gated and non-gated communities. The main problem concerned the proper usage and maintenance of the gates and security systems. Damaged and nonfunctioning gates, broken security cameras, a lack of proper patrolling, and low walls all permitted criminals easily to enter gated communities. Additionally, gates that require access codes are no barrier to keeping nonresidents out

since many of them know the codes. For example, family members of the residents almost always know the codes as do individuals working for the residents. Among these people are maids, babysitters, and gardeners. Lastly, delivery personnel from the post office, restaurants, and other places almost always know the proper codes to gain access. With so many people cognizant of the entry codes, it is no surprise that they often end up in the hands of criminals.

Despite these drawbacks, the number of gated communities is growing around the world. In the United States, nearly eleven million households were located inside gated communities in 2009. In other nations, there are wide gaps between the rich and the poor, and crime is rampant, so gated communities are frequently the only bastions of safety for worried citizens. In Brazil, gated communities are popular on the peripheries of the crime-ridden urban areas of Rio de Janeiro and Sao Paulo. Mexico and South Africa, which both have high crime rates, are seeing many members of their middle and upper classes hiding themselves behind the walls of gated communities. While these places do not always provide the protection that people seek, they at least comfort people by providing them with the perception that they are safe.

*Glossary

enclave: a distinct area that is located inside another region but which is physically separated from it
periphery: a border; an edge

11 Which of the following can be inferred from paragraph 1 about gated communities?

(A) The only nations in which they currently exist are developed countries.

(B) The people who live in them frequently have their workplaces in them, too.

(C) A limited number of people are permitted to gain access to them.

(D) The vast majority of people who live in them are childless retirees.

Paragraph 1 is marked with an arrow (➡).

12 In stating that most criminals are "deterred" from even entering gated communities, the author means that criminals

(A) will rob homes in them

(B) consider stealing from them

(C) never enter them

(D) are discouraged to go into them

13 According to paragraph 2, which of the following is NOT true about the advantages of gated communities?

(A) There are not as many car accidents in them as there are in other places.

(B) The families living in them often spend time socializing together with one another.

(C) Children have many places where they can spend time playing with their friends.

(D) Their emphasis on safety means that they do not have to deal with many criminals.

Paragraph 2 is marked with an arrow (⇨).

Gated Communities

➡ Around the world, there are areas in cities in which some residences are surrounded by walls accessed solely by gates in various locations. Only the residents and their invited guests are permitted entry into these gated communities, as they are called. The gates themselves are manned by security personnel, who also patrol the community. Most gated communities, which offer protection from crime, are enclaves for the wealthy or retirement villages for the elderly. Within them, there are normally amenities such as health clubs, swimming pools, tennis courts, golf courses, beaches, playgrounds, and even restaurants and stores. While gated communities have a great amount of appeal to many people, they have a few drawbacks as well.

⇨ The greatest advantage gated communities offer is that they increase the safety of the people living in them in numerous ways. With no through traffic, there are fewer traffic accidents, which provides parents with children more peace of mind when their young ones are playing outside or returning home from school. Gated communities further provide more protection from criminals. Thanks to their gates, walls, cameras, and security personnel, most criminals are deterred from entering gated communities, so their crime rates are lower than those in neighboring districts. The people who live in gated communities tend to be close to one another, too. One reason is that the communities sponsor frequent social events, so there are chances for families to meet one another and to become friends who look out for the welfare of their neighbors.

*Glossary

enclave: a distinct area that is located inside another region but which is physically separated from it

Actual Test 03   69

14 In paragraph 3, the author implies that the usage of key codes in gated communities

- Ⓐ is the primary reason that they have lower crime rates than other areas
- Ⓑ is considered to be more convenient than having residents use access cards
- Ⓒ should not be required when residents are trying to leave the areas
- Ⓓ is regarded as an annoyance by some of the people who live in them

Paragraph 3 is marked with an arrow (➡).

15 According to paragraph 4, which of the following is true about the study carried out in Florida in 2005?

- Ⓐ Gated communities saw an increase in the number of car accidents.
- Ⓑ There were more murders in gated communities than in other areas.
- Ⓒ Gated communities had fewer traffic violations than other regions.
- Ⓓ There were fewer car thefts in gated communities than in other places.

Paragraph 4 is marked with an arrow (⇨).

16 In paragraph 4, the author uses "delivery personnel" as an example of

- Ⓐ individuals who may give key codes for gated communities to criminals
- Ⓑ laborers who can be trusted to move around by themselves in gated communities
- Ⓒ people who know how to gain access to gated communities
- Ⓓ workers who visit gated communities more often than maids and gardeners

Paragraph 4 is marked with an arrow (⇨).

➡ On the other hand, the homes in gated communities are typically much more expensive than others, so houses are often out of the price ranges of all but the wealthiest members of society. Furthermore, the cost of maintaining the gates, walls, and security is borne by the people living in the communities. There is also the bothersome task of having to use an access card or key code to open and close the gates to enter and depart the community. Finally, most gated communities have strict rules on what people can and cannot do with their property. Any renovations and landscaping changes must usually be approved by a committee of community representatives.

⇨ Gated communities are occasionally criticized for the fact that they may appear safer than they actually are. While they offer the perception of safety, some do not have lower crime rates than non-gated communities. A study carried out in the American state of Florida in 2005 showed that even though there were fewer traffic violations and accidents in gated communities, there were similar rates of car theft and burglary in gated and non-gated communities. The main problem concerned the proper usage and maintenance of the gates and security systems. Damaged and nonfunctioning gates, broken security cameras, a lack of proper patrolling, and low walls all permitted criminals easily to enter gated communities. Additionally, gates that require access codes are no barrier to keeping nonresidents out since many of them know the codes. For example, family members of the residents almost always know the codes as do individuals working for the residents. Among these people are maids, babysitters, and gardeners. Lastly, delivery personnel from the post office, restaurants, and other places almost always know the proper codes to gain access. With so many people cognizant of the entry codes, it is no surprise that they often end up in the hands of criminals.

17 The word "rampant" in the passage is closest in meaning to

   Ⓐ worrisome

   Ⓑ widespread

   Ⓒ unsolved

   Ⓓ violent

18 According to paragraph 5, people in Brazil often live in gated communities because

   Ⓐ they appear to provide safe havens from nearby areas with many criminals

   Ⓑ the murder rates in other parts of large cities there are very high

   Ⓒ wealthy members of the upper class there are expected to reside in them

   Ⓓ these neighborhoods receive the most patrolling by local police

Paragraph 5 is marked with an arrow (➡).

➡ Despite these drawbacks, the number of gated communities is growing around the world. In the United States, nearly eleven million households were located inside gated communities in 2009. In other nations, there are wide gaps between the rich and the poor, and crime is rampant, so gated communities are frequently the only bastions of safety for worried citizens. In Brazil, gated communities are popular on the peripheries of the crime-ridden urban areas of Rio de Janeiro and São Paulo. Mexico and South Africa, which both have high crime rates, are seeing many members of their middle and upper classes hiding themselves behind the walls of gated communities. While these places do not always provide the protection that people seek, they at least comfort people by providing them with the perception that they are safe.

*Glossary

periphery: a border; an edge

19 Look at the four squares [■] that indicate where the following sentence could be added to the passage.

This can create bad feelings at times when requests made by homeowners are rejected by the group for whatever reasons.

Where would the sentence best fit?

Click on a square [■] to add the sentence to the passage.

On the other hand, the homes in gated communities are typically much more expensive than others, so houses are often out of the price ranges of all but the wealthiest members of society. Furthermore, the cost of maintaining the gates, walls, and security is borne by the people living in the communities. **1** There is also the bothersome task of having to use an access card or key code to open and close the gates to enter and depart the community. **2** Finally, most gated communities have strict rules on what people can and cannot do with their property. **3** Any renovations and landscaping changes must usually be approved by a committee of community representatives. **4**

20 **Directions:** An introductory sentence for a brief summary of the passage is provided below. Complete the summary by selecting the THREE answer choices that express the most important ideas of the passage. Some sentences do not belong because they express ideas that are not presented in the passage or are minor ideas in the passage. **This question is worth 2 points.**

Drag your answer choices to the spaces where they belong. To remove an answer choice, click on it. To review the passage, click on **VIEW TEXT**.

Although gated communities have been growing in popularity in recent years, they have some drawbacks in addition to their many benefits.

-

-

-

ANSWER CHOICES

1 While most gated communities claim to have lower crime rates, a study has shown that is not always true of them.

2 The United States has the greatest number of people living in gated communities, but they are popular in South Africa as well.

3 Because living in gated communities is an expensive venture, only people with access to a lot of money can move into them.

4 A large number of gated communities function as retirement homes for the elderly and allow them to live in relative comfort.

5 People in countries around the world are moving into gated communities in order to escape from nearby areas with high crime rates.

6 Security guards often man the gates and also patrol the streets of most gated communities in the United States.

Ganymede and Callisto

Ganymede   Callisto

The four largest moons of the planet Jupiter are called the Galilean moons because they were discovered by Italian astronomer Galileo Galilei in 1601. The two smallest, Io and Europa, orbit closer to Jupiter than Ganymede and Callisto, the two largest. Ganymede and Callisto are similar in several ways but also have some profound differences. Several, particularly the dissimilarity between their surfaces, were first noticed when the *Voyager 1* and *Voyager* 2 space probes passed through the Jovian system in 1979 and closely observed Jupiter and its moons.

With a diameter of 5,268 kilometers, Ganymede is the largest moon in the solar system and is bigger than Mercury and nearly as large as Mars. Were it not for the fact that Ganymede orbits Jupiter, it would likely be classified as a planet. Ganymede is extremely old, having formed around 4.5 billion years ago, which was roughly when Jupiter itself came into being. Primarily composed of ice and rock, Ganymede has a surface that is mainly ice. Yet its surface is not even in composition, for large areas of it are darker than other parts. These dark regions comprise about forty percent of the moon's surface and have many impact craters whereas the lighter regions have fewer craters despite being the majority of the moon's surface. The light regions show evidence of recent geological activity, which may explain why they are less cratered. As for Ganymede's interior, it is believed to have a solid, rocky core with layers of rock and ice between the core and the surface. Ganymede has a thin oxygen atmosphere insufficient to support life and is the only moon in the solar system to have its own magnetosphere.

At 4,820 kilometers in diameter, Callisto is smaller than Ganymede, but the two are the same age. Similar to Ganymede, it is made of rock and ice and has a predominantly ice surface. Nevertheless, Callisto's surface is much darker than Ganymede's and reflects little light. Callisto is one of the most heavily cratered celestial objects in the solar system. The presence of so many craters indicates that

Callisto has no tectonic forces changing its surface, a fact that induces most astronomers to regard it as a dead world. However, the craters on Callisto have not been totally unaffected; they are smoother than those on other worlds and lack the deep depressions and high perimeter walls the craters on Earth's moon have. These characteristics may be a result of Callisto's icy surface smoothing out the craters as the ice moves, something which also happens on Ganymede. Additionally, like Ganymede, Callisto has a thin atmosphere, but it is composed mainly of carbon dioxide.

Another characteristic both moons share is that it is likely that at least one internal ocean exists on each of them. Ganymede is believed to have one or more oceans stacked between the layers of ice making up its interior. Furthermore, there is evidence suggesting that Callisto may have an internal ocean of unfrozen salt water between fifty and 200 kilometers beneath its surface. Some astronomers speculate that each moon may contain alien life in its subsurface waters.

As for the primary difference between the two moons, it is their surfaces, which were photographed up close by the *Voyager* probes. The high number of craters on Callisto is most likely the result of it—as well as many other objects in the solar system—being subjected to a massive series of impacts during the Late Heavy Bombardment Period approximately 3.8 billion years ago. Ganymede was also caught in this bombardment of celestial objects, yet it orbits closer to Jupiter, so as the giant planet's gravity pulled many meteorites toward it, an even larger number managed to strike Ganymede. These impacts forced the icy surface to melt and pushed rocks deep into its core. The impacts drove heat into the core. This heat is still creating internal tectonic forces on Ganymede, which, in turn, cause its surface to change and many craters to disappear over time. Callisto, being further away from Jupiter, was hit with fewer impacts, which drove fewer rocks and less heat into its core. Resultantly, Callisto has had virtually no tectonic forces at work, so its surface has remained mostly unchanged for billions of years.

*Glossary

Jovian: relating to the planet Jupiter
magnetosphere: an area of space around a celestial object that contains charged particles due to its magnetic field

21 In paragraph 1, why does the author mention "Italian astronomer Galileo Galilei"?

  (A) To point out an astronomical discovery that he made

  (B) To focus on his dispute with the Catholic Church

  (C) To claim that he named the largest of Jupiter's moons

  (D) To emphasize his role in the history of astronomy

Paragraph 1 is marked with an arrow (➡).

22 The word "profound" in the passage is closest in meaning to

  (A) traumatic

  (B) sincere

  (C) stark

  (D) potential

Ganymede and Callisto

➡ The four largest moons of the planet Jupiter are called the Galilean moons because they were discovered by Italian astronomer Galileo Galilei in 1601. The two smallest, Io and Europa, orbit closer to Jupiter than Ganymede and Callisto, the two largest. Ganymede and Callisto are similar in several ways but also have some profound differences. Several, particularly the dissimilarity between their surfaces, were first noticed when the *Voyager 1* and *Voyager* 2 space probes passed through the Jovian system in 1979 and closely observed Jupiter and its moons.

*Glossary

Jovian: relating to the planet Jupiter

23 The word "it" in the passage refers to

(A) Ganymede

(B) Callisto

(C) a thin atmosphere

(D) carbon dioxide

24 Which of the following can be inferred from paragraphs 2 and 3 about Callisto?

(A) The atmosphere on it is capable of supporting some life found on Earth.

(B) It first came into existence sometime around 4.5 billion years in the past.

(C) Earth's moon has roughly the same number of craters as it does.

(D) The internal ocean lying close to the moon's surface causes it to be so dark.

Paragraphs 2 and 3 are marked with arrows (➡) and (⇨).

25 In paragraph 3, the author's description of Callisto mentions all of the following EXCEPT:

(A) the amount of time it takes to complete an orbit of Jupiter

(B) the reason that it has so many craters on its surface

(C) the gas that makes up the main portion of its atmosphere

(D) how large it is in comparison with another Jovian moon

Paragraph 3 is marked with an arrow (⇨).

➡ With a diameter of 5,268 kilometers, Ganymede is the largest moon in the solar system and is bigger than Mercury and nearly as large as Mars. Were it not for the fact that Ganymede orbits Jupiter, it would likely be classified as a planet. Ganymede is extremely old, having formed around 4.5 billion years ago, which was roughly when Jupiter itself came into being. Primarily composed of ice and rock, Ganymede has a surface that is mainly ice. Yet its surface is not even in composition, for large areas of it are darker than other parts. These dark regions comprise about forty percent of the moon's surface and have many impact craters whereas the lighter regions have fewer craters despite being the majority of the moon's surface. The light regions show evidence of recent geological activity, which may explain why they are less cratered. As for Ganymede's interior, it is believed to have a solid, rocky core with layers of rock and ice between the core and the surface. Ganymede has a thin oxygen atmosphere insufficient to support life and is the only moon in the solar system to have its own magnetosphere.

⇨ At 4,820 kilometers in diameter, Callisto is smaller than Ganymede, but the two are the same age. Similar to Ganymede, it is made of rock and ice and has a predominantly ice surface. Nevertheless, Callisto's surface is much darker than Ganymede's and reflects little light. Callisto is one of the most heavily cratered celestial objects in the solar system. The presence of so many craters indicates that Callisto has no tectonic forces changing its surface, a fact that induces most astronomers to regard it as a dead world. However, the craters on Callisto have not been totally unaffected; they are smoother than those on other worlds and lack the deep depressions and high perimeter walls the craters on Earth's moon have. These characteristics may be a result of Callisto's icy surface smoothing out the craters as the ice moves, something which also happens on Ganymede. Additionally, like Ganymede, Callisto has a thin atmosphere, but it is composed mainly of carbon dioxide.

*Glossary

magnetosphere: an area of space around a celestial object that contains charged particles due to its magnetic field

26 The word "stacked" in the passage is closest in meaning to

Ⓐ dispersed

Ⓑ trapped

Ⓒ organized

Ⓓ layered

27 According to paragraph 4, which of the following is true about Ganymede and Callisto?

Ⓐ Most scientists agree that they harbor extraterrestrial life in their oceans.

Ⓑ There is a strong chance that both of them have oceans under their surfaces.

Ⓒ Each of them has liquid water, but Callisto has more of it than Ganymede does.

Ⓓ The amount of water located on each moon is equivalent to the amount on Earth.

Paragraph 4 is marked with an arrow (➡).

28 According to paragraph 5, there are tectonic forces at work on Ganymede because

Ⓐ meteorites colliding with it heated the core of the moon

Ⓑ there is still a great amount of volcanic activity happening on it

Ⓒ the effect of Jupiter's gravity on the moon is so powerful

Ⓓ a great amount of ice was once pushed into its center

Paragraph 5 is marked with an arrow (⇨).

➡ Another characteristic both moons share is that it is likely that at least one internal ocean exists on each of them. Ganymede is believed to have one or more oceans stacked between the layers of ice making up its interior. Furthermore, there is evidence suggesting that Callisto may have an internal ocean of unfrozen salt water between fifty and 200 kilometers beneath its surface. Some astronomers speculate that each moon may contain alien life in its subsurface waters.

⇨ As for the primary difference between the two moons, it is their surfaces, which were photographed up close by the *Voyager* probes. The high number of craters on Callisto is most likely the result of it—as well as many other objects in the solar system—being subjected to a massive series of impacts during the Late Heavy Bombardment Period approximately 3.8 billion years ago. Ganymede was also caught in this bombardment of celestial objects, yet it orbits closer to Jupiter, so as the giant planet's gravity pulled many meteorites toward it, an even larger number managed to strike Ganymede. These impacts forced the icy surface to melt and pushed rocks deep into its core. The impacts drove heat into the core. This heat is still creating internal tectonic forces on Ganymede, which, in turn, cause its surface to change and many craters to disappear over time. Callisto, being further away from Jupiter, was hit with fewer impacts, which drove fewer rocks and less heat into its core. Resultantly, Callisto has had virtually no tectonic forces at work, so its surface has remained mostly unchanged for billions of years.

29 Look at the four squares [■] that indicate where the following sentence could be added to the passage.

It is highly unlikely that this theory will be proven until probes—or perhaps even manned missions—are sent to explore the surfaces of the moons themselves.

Where would the sentence best fit?

Click on a square [■] to add the sentence to the passage.

Another characteristic both moons share is that it is likely that at least one internal ocean exists on each of them. ■ Ganymede is believed to have one or more oceans stacked between the layers of ice making up its interior. ■ Furthermore, there is evidence suggesting that Callisto may have an internal ocean of unfrozen salt water between fifty and 200 kilometers beneath its surface. ■ Some astronomers speculate that each moon may contain alien life in its subsurface waters. ■

30 Directions: Select the appropriate statements from the answer choices and match them to the moon of Jupiter to which they relate. TWO of the answer choices will NOT be used. **This question is worth 3 points.**

Drag your answer choices to the spaces where they belong. To remove an answer choice, click on it. To review the passage, click on **VIEW TEXT**.

ANSWER CHOICES

1. Is thought to have a saltwater ocean around 200 kilometers beneath its surface

2. Has some parts with many craters and other parts with smaller numbers of them

3. Has craters that have deep depressions and high walls around their perimeters

4. Has a dark surface from which only a small amount of light is reflected

5. Is larger in diameter than one of the planets in the solar system

6. Orbits the planet Jupiter closer than either the moons Io and Europa do

7. Has tectonic forces that are at work changing the face of its surface

MOON OF JUPITER

Ganymede (Select 3)

-
-
-

Callisto (Select 2)

-
-

80

Actual Test

04

Reading Section Directions

This section measures your ability to understand academic passages in English. You will have **54 minutes** to read and answer questions about **3 passages**. A clock at the top of the screen will show you how much time is remaining.

Most questions are worth 1 point but the last question for each passage is worth more than 1 point. The directions for the last question indicate how many points you may receive.

Some passages include a word or phrase that is underlined in blue. Click on the word or phrase to see a definition or an explanation.

When you want to move to the next question, click on **NEXT**. You may skip questions and go back to them later. If you want to return to previous questions, click on **BACK**. You can click on **REVIEW** at any time, and the review screen will show you which questions you have answered and which you have not answered. From this review screen, you may go directly to any question you have already seen in the Reading section.

Click on **CONTINUE** to go on.

The Influence of Greece on the Roman Republic

Two of the greatest civilizations in the ancient world were Greece and Rome. While culturally far apart, by the time the Romans had seized control of the entire Italian peninsula and founded their republic, the Greeks were already having a lasting impact on them. This influence was further boosted when the Romans conquered Greece in the second century B.C. and imported multitudes of Greek slaves to Rome. Over time, the Romans came to emulate the Greeks in many fields, including literature, science, education, religion, art, architecture, and philosophy. The Romans may have conquered the Greeks in battle, but, ultimately, the Greeks dramatically influenced their Roman masters.

Rome was founded on seven hills alongside the Tiber River around when the Greeks were dominating the eastern part of the Mediterranean Sea. In the eighth century B.C., Greek colonists began establishing city-states modeled on those at home in both southern Italy and Sicily, and these city-states served as the places of first contact between the Greeks and the fledgling Romans. At that time, there existed a tremendous gap between the two cultures. Most Romans were hardworking farmers wary of the literate, artistic, and intellectual Greeks, who took pleasure in the decadent aspects of life. Despite these feelings, some Greek influence began being felt in Rome. Exchanges between the Greek city-states and Rome were initially mostly made by merchants; however, after the Romans subjugated the Italian peninsula by the beginning of the third century B.C., Greek and Roman contact became more direct.

Among the earliest Greek influences were in the arts and architecture. Romans in the early years of the republic were enamored of Greek art, and by the third century B.C., they were importing Greek sculptures and paintings. Soon afterward, they were imitating some Greek artistic styles. For instance, the Romans adopted the Greek technical aspects of creating sculptures, yet they tended more toward making realistic sculptures of people whereas Greek sculptures concentrated more on beauty and form. This desire to imitate Hellenic methods extended to the field of architecture. Roman builders copied Greek columns and similarly built grand temples. Nevertheless, the Romans added their own stylistic elements and also came up with the dome and the arch, two architectural achievements never employed by the Greeks.

Arguably the greatest influence the Greeks had upon the Romans came in the field of education. Among the slaves taken to Rome after the conquest of Greece were numerous teachers, who became the tutors of the children of the Roman elites. In time, these children, who had learned the Greek language as well as Greek history and literature, joined the leadership of the republic. Future generations came to revere having a Greek education so much that they sent their sons to Athens to be schooled and therefore caused Athens to transform into a center of education in the eastern Mediterranean. The Greek language became the language of education in the Roman Republic and later in the empire. Many Romans were

so inspired by the Greeks that they aspired to become writers and attempted to follow in the footsteps of noted Greeks such as Homer and Herodotus. Among these men were Plautus, Terence, Lucretius, and the greatest of all Roman writers and the author of the epic poem the *Aeneid*, Virgil.

The Greeks further heavily influenced the Romans in religious matters. The early Romans were a highly superstitious people whose beliefs originated from the historical founding of Rome as well as the Etruscans, who had previously dominated the region around Rome. The Romans had a mythos relating to Romulus and Remus, the legendary founders of Rome, and attributed semi-deity status to their kings, but, as they came under Hellenic influence, they began mimicking the Greek pantheon of deities and adopted many Greek gods as their own. For example, the Greek supreme god Zeus became Jupiter in the Roman pantheon while the Greek god of war Ares became the Roman Mars. In spite of the Greek influence, the Romans maintained their own distinct religious characteristics: They remained extremely superstitious, engaged in animal sacrifices, and allowed the Roman state to control various aspects of their religion. Thus the Romans accepted certain imports from Greece yet managed to keep from being Hellenized entirely.

*Glossary

city-state: a city that rules itself and controls the area around it
Hellenic: Greek; relating to Greece in some manner

1   The word "boosted" in the passage is closest in meaning to

   Ⓐ appreciated

   Ⓑ enhanced

   Ⓒ announced

   Ⓓ launched

2   According to paragraph 1, which of the following is NOT true about the Romans?

   Ⓐ They defeated the Greeks in battle and took over their lands.

   Ⓑ They imitated Greek practices in a large number of different fields.

   Ⓒ They allowed captured Greeks to have direct roles in their government.

   Ⓓ They permitted the practice of slavery during the time of the republic.

Paragraph 1 is marked with an arrow (➡).

3   In paragraph 2, the author implies that the Romans

   Ⓐ lived lives that were quite different than those led by the Greeks

   Ⓑ created a city that would become the greatest in the Mediterranean area

   Ⓒ permitted the Greeks to found city-states in places near their capital

   Ⓓ believed that they should not trust the Greeks when trading with them

Paragraph 2 is marked with an arrow (⇨).

The Influence of Greece on the Roman Republic

➡ Two of the greatest civilizations in the ancient world were Greece and Rome. While culturally far apart, by the time the Romans had seized control of the entire Italian peninsula and founded their republic, the Greeks were already having a lasting impact on them. This influence was further boosted when the Romans conquered Greece in the second century B.C. and imported multitudes of Greek slaves to Rome. Over time, the Romans came to emulate the Greeks in many fields, including literature, science, education, religion, art, architecture, and philosophy. The Romans may have conquered the Greeks in battle, but, ultimately, the Greeks dramatically influenced their Roman masters.

⇨ Rome was founded on seven hills alongside the Tiber River around when the Greeks were dominating the eastern part of the Mediterranean Sea. In the eighth century B.C., Greek colonists began establishing city-states modeled on those at home in both southern Italy and Sicily, and these city-states served as the places of first contact between the Greeks and the fledgling Romans. At that time, there existed a tremendous gap between the two cultures. Most Romans were hardworking farmers wary of the literate, artistic, and intellectual Greeks, who took pleasure in the decadent aspects of life. Despite these feelings, some Greek influence began being felt in Rome. Exchanges between the Greek city-states and Rome were initially mostly made by merchants; however, after the Romans subjugated the Italian peninsula by the beginning of the third century B.C., Greek and Roman contact became more direct.

*Glossary

city-state: a city that rules itself and controls the area around it

4 The phrase "enamored of" in the passage is closest in meaning to

Ⓐ captivated by

Ⓑ critical of

Ⓒ considerate of

Ⓓ competitive in

5 The author uses "the dome and the arch" as examples of

Ⓐ two forms that the Greeks invented and the Romans borrowed from them

Ⓑ the two most notable developments in Roman architecture

Ⓒ structures that enabled the Romans to erect long-lasting buildings

Ⓓ Roman architectural elements that the Greeks never used

6 In paragraph 3, the author's description of Greek sculpture mentions which of the following?

Ⓐ The technical features that Greek sculptors utilized

Ⓑ The way that it compared in quality with Greek painting

Ⓒ The aspects of it that the Greeks emphasized the most

Ⓓ The names of some of the better-known Greek sculptors

Paragraph 3 is marked with an arrow (➡).

➡ Among the earliest Greek influences were in the arts and architecture. Romans in the early years of the republic were enamored of Greek art, and by the third century B.C., they were importing Greek sculptures and paintings. Soon afterward, they were imitating some Greek artistic styles. For instance, the Romans adopted the Greek technical aspects of creating sculptures, yet they tended more toward making realistic sculptures of people whereas Greek sculptures concentrated more on beauty and form. This desire to imitate Hellenic methods extended to the field of architecture. Roman builders copied the Greek usage of columns and similarly built grand temples. Nevertheless, the Romans added their own stylistic elements and also came up with the dome and the arch, two architectural achievements never employed by the Greeks.

*Glossary

Hellenic: Greek; relating to Greece in some manner

7 According to paragraph 4, Greek teachers influenced the Romans because

    Ⓐ they encouraged their students to adopt Greek as their primary language

    Ⓑ they helped the Romans imitate the writing styles of famous Greek poets

    Ⓒ they taught many Romans who went on to have positions in the government

    Ⓓ they made the Romans more interested in learning than they had ever been

Paragraph 4 is marked with an arrow (➡).

8 Which of the sentences below best expresses the essential information in the highlighted sentence in the passage? Incorrect answer choices change the meaning in important ways or leave out essential information.

The Romans had a mythos relating to Romulus and Remus, the legendary founders of Rome, and attributed semi-deity status to their kings, but, as they came under Greek influence, they began mimicking the Greek pantheon of deities and adopted many Greek gods as their own.

    Ⓐ The Romans once believed that their kings were gods, but they stopped thinking that way due to the influence of the Greeks.

    Ⓑ The Romans had their own mythology, but they later took many gods from the Greeks and made them their own.

    Ⓒ The Greeks had a number of gods in their pantheon, and the Romans took many of those gods and worshipped them.

    Ⓓ The Greeks and Romans had separate outlooks on religion, so they worshipped their gods in different ways.

➡ Arguably the greatest influence the Greeks had upon the Romans came in the field of education. Among the slaves taken to Rome after the conquest of Greece were numerous teachers, who became the tutors of the children of the Roman elites. In time, these children, who had learned the Greek language as well as Greek history and literature, joined the leadership of the republic. Future generations came to revere having a Greek education so much that they sent their sons to Athens to be schooled and therefore caused Athens to transform into a center of education in the eastern Mediterranean. The Greek language became the language of education in the Roman Republic and later in the empire. Many Romans were so inspired by the Greeks that they aspired to become writers and attempted to follow in the footsteps of noted Greeks such as Homer and Herodotus. Among these men were Plautus, Terence, Lucretius, and the greatest of all Roman writers and the author of the epic poem the *Aeneid*, Virgil.

The Greeks further heavily influenced the Romans in religious matters. The early Romans were a highly superstitious people whose beliefs originated from the historical founding of Rome as well as the Etruscans, who had previously dominated the region around Rome. The Romans had a mythos relating to Romulus and Remus, the legendary founders of Rome, and attributed semi-deity status to their kings, but, as they came under Hellenic influence, they began mimicking the Greek pantheon of deities and adopted many Greek gods as their own. For example, the Greek supreme god Zeus became Jupiter in the Roman pantheon while the Greek god of war Ares became the Roman Mars. In spite of the Greek influence, the Romans maintained their own distinct religious characteristics: They remained extremely superstitious, engaged in animal sacrifices, and allowed the Roman state to control various aspects of their religion. Thus the Romans accepted certain imports from Greece yet managed to keep from being Hellenized entirely.

More Available ▲

9   Look at the four squares [■] that indicate where the following sentence could be added to the passage.

Art dealers found a ready market for these items in the form of wealthy Romans residing in and around Rome.

Where would the sentence best fit?

Click on a square [■] to add the sentence to the passage.

Among the earliest Greek influences were in the arts and architecture. Romans in the early years of the republic were enamored of Greek art, and by the third century B.C., they were importing Greek sculptures and paintings. **1** Soon afterward, they were imitating some Greek artistic styles. **2** For instance, the Romans adopted the Greek technical aspects of creating sculptures, yet they tended more toward making realistic sculptures of people whereas Greek sculptures concentrated more on beauty and form. **3** This desire to imitate Hellenic methods extended to the field of architecture. **4** Roman builders copied Greek columns and similarly built grand temples. Nevertheless, the Romans added their own stylistic elements and also came up with the dome and the arch, two architectural achievements never employed by the Greeks.

*Glossary

Hellenic: Greek; relating to Greece in some manner

88

10 **Directions:** Select the appropriate statements from the answer choices and match them to the ancient civilization to which they relate. TWO of the answer choices will NOT be used. **This question is worth 3 points.**

Drag your answer choices to the spaces where they belong. To remove an answer choice, click on it. To review the passage, click on **VIEW TEXT**.

ANSWER CHOICES

1 Was influenced in some manner by the Etruscan people

2 Conquered most of the land around the Mediterranean Sea

3 Had its language come to be associated with education

4 Defeated the other in war during the second century B.C.

5 Focused on beauty and style in the sculptures its people made

6 Had many of its enslaved people go on to influence their masters

7 Existed as a civilization for centuries longer than the other

ANCIENT CIVILIZATION

Greece (Select 3)

-
-
-

Rome (Select 2)

-
-

Pesticides

Pesticides are chemical and biological agents utilized to control pests, some of which are insects, mice, weeds, fungi, bacteria, and viruses. The most common usage of pesticides is to protect crops from harmful insects, yet they are not limited to that activity. Due to the fact that they are designed to kill or limit the activity of certain organisms, pesticides constitute a danger to all living things, including large animals and humans. As such, the use of pesticides has been a matter of debate for a long time. It centers upon the benefits of using pesticides versus the harmful side effects they may have on other organisms as well as the environment.

During the late 1900s, approximately 2.5 million tons of pesticides were used around the world at a cost of roughly twenty billion dollars each year. The justification for the high cost was that those employing the pesticides benefitted an even greater amount. One study estimated that for every dollar spent spraying crops with pesticides, close to four dollars' worth of crops were saved worldwide. By protecting food crops from harmful pests, pesticides increased crop yields. This made fewer people suffer from starvation or malnutrition. Without pesticides, some experts believe that worldwide crop yields would decline around ten percent, and, in some extreme cases, farmers might experience the complete loss of their crops, which could lead to widespread food shortages and famines in some regions.

Another frequently cited benefit of pesticides is that they destroy organisms carrying deadly diseases. The mosquito has plagued humanity with diseases such as malaria, yellow fever, and dengue fever for millennia. During the construction of the Panama Canal, for instance, thousands of workers were sickened and killed by mosquito-borne illnesses. Pesticides later managed to reduce the mosquito population and enabled the canal to be built while saving countless lives. In 1939, the discovery of the insecticidal properties of the chemical agent DDT led to its widespread use to kill mosquitoes to prevent malaria. But by the late 1960s, accusations that DDT harmed the environment led to its banning in nearly every nation worldwide. This resulted in mosquito-borne illnesses, particularly malaria, killing millions of people in subsequent years since DDT was the only affordable method of eliminating mosquitoes in many countries. In 2004, the Stockholm Convention on Persistent Organic Pollutants permitted DDT to be used for disease-carrying insect control. This led to a renewal in its usage, particularly in Africa, which has caused fewer people to get malaria.

Unfortunately, the benefits of pesticides are more than countered by their harmful effects. For instance, when farmers spray their crops with pesticides, both the crops and the environment must be cleansed of the chemicals. In addition, in the late 1900s, it was estimated that roughly one million people around the world were harmed by pesticides in some way each year while about 20,000 of them died directly due to pesticide poisoning. Some typical side effects of those exposed to pesticides include

irritated eyes, skin rashes, and respiratory problems. Long-term exposure can harm both male and female reproductive systems. It can also cause pregnant women to suffer miscarriages. More severe effects of pesticides include causing life-threatening illnesses such as diabetes and cancer. The majority of those harmed by pesticides are the workers who apply them, especially if they fail to wear protective clothing and masks.

The environmental damage caused by pesticides is more difficult to witness because the effects either do not manifest for long periods of time or are difficult to observe. For instance, many pesticides seep into the soil underneath the crops they are sprayed on. There, they may enter both the roots of the crops and the groundwater beneath the soil. Plant size may be reduced by exposure to pesticides. A plant's ability to produce seeds that germinate may also be affected. Farm animals and wild animals absorb the pesticides when consuming these plants, and the poisons are passed up the food chain to humans and apex predators, which causes them harm. The end result is a tradeoff of sorts: Saving food from pests and killing deadly disease-carrying insects help humans live longer, but humans and other animals are eventually harmed in other ways.

*Glossary

miscarriage: an event in which a pregnancy is terminated so that a live baby is not born
apex predator: an animal that, when it is an adult, has no natural predators of its own; an animal at the top of the food chain

11   In paragraph 1, the author implies that pesticides

    Ⓐ must be applied a number of time in order to be effective

    Ⓑ are more effective against animals than they are against viruses

    Ⓒ can take a long time to kill their intended targets

    Ⓓ may unintentionally cause harm to animals other than pests

Paragraph 1 is marked with an arrow (➡).

12   The word "justification" in the passage is closest in meaning to

    Ⓐ rationalization   Ⓑ appreciation

    Ⓒ consent   Ⓓ discussion

13   Which of the sentences below best expresses the essential information in the highlighted sentence in the passage? Incorrect answer choices change the meaning in important ways or leave out essential information.

Without pesticides, some experts believe that worldwide crop yields would decline around ten percent, and, in some extreme cases, farmers might experience the complete loss of their crops, which could lead to widespread food shortages and famines in some regions.

    Ⓐ It is possible that fewer crops would grow and that many people would starve if there were no pesticides being used.

    Ⓑ Food shortages and famines are two of the problems that would occur if pesticides were not sprayed on crops.

    Ⓒ When farmers stopped using pesticides, their crop yields declined, and some places suffered from famines.

    Ⓓ Experts claim that the usage of pesticides is necessary to prevent crop yields around the world from being decimated.

Pesticides

➡ Pesticides are chemical and biological agents utilized to control pests, some of which are insects, mice, weeds, fungi, bacteria, and viruses. The most common usage of pesticides is to protect crops from harmful insects, yet they are not limited to that activity. Due to the fact that they are designed to kill or limit the activity of certain organisms, pesticides constitute a danger to all living things, including large animals and humans. As such, the use of pesticides has been a matter of debate for a long time. It centers upon the benefits of using pesticides versus the harmful side effects they may have on other organisms as well as the environment.

During the late 1900s, approximately 2.5 million tons of pesticides were used around the world at a cost of roughly twenty billion dollars each year. The justification for the high cost was that those employing the pesticides benefitted an even greater amount. One study estimated that for every dollar spent spraying crops with pesticides, close to four dollars' worth of crops were saved worldwide. By protecting food crops from harmful pests, pesticides increased crop yields. This made fewer people suffer from starvation or malnutrition. Without pesticides, some experts believe that worldwide crop yields would decline around ten percent, and, in some extreme cases, farmers might experience the complete loss of their crops, which could lead to widespread food shortages and famines in some regions.

92

14 The author discusses "the Panama Canal" in paragraph 3 in order to

   (A) argue that pesticides should be used and should not be made illegal

   (B) claim that it has had a tremendous effect on the global economy

   (C) state that pesticides could have prevented thousands of workers from becoming sick

   (D) describe the effect that pesticides had on it during its construction

Paragraph 3 is marked with an arrow (➡).

15 According to paragraph 3, DDT was banned in many countries because

   (A) it caused birth defects in children whose parents had been exposed to it

   (B) people used faulty science to claim that it negatively affected some animals

   (C) there were accusations that it was causing damage to the environment

   (D) it was responsible for the deaths of millions of people in Africa

Paragraph 3 is marked with an arrow (➡).

➡ Another frequently cited benefit of pesticides is that they destroy organisms carrying deadly diseases. The mosquito has plagued humanity with diseases such as malaria, yellow fever, and dengue fever for millennia. During the construction of the Panama Canal, for instance, thousands of workers were sickened and killed by mosquito-borne illnesses. Pesticides later managed to reduce the mosquito population and enabled the canal to be built while saving countless lives. In 1939, the discovery of the insecticidal properties of the chemical agent DDT led to its widespread use to kill mosquitoes to prevent malaria. But by the late 1960s, accusations that DDT harmed the environment led to its banning in nearly every nation worldwide. This resulted in mosquito-borne illnesses, particularly malaria, killing millions of people in the subsequent years since DDT was the only affordable method of eliminating mosquitoes in many countries. In 2004, the Stockholm Convention on Persistent Organic Pollutants permitted DDT to be used for disease-carrying insect control. This led to a renewal in its usage, particularly in Africa, which has caused fewer people to get malaria.

End ▲

16 In paragraph 4, why does the author mention "irritated eyes, skin rashes, and respiratory problems"?

　Ⓐ To name some problems people exposed to pesticides commonly experience

　Ⓑ To state that people with those problems need to seek medical attention at once

　Ⓒ To claim that 20,000 people get these side effects from pesticides each year

　Ⓓ To compare them with the long-term problems some individuals suffer from

Paragraph 4 is marked with an arrow (➡).

17 According to paragraph 4, which of the following is true about the negative effects of pesticides?

　Ⓐ They are responsible for both miscarriages and babies born with deformations.

　Ⓑ They have killed around one million people ever since they started being used.

　Ⓒ They may cause people to get illnesses of both a physical and mental nature.

　Ⓓ The people that they have harmed the most are those who work with them.

Paragraph 4 is marked with an arrow (➡).

18 The word "tradeoff" in the passage is closest in meaning to

　Ⓐ dilemma

　Ⓑ enigma

　Ⓒ delay

　Ⓓ compromise

➡ Unfortunately, the benefits of pesticides are more than countered by their harmful effects. For instance, when farmers spray their crops with pesticides, both the crops and the environment must be cleansed of the chemicals. In addition, in the late 1900s, it was estimated that roughly one million people around the world were harmed by pesticides in some way each year while about 20,000 of them died directly due to pesticide poisoning. Some typical side effects of those exposed to pesticides include irritated eyes, skin rashes, and respiratory problems. Long-term exposure can harm both male and female reproductive systems. It can also cause pregnant women to suffer miscarriages. More severe effects of pesticides include causing life-threatening illnesses such as diabetes and cancer. The majority of those harmed by pesticides are the workers who apply them, especially if they fail to wear protective clothing and masks.

➡ The environmental damage caused by pesticides is more difficult to witness because the effects either do not manifest for long periods of time or are difficult to observe. For instance, many pesticides seep into the soil underneath the crops they are sprayed on. There, they may enter both the roots of the crops and the groundwater beneath the soil. Plant size may be reduced by exposure to pesticides. A plant's ability to produce seeds that germinate may also be affected. Farm animals and wild animals absorb the pesticides when consuming these plants, and the poisons are passed up the food chain to humans and apex predators, which causes them harm. The end result is a tradeoff of sorts: Saving food from pests and killing deadly disease-carrying insects help humans live longer, but humans and other animals are eventually harmed in other ways.

*Glossary

miscarriage: an event in which a pregnancy is terminated so that a live baby is not born

apex predator: an animal that, when it is an adult, has no natural predators of its own; an animal at the top of the food chain

19 Look at the four squares [■] that indicate where the following sentence could be added to the passage.

Without their usage, it is highly likely that ships would be sailing the long way around South America to get from one ocean to another as the canal never would have been completed.

Where would the sentence best fit?

Click on a square [■] to add the sentence to the passage.

Another frequently cited benefit of pesticides is that they destroy organisms carrying deadly diseases. The mosquito has plagued humanity with diseases such as malaria, yellow fever, and dengue fever for millennia. During the construction of the Panama Canal, for instance, thousands of workers were sickened and killed by mosquito-borne illnesses. ■ Pesticides later managed to reduce the mosquito population and enabled the canal to be built while saving countless lives. ■ In 1939, the discovery of the insecticidal properties of the chemical agent DDT led to its widespread use to kill mosquitoes to prevent malaria. ■ But by the late 1960s, accusations that DDT harmed the environment led to its banning in nearly every nation worldwide. ■ This resulted in mosquito-borne illnesses, particularly malaria, killing millions of people in the subsequent years since DDT was the only affordable method of eliminating mosquitoes in many countries. In 2004, the Stockholm Convention on Persistent Organic Pollutants permitted DDT to be used for disease-carrying insect control. This led to a renewal in its usage, particularly in Africa, which has caused fewer people to get malaria.

20 Directions: An introductory sentence for a brief summary of the passage is provided below. Complete the summary by selecting the THREE answer choices that express the most important ideas of the passage. Some sentences do not belong because they express ideas that are not presented in the passage or are minor ideas in the passage. **This question is worth 2 points.**

Drag your answer choices to the spaces where they belong. To remove an answer choice, click on it. To review the passage, click on **VIEW TEXT**.

While pesticides have provided people with a number of benefits, their use can cause harm to humans, animals, and the environment.

-
-
-

ANSWER CHOICES

1. Even though it was highly effective at killing mosquitoes, DDT was banned as a pesticide in the 1960s.

2. Thanks to pesticides, the amount of crops that farmers grow has increased in many places.

3. Pesticides sometimes seep into the ground, where they can then pose problems to both plants and animals.

4. People who are exposed to some pesticides may develop both short-term and long-term health problems.

5. Most pesticides are designed to eliminate a variety of pests rather than being made for a specific one.

6. In places that have serious pest problems, the usage of pesticide is the only way to solve the issue.

Rainforest Animal Camouflage

A leaf-tailed gecko

Animals possess a multitude of ways to avoid detection by other animals, and camouflage is among the most effective. This is especially true in the world's rainforests in hot, humid climates in the tropical regions of South America, Africa, Southeast Asia, and Northern Australia. The great amount of rainfall and the high temperatures in these regions resulted in the appearing of massive rainforests that provide homes for large, diverse populations of animals. Like in all ecosystems, there are prey animals and predators in rainforests, and those that are hunted will do nearly anything to avoid becoming meals for other animals. One effective means of obtaining protection is to disguise themselves like the background so that predators will never see them. However, in response, most rainforest predators have correspondingly evolved so that they either utilize camouflage themselves or can see through animals' attempts to hide themselves.

Rainforests have a combination of backgrounds, such as green leaves, brown deadfall, grayish and brownish tree trunks, and sometimes even tall grasses and low shrubs, and many animals living within them have evolved to blend into these backgrounds. They generally do this in two ways: by having similar-colored skin, fur, or feathers and by imitating something else. The leaf-tailed gecko, for example, has skin resembling gray tree bark, so, when it is sitting still on a tree trunk with the same color, it is difficult to observe. The green-eyed tree frog takes camouflage one step further. It has greenish skin, which is the same as the mossy background in which it lives, and it additionally has a body shape broken up by a fringe of skin all around the frog. This helps break up the visual outline of the frog so that it blends in more easily with its background. While those two are small animals, even large animals employ camouflage to avoid predators. The cassowary, one of the biggest birds in the world, has alternating dark and light brown stripes as a chick. These stripes enable young cassowaries to blend in with the background deep in the dark rainforest, where there is little light but many shadows.

Imitation is another popular way some animals avoid predators in rainforests. The walking stick insect looks like a green branch that can be found on many plants while another insect, the katydid, resembles a green tree leaf. Some animals combine both camouflage and imitation. For instance, many butterflies have the same shapes and colors of leaves, and the pygmy chameleon of Madagascar is brown and leaf shaped, making it look like the leaves lying dead on the rainforest floor. Some prey animals appear more fearsome and dangerous than they actually are to frighten away predators. The owl butterfly has what appears to be large eyes on its wings. When its wings are spread, it look as though it has the face of a large animal, which prevents some predators from attacking it.

Despite the various attempts at camouflage, rainforest predators are not completely fooled and can still track and kill animals utilizing it. Many species of snakes have sensitive tongues that can pick up scents in the air and transmit them to their brains. Furthermore, they can detect heat from animals' bodies at night, so camouflage is useless against snakes hunting after sundown. Many species of birds have sharp eyes that can detect even the slightest difference in the background vegetation or ground they are observing. The kookaburra bird of Australia, for instance, is a carnivore with excellent eyesight that sits in trees and remains absolutely still while staring at the ground and looking for prey that may be hiding.

Some rainforest predators utilize camouflage while lying in wait for prey as well. The green coloring of the praying mantis permits it to lie hidden until it ambushes passing animals. Many snakes are colored like the rainforest vegetation they live amongst. For example, the green tree snake looks exactly like a green vine hanging from a tree. Large predators may also use camouflage while stalking their prey. Tigers have alternating colored stripes, so they can blend into the background and surprise potential prey. Ultimately, camouflage assists both prey animals and predators in the never-ending struggle for life in the world's rainforests.

*Glossary

gecko: a species of lizard
ambush: to lie in wait and then to attack someone or something while it is unaware

98

Beginning

Rainforest Animal Camouflage

➡ Animals possess a multitude of ways to avoid detection by other animals, and camouflage is among the most effective. This is especially true in the world's rainforests in hot, humid climates in the tropical regions of South America, Africa, Southeast Asia, and Northern Australia. The great amount of rainfall and the high temperatures in these regions resulted in the appearing of massive rainforests that provide homes for large, diverse populations of animals. Like in all ecosystems, there are prey animals and predators in rainforests, and those that are hunted will do nearly anything to avoid becoming meals for other animals. One effective means of obtaining protection is to disguise themselves like the background so that predators will never see them. However, in response, most rainforest predators have correspondingly evolved so that they either utilize camouflage themselves or can see through animals' attempts to hide themselves.

21 The word "correspondingly" in the passage is closest in meaning to

Ⓐ similarly

Ⓑ relevantly

Ⓒ conditionally

Ⓓ apparently

22 Which of the following can be inferred from paragraph 1 about rainforests?

Ⓐ They are found in great numbers on all of the continents on the planet.

Ⓑ A large number of species of animals live within them.

Ⓒ They can be dangerous places for both prey animals and predators.

Ⓓ Few of them have been thoroughly investigated by people.

Paragraph 1 is marked with an arrow (➡).

PASSAGE 3

REVIEW

HELP

BACK

NEXT

HIDE TIME 00:54:00

More Available

➡ Rainforests have a combination of backgrounds, such as green leaves, brown deadfall, grayish and brownish tree trunks, and sometimes even tall grasses and low shrubs, and many animals living within them have evolved to blend into these backgrounds. They generally do this in two ways: by having similar-colored skin, fur, or feathers and by imitating something else. The leaf-tailed gecko, for example, has skin resembling gray tree bark, so, when it is sitting still on a tree trunk with the same color, it is difficult to observe. The green-eyed tree frog takes camouflage one step further. It has greenish skin, which is the same as the mossy background in which it lives, and it additionally has a body shape broken up by a fringe of skin all around the frog. This helps break up the visual outline of the frog so that it blends in more easily with its background. While those two are small animals, even large animals employ camouflage to avoid predators. The cassowary, one of the biggest birds in the world, has alternating dark and light brown stripes as a chick. These stripes enable young cassowaries to blend in with the background deep in the dark rainforest, where there is little light but many shadows.

23 In paragraph 2, why does the author mention "The green-eyed tree frog"?

Ⓐ To compare its type of camouflage with that of the cassowary

Ⓑ To argue that its small size enables it to hide easily from predators

Ⓒ To explain the forces that made it evolve the way that it did

Ⓓ To describe the manner in which it hides itself from others

Paragraph 2 is marked with an arrow (➡).

24 According to paragraph 2, rainforest animals manage to hide from others by

Ⓐ finding small places and then remaining within them for long periods of time

Ⓑ having body parts that are the same colors as the background where they live

Ⓒ residing in places where few of the predators in rainforests ever go

Ⓓ changing the shapes of their bodies so that they resemble dangerous animals

Paragraph 2 is marked with an arrow (➡).

*Glossary

gecko: a species of lizard

REVIEW

HELP

BACK

NEXT

HIDE TIME 00:54:00

More Available ▲

25 The word "fearsome" in the passage is closest in meaning to

Ⓐ lethal

Ⓑ formidable

Ⓒ impressive

Ⓓ enormous

26 According to paragraph 3, which of the following is NOT true about the imitation methods that rainforest animals utilize?

Ⓐ A few animals use two types of camouflage in concert with each other.

Ⓑ The owl butterfly can make itself appear to be a different animal at times.

Ⓒ One species of chameleon has the shape of a dead tree branch.

Ⓓ Some species of animals resemble the green parts of various plants.

Paragraph 3 is marked with an arrow (➡).

27 According to paragraph 4, animals cannot hide themselves from snakes at night because

Ⓐ snakes have extremely good night vision

Ⓑ snakes can sense the animals when they move

Ⓒ snakes rely upon their sense of touch when they are hunting

Ⓓ snakes are capable of sensing the animals' body heat

Paragraph 4 is marked with an arrow (⇨).

➡ Imitation is another popular way some animals avoid predators in rainforests. The walking stick insect looks like a green branch that can be found on many plants while another insect, the katydid, resembles a green tree leaf. Some animals combine both camouflage and imitation. For instance, many butterflies have the same shapes and colors of leaves, and the pygmy chameleon of Madagascar is brown and leaf shaped, making it look like the leaves lying dead on the rainforest floor. Some prey animals appear more fearsome and dangerous than they actually are to frighten away predators. The owl butterfly has what appears to be large eyes on its wings. When its wings are spread, it looks as though it has the face of a large animal, which prevents some predators from attacking it.

⇨ Despite the various attempts at camouflage, rainforest predators are not completely fooled and can still track and kill animals utilizing it. Many species of snakes have sensitive tongues that can pick up scents in the air and transmit them to their brains. Furthermore, they can detect heat from animals' bodies at night, so camouflage is useless against snakes hunting after sundown. Many species of birds have sharp eyes that can detect even the slightest difference in the background vegetation or ground they are observing. The kookaburra bird of Australia, for instance, is a carnivore with excellent eyesight that sits in trees and remains absolutely still while staring at the ground and looking for prey that may be hiding.

End ▲

28 The author discusses "Tigers" in paragraph 5 in order to

(A) explain how they utilize camouflage so that it benefits them

(B) describe why many rainforest animals cannot hide from them

(C) contrast their type of camouflage with that of the green tree snake

(D) show how they have evolved to be one of nature's most effective hunters

Paragraph 5 is marked with an arrow (➡).

➡ Some rainforest predators utilize camouflage while lying in wait for prey as well. The green coloring of the praying mantis permits it to lie hidden until it ambushes passing animals. Many snakes are colored like the rainforest vegetation they live amongst. For example, the green tree snake looks exactly like a green vine hanging from a tree. Large predators may also use camouflage while stalking their prey. Tigers have alternating colored stripes, so they can blend into the background and surprise potential prey. Ultimately, camouflage assists both prey animals and predators in the never-ending struggle for life in the world's rainforests.

*Glossary

ambush: to lie in wait and then to attack someone or something while it is unaware

29 Look at the four squares [■] that indicate where the following sentence could be added to the passage.

Another big cat, the leopard, is mostly the color of the grass it prefers to hide in, letting it get close to the animals it hunts.

Where would the sentence best fit?

Click on a square [■] to add the sentence to the passage.

Some rainforest predators utilize camouflage while lying in wait for prey as well. The green coloring of the praying mantis permits it to lie hidden until it <u>ambushes</u> passing animals. Many snakes are colored like the rainforest vegetation they live amongst. For example, the green tree snake looks exactly like a green vine hanging from a tree. **1** Large predators may also use camouflage while stalking their prey. **2** Tigers have alternating colored stripes, so they can blend into the background and surprise potential prey. **3** Ultimately, camouflage assists both prey animals and predators in the never-ending struggle for life in the world's rainforests. **4**

*Glossary

ambush: to lie in wait and then to attack someone or something while it is unaware

30 **Directions:** An introductory sentence for a brief summary of the passage is provided below. Complete the summary by selecting the THREE answer choices that express the most important ideas of the passage. Some sentences do not belong because they express ideas that are not presented in the passage or are minor ideas in the passage. **This question is worth 2 points.**

> Drag your answer choices to the spaces where they belong. To remove an answer choice, click on it. To review the passage, click on **VIEW TEXT**.

Many rainforest animals, including prey animals and predators, use various types of camouflage to keep themselves hidden from others.

-
-
-

ANSWER CHOICES

1. There are all kinds of background colors in rainforests, but green and brown are the most common ones.

2. There are a number of insects that resemble other objects and which are found in rainforests.

3. The cassowary has different-colored stripes when it is a chick, so it can easily hide from other animals.

4. A large number of animals have coloring on their bodies that lets them blend in with the background in rainforests.

5. There are some animals, such as snakes and birds, that camouflage does not work well against.

6. Many rainforest predators have camouflage of their own that allows them to ambush unsuspecting prey.

Actual Test

05

CONTINUE

Reading Section Directions

This section measures your ability to understand academic passages in English. You will have **54 minutes** to read and answer questions about **3 passages**. A clock at the top of the screen will show you how much time is remaining.

Most questions are worth 1 point but the last question for each passage is worth more than 1 point. The directions for the last question indicate how many points you may receive.

Some passages include a word or phrase that is underlined in blue. Click on the word or phrase to see a definition or an explanation.

When you want to move to the next question, click on **NEXT**. You may skip questions and go back to them later. If you want to return to previous questions, click on **BACK**. You can click on **REVIEW** at any time, and the review screen will show you which questions you have answered and which you have not answered. From this review screen, you may go directly to any question you have already seen in the Reading section.

Click on **CONTINUE** to go on.

Diseases and the Decline of Native Americans

When Europeans began sailing across the Atlantic Ocean and arriving in North and South America, they brought many things unknown to the natives. These included horses, gunpowder, and iron and steel weapons. While each had varying degrees of influence in the New World, the import with the greatest impact was European diseases. The natives of the Americas had no experience with diseases such as smallpox and measles, so they quickly succumbed to them in huge numbers. It is believed that millions were killed within a few decades of the Europeans' arrival. According to one estimate, nearly half of all natives of the two continents died because of European diseases. The end result was that numerous American tribes were weakened so much that a handful of Europeans were able to conquer much of South and Central America in a few years.

There had been contact between Native Americans and the Vikings in Newfoundland in North America as early as 1000 A.D. But the first sustained contact between the natives and Europeans began on some islands in the Caribbean Sea when Christopher Columbus arrived in October 1492. Shortly after first contact was made, diseases began spreading, with smallpox being the biggest killer. In the late fifteenth century, smallpox was well known in Europe and had a mortality rate of roughly thirty percent. Smallpox spread due to close contact with an infected person. It could be transferred either through the air from a sick person's breath or from scabs that grew over the pustules that burst on a sufferer's skin. Studies have indicated that natives exposed to smallpox died in greater numbers than the Europeans did. The Aztecs of Central Mexico suffered a mortality rate greater than thirty-eight percent while the Iroquois of North America died at a rate of around sixty-six percent. One unlucky tribe—the Taino—who lived on several Caribbean islands, including Hispaniola, suffered a 100% mortality rate from smallpox.

The first wave of diseases that struck North and South America was not intentional so was not a type of primitive biological warfare waged by the Europeans. Instead, it was a combination of unfortunate circumstances that doomed millions of people. The Europeans carried diseases that many of them had become immune to thanks to Europe's centuries-long exposure to them. Among these diseases were the bubonic plague, influenza, measles, and smallpox. When they encountered a population of people who had never been exposed to them and therefore lacked any kind of protection, they spread rapidly from person to person and from village to village. In most cases, these diseases infected people in vast areas relatively quickly.

The spread of these diseases was aided by the natives' ignorance of their afflictions. By trying to assist their stricken family members, more people came into close contact with the diseases and then caught them. By not understanding that sick people and even entire villages needed to be quarantined, the natives enabled the diseases to spread further. Travelers carried these illnesses along trade routes,

especially up and down the great river systems that served as highways for the natives in North and South America.

Ultimately, the natives were not wiped out, but their population levels declined severely. One immediate effect was that a fairly small number of Europeans conquered enormous swaths of land. For instance, smallpox spread from the Spanish conquistadors into the interiors of modern-day Mexico and Peru, where the Aztec and Incan empires were located, respectively. Rather small Spanish armies handily defeated both empires and made the lands the natives had once ruled colonies of Spain. Similar events took place on many Caribbean islands as well as among the widespread tribes living in North America.

Over time, the population levels of many tribes recovered, and the people developed their own immunities to various diseases. When there were later outbreaks in the Americas, most of them suffered only minimal losses. Nonetheless, while the tribes did not vanish entirely, they never recovered their empires and native lands. European incursions continued unabated, and those invaders established colonies and states of their own. They eventually marginalized the Native American populations to such an extent that they became second-class citizens in the very lands they had once controlled.

*Glossary

pustule: a small raised collection of pus beneath the skin
conquistador: a Spanish conqueror who visited the New World in the 1500s and 1600s

1 According to paragraph 1, which of the following is true about European diseases in the Americas?

Ⓐ The Spanish and other Europeans intentionally spread them to the natives.

Ⓑ Other European imports such as gunpowder were more influential than them.

Ⓒ They were responsible for killing around half of all of the American natives.

Ⓓ Some American empires were completely wiped out by certain diseases.

Paragraph 1 is marked with an arrow (➡).

Diseases and the Decline of Native Americans

➡ When Europeans began sailing across the Atlantic Ocean and arriving in North and South America, they brought many things unknown to the natives. These included horses, gunpowder, and iron and steel weapons. While each had varying degrees of influence in the New World, the import with the greatest impact was European diseases. The natives of the Americas had no experience with diseases such as smallpox and measles, so they quickly succumbed to them in huge numbers. It is believed that millions were killed within a few decades of the Europeans' arrival. According to one estimate, nearly half of all natives of the two continents died because of European diseases. The end result was that numerous American tribes were weakened so much that a handful of Europeans were able to conquer much of South and Central America in a few years.

More Available ▲

2   The author uses "the Taino" as an example of

    Ⓐ a Native American tribe that died at the same rate as the Aztecs

    Ⓑ a group of natives that were entirely eliminated by imported diseases

    Ⓒ one of the most powerful of all of the native tribes in the Americas

    Ⓓ a tribe in the Americas that was greatly affected by measles

3   In paragraph 2, which of the following can be inferred about smallpox?

    Ⓐ It killed fewer than half of the Europeans it infected.

    Ⓑ It was nearly as fatal to American tribes as measles was.

    Ⓒ It was the first of all European diseases to reach the Americas.

    Ⓓ The Europeans discovered a way to cure the disease.

Paragraph 2 is marked with an arrow (➡).

➡ There had been contact between Native Americans and the Vikings in Newfoundland in North America as early as 1000 A.D. But the first sustained contact between the natives and Europeans began on some islands in the Caribbean Sea when Christopher Columbus arrived in October 1492. Shortly after first contact was made, diseases began spreading, with smallpox being the biggest killer. In the late fifteenth century, smallpox was well known in Europe and had a mortality rate of roughly thirty percent. Smallpox spread due to close contact with an infected person. It could be transferred either through the air from a sick person's breath or from scabs that grew over the pustules that burst on a sufferer's skin. Studies have indicated that natives exposed to smallpox died in greater numbers than the Europeans did. The Aztecs of Central Mexico suffered a mortality rate greater than thirty-eight percent while the Iroquois of North America died at a rate of around sixty-six percent. One unlucky tribe—the Taino—who lived on several Caribbean islands, including Hispaniola, suffered a 100% mortality rate from smallpox.

The first wave of diseases that struck North and South America was not intentional so was not a type of primitive biological warfare waged by the Europeans. Instead, it was a combination of unfortunate circumstances that doomed millions of people. The Europeans carried diseases that many of them had become immune to thanks to Europe's centuries-long exposure to them. Among these diseases were the bubonic plague, influenza, measles, and smallpox. When they encountered a population of people who had never been exposed to them and therefore lacked any kind of protection, they spread rapidly from person to person and from village to village. In most cases, these diseases infected people in vast areas in relatively quickly.

*Glossary

pustule: a small raised collection of pus beneath the skin

4 The word "quarantined" in the passage is closest in meaning to

(A) healed

(B) incinerated

(C) medicated

(D) isolated

5 According to paragraph 4, how did the natives' ignorance of European diseases affect them?

(A) Sick individuals continued to travel and thus spread the diseases further.

(B) They were unable to come up with any medicines to help the sufferers.

(C) Many natives believed their gods were punishing them with these diseases.

(D) Travelers with the diseases were not avoided by healthy natives.

Paragraph 4 is marked with an arrow (➡).

6 According to paragraph 5, which of the following is NOT true about the effects of the European diseases?

(A) They caused many islands in the Caribbean Sea to become European colonies.

(B) They reduced the sizes of the lands that many tribes were able to control.

(C) They enabled the fall of two great American empires in Mexico and Peru.

(D) They made many lands vulnerable to European invaders.

Paragraph 5 is marked with an arrow (⇨).

➡ The spread of these diseases was aided by the natives' ignorance of their afflictions. By trying to assist their stricken family members, more people came into close contact with the diseases and then caught them. By not understanding that sick people and even entire villages needed to be quarantined, the natives enabled the diseases to spread further. Travelers carried these illnesses along trade routes, especially up and down the great river systems that served as highways for the natives in North and South America.

⇨ Ultimately, the natives were not wiped out, but their population levels declined severely. One immediate effect was that a fairly small number of Europeans conquered enormous swaths of land. For instance, smallpox spread from the Spanish conquistadors into the interiors of modern-day Mexico and Peru, where the Aztec and Incan empires were located, respectively. Rather small Spanish armies handily defeated both empires and made the lands the natives had once ruled colonies of Spain. Similar events took place on many Caribbean islands as well as among the widespread tribes living in North America.

*Glossary

conquistador: a Spanish conqueror who visited the New World in the 1500s and 1600s

7   In stating that Europeans eventually "marginalized" the Native American populations, the author means that the Native Americans

    (A) made a comeback

    (B) lost power

    (C) remained neutral

    (D) were revitalized

8   According to paragraph 6, the natives of the Americas were unable to regain their lands because

    (A) their populations never increased to acceptable numbers

    (B) European colonists often made war on them to keep them from regaining power

    (C) large numbers of Europeans continued to move to the Americas

    (D) they were forced to live on small areas of land called reservations

Paragraph 6 is marked with an arrow (➡).

➡ Over time, the population levels of many tribes recovered, and the people developed their own immunities to various diseases. When there were later outbreaks in the Americas, most of them suffered only minimal losses. Nonetheless, while the tribes did not vanish entirely, they never recovered their empires and native lands. European incursions continued unabated, and those invaders established colonies and states of their own. They eventually marginalized the Native American populations to such an extent that they became second-class citizens in the very lands they had once controlled.

REVIEW

HELP

BACK

NEXT

HIDE TIME 00:54:00

More Available

9   Look at the four squares [■] that indicate where the following sentence could be added to the passage.

The natives were then treated horridly by the Spanish, who enslaved masses of them and forced them to work on plantations and in mines.

Where would the sentence best fit?

Click on a square [■] to add the sentence to the passage.

Ultimately, the natives were not wiped out, but their population levels declined severely. **1** One immediate effect was that a fairly small number of Europeans conquered enormous swaths of land. **2** For instance, smallpox spread from the Spanish conquistadors into the interiors of modern-day Mexico and Peru, where the Aztec and Incan empires were located, respectively. **3** Rather small Spanish armies handily defeated both empires and made the lands the natives had once ruled colonies of Spain. **4** Similar events took place on many Caribbean islands as well as among the widespread tribes living in North America.

*Glossary

conquistador: a Spanish conqueror who visited the New World in the 1500s and 1600s

10 **Directions:** An introductory sentence for a brief summary of the passage is provided below. Complete the summary by selecting the THREE answer choices that express the most important ideas of the passage. Some sentences do not belong because they express ideas that are not presented in the passage or are minor ideas in the passage. **This question is worth 2 points.**

> Drag your answer choices to the spaces where they belong. To remove an answer choice, click on it. To review the passage, click on **VIEW TEXT**.

When Europeans began to visit the Americas after 1492, they brought many diseases that resulted in the deaths of millions of people who were natives of the lands.

-

-

-

ANSWER CHOICES

1 The members of the American tribes had no natural immunities to the diseases, so they suffered high mortality rates.

2 The Europeans were able to conquer large amounts of lands in the Americas because so many natives were killed by diseases.

3 After suffering many deaths, the natives of the Americas eventually developed some amount of immunity to a few of the imported diseases.

4 The Vikings made contact with people in the Americas around 1000 A.D., but they are not known to have spread any illnesses.

5 Because of their ignorance of these diseases, the natives unintentionally spread them to people living in other regions.

6 The Aztecs and the Incas once had large and powerful empires, but both of them were conquered by the Spanish.

Music Texture

In music, the term texture refers to the pattern of music and how many layers of it are found in a particular musical composition as well as how they are arranged and played at any particular moment. For instance, there may be one voice singing or one instrument playing, or there may be a full orchestra performing while accompanied by a choral group. The possible ways music can be layered and combined are vast, yet the texture of most musical pieces falls within one of four basic types: monophonic, homophonic, polyphonic, and heterophonic. While monophonic music, the simplest form, is typically easily recognizable, there is some overlap between the other three. As a result, despite there being clear definitions of each kind of music texture, they are not always easy to identify, and the texture of many musical works often seems as though it could be two separate types.

The most basic type of music texture is monophonic music, which consists of a single voice singing or one musical instrument playing alone. It is arguably the oldest form of music as it originated the first time a human learned to produce melodic noises from his or her vocal cords. That first singing voice, in addition to music produced by someone whistling or humming a tune, has monophonic texture. There is no harmony or counterpoint in monophonic music. Even if a group of people sing together, so long as they have no accompanying instruments and all of the singers maintain the same rhythm, then the piece is considered monophonic music. This form of music texture was the dominant type of church music in Europe for centuries subsequent to the fall of Rome. Its basic method was called plainchant, a style in which groups of singers performed chants in monophonic form.

Homophonic music is the next most basic form of music texture. It usually has only two layers, most commonly a main melody with an accompaniment of chords. One example is a musician singing while playing an instrument such as the guitar or piano. There is one primary melodic layer while the other is played in support of the main melody. The chords played do not comprise an independent piece of music but are instead a vital component of the main melody. Homophonic music evolved during the Baroque Period, which lasted from around 1600 to 1750. During it, keyboard instruments such as the harpsichord, organ, and piano became prominent in music composition. A more modern example of this type is ragtime music, which was popular in the United States during the early 1900s and whose most famous composer was Scott Joplin. Today, homophonic music is one of the most common music textures and is a part of the mainstream music scene in pop, rock, and country music performances.

Polyphonic music texture, which is sometimes called counterpoint, has multiple layers independent of one another. Common examples are rondos and fugues, which Johann Sebastian Bach was noted for. Music played by a large orchestra is typically polyphonic. This type of music texture's origin is uncertain, but the earliest recorded evidence of it comes from Europe around 1000 A.D. At that time, the Church

disapproved of it. People found it too jarring when singers began experimenting with different voices in various layers, especially since they were used to the monophonic chanting popular then. Over time, however, the Church began to approve of this music form, so when the Renaissance was underway in the 1400s, it had become an accepted type of music and has remained that way up to the present day.

The last form of music texture—heterophonic—is the rarest. This music texture has only one melody but is played in different ways by a variety of instruments. For example, if a band plays this type of music, the lead singer sings the melody one way while the lead guitarist plays it another. The accompanying bassist and keyboardist play it with various embellishments or minor variations. This is typical of American bluegrass and Cajun music. It is more common in Native American, Middle Eastern, and South Asian music traditions than in traditional European forms of music.

*Glossary

counterpoint: musical material added to a piece of music that already exists
rondo: an instrumental musical composition

Beginning

Music Texture

➡ In music, the term texture refers to the pattern of music and how many layers of it are found in a particular musical composition as well as how they are arranged and played at any particular moment. For instance, there may be one voice singing or one instrument playing, or there may be a full orchestra performing while accompanied by a choral group. The possible ways music can be layered and combined is vast, yet the texture of most musical pieces falls within one of four basic types: monophonic, homophonic, polyphonic, and heterophonic. While monophonic music, the simplest form, is typically easily recognizable, there is some overlap between the other three. As a result, despite there being clear definitions of each kind of music texture, they are not always easy to identify, and the texture of many musical works often seems as though it could be two separate types.

⇨ The most basic type of music texture is monophonic music, which consists of a single voice singing or one musical instrument playing alone. It is arguably the oldest form of music as it originated the first time a human learned to produce melodic noises from his or her vocal cords. That first singing voice, in addition to music produced by someone whistling or humming a tune, has monophonic texture. There is no harmony or counterpoint in monophonic music. Even if a group of people sing together, so long as they have no accompanying instruments and all of the singers maintain the same rhythm, then the piece is considered monophonic music. This form of music texture was the dominant type of church music in Europe for centuries subsequent to the fall of Rome. Its basic method was called plainchant, a style in which groups of singers performed chants in monophonic form.

*Glossary

counterpoint: musical material added to a piece of music that already exists

11 According to paragraph 1, which of the following is NOT true about music texture?

Ⓐ Determining the type of texture in some musical compositions can be challenging.

Ⓑ Monophonic music is the most basic of the four types of music texture.

Ⓒ It is possible for a composer to layer music in a wide variety of manners.

Ⓓ The majority of modern musical pieces are either homophonic or polyphonic.

Paragraph 1 is marked with an arrow (➡).

12 The word "dominant" in the passage is closest in meaning to

Ⓐ overbearing   Ⓑ repeating

Ⓒ prevailing   Ⓓ foreboding

13 In paragraph 2, the author uses "plainchant" as an example of

Ⓐ the primary kind of monophonic music played nowadays

Ⓑ a type of monophonic music that was once popular for many years

Ⓒ a form of music which was developed during Roman times

Ⓓ a style of chanting that humans developed thousands of years ago

Paragraph 2 is marked with an arrow (⇨).

14 In paragraph 2, the author's description of monophonic texture mentions which of the following?

Ⓐ The types of effects it has on people who listen to it

Ⓑ Some different kinds of sounds that can produce it

Ⓒ How the Romans made use of it in their music

Ⓓ The type of harmony that appears in it

Paragraph 2 is marked with an arrow (⇨).

15 The word "whose" in the passage refers to

    Ⓐ music composition

    Ⓑ ragtime music

    Ⓒ the United States

    Ⓓ the early 1900s

16 According to paragraph 3, what happened during the Baroque Period?

    Ⓐ Homophonic music lost some of the popularity it once had in the Middle Ages.

    Ⓑ Ragtime music became the most popular music during that period.

    Ⓒ The harpsichord, organ, and piano were all invented by musicians then.

    Ⓓ Musical compositions that employed members of the keyboard family were popular.

Paragraph 3 is marked with an arrow (➡).

➡ Homophonic music is the next most basic form of music texture. It usually has only two layers, most commonly a main melody with an accompaniment of chords. One example is a musician singing while playing an instrument such as the guitar or piano. There is one primary melodic layer while the other is played in support of the main melody. The chords played do not comprise an independent piece of music but are instead a vital component of the main melody. Homophonic music evolved during the Baroque Period, which lasted from around 1600 to 1750. During it, keyboard instruments such as the harpsichord, organ, and piano became prominent in music composition. A more modern example of this type is ragtime music, which was popular in the United States during the early 1900s and whose most famous composer was Scott Joplin. Today, homophonic music is one of the most common music textures and is a part of the mainstream music scene in pop, rock, and country music performances.

118

REVIEW

HELP

BACK

NEXT

HIDE TIME   00:54:00

End ▲

17 According to paragraph 4, which of the following is true about polyphonic music?

(A) Johann Sebastian Bach is the composer who is usually credited with inventing it.

(B) When it first appeared, there were many people who did not like the way it sounded.

(C) It is the type of music texture which is the least common of all four of them.

(D) Fugues and rondos are the only two types of musical compositions in which it is used.

Paragraph 4 is marked with an arrow (➡).

18 The word "embellishments" in the passage is closest in meaning to

(A) additions

(B) styles

(C) cadences

(D) renditions

➡ Polyphonic music texture, which is sometimes called counterpoint, has multiple layers independent of one another. Common examples are rondos and fugues, which Johann Sebastian Bach was noted for. Music played by a large orchestra is typically polyphonic. This type of music texture's origin is uncertain, but the earliest recorded evidence of it comes from Europe around 1000 A.D. At that time, the Church disapproved of it. People found it too jarring when singers began experimenting with different voices in various layers, especially since they were used to the monophonic chanting popular then. Over time, however, the Church began to approve of this music form, so when the Renaissance was underway in the 1400s, it had become an accepted type of music and has remained that way up to the present day.

The last form of music texture—heterophonic— is the rarest. This music texture has only one melody but is played in different ways by a variety of instruments. For example, if a band plays this type of music, the lead singer sings the melody one way while the lead guitarist plays it another. The accompanying bassist and keyboardist play it with various embellishments or minor variations. This is typical of American bluegrass and Cajun music. It is more common in Native American, Middle Eastern, and South Asian music traditions than in traditional European forms of music.

*Glossary

rondo: an instrumental musical composition

19 Look at the four squares [■] that indicate where the following sentence could be added to the passage.

Furthermore, when people first made simple instruments such as flutes and drums and then played them, they were performing monophonic music.

Where would the sentence best fit?

Click on a square [■] to add the sentence to the passage.

The most basic type of music texture is monophonic music, which consists of a single voice singing or one musical instrument playing alone. **1** It is arguably the oldest form of music as it originated the first time a human learned to produce melodic noises from his or her vocal cords. **2** That first singing voice, in addition to music produced by someone whistling or humming a tune, has monophonic texture. **3** There is no harmony or counterpoint in monophonic music. **4** Even if a group of people sing together, so long as they have no accompanying instruments and all of the singers maintain the same rhythm, then the piece is considered monophonic music. This form of music texture was the dominant type of church music in Europe for centuries subsequent to the fall of Rome. Its basic method was called plainchant, a style in which groups of singers performed chants in monophonic form.

*Glossary

counterpoint: musical material added to a piece of music that already exists

20 **Directions:** An introductory sentence for a brief summary of the passage is provided below. Complete the summary by selecting the THREE answer choices that express the most important ideas of the passage. Some sentences do not belong because they express ideas that are not presented in the passage or are minor ideas in the passage. . **This question is worth 2 points.**

Drag your answer choices to the spaces where they belong. To remove an answer choice, click on it. To review the passage, click on **VIEW TEXT**.

There are four basic types of music texture, which nearly all musical compositions can be categorized into.

-

-

-

ANSWER CHOICES

1 Music that contains two layers, such as a musician singing while accompanied by an instrument, is homophonic music.

2 Monophonic music is the simplest type of texture as it involves either a single voice or a lone instrument.

3 The most complicated music of all is polyphonic music texture, which features multiple layers of music that are independent of one another.

4 The types of music texture that are popular with people tend to change during the passage of time.

5 American bluegrass and Cajun music are often played in the style of heterophonic music texture, which is the rarest type.

6 It is believed that the oldest form of music that was ever played was monophonic music.

Japanese Architecture

A *minka* house in Shirakawa, Gifu

Modern Japanese architecture employs steel, glass, cement, stone, and brick as building materials for immense structures reaching high into the sky. However, Japan has its own unique architectural style that developed throughout its past. From ancient times until the mid-nineteenth century, Japanese architecture underwent numerous transformations. The Japanese developed their own special architectural styles for simple farmers' huts, enormous temples, and powerful fortresses. Yet Japanese architecture did not develop in a vacuum but was instead influenced by several outside factors, among them being the spread of Buddhism, the fighting of a civil war, and the Western world once contact with it was established.

Many factors in Japanese architecture were common during all ages. For instance, wood was the dominant building material in every period thanks to the ease with which it was attained. In addition, the Japanese used stone for foundations, thatching and clay tiles for roofs, and stiffened paper in wooden frames for interior walls and sliding screens. Roofs were large with sharp peaks and steep, sloping sides ending in curved eaves, and thick, square wooden posts supported the roofs. The interiors of buildings contained a central main room with smaller rooms branching off from it. Japanese structures in the past had movable paper interior walls, allowing them to be reconfigured if the need arose. Some exterior walls could be moved to permit access to gardens or verandas. In ancient times, many Japanese homes were built on raised stilts, ostensibly to keep out mice and other small creatures. In later periods, the stilts were abandoned, but the main floor was often raised above the level of the foundation. As for the foundations, they were initially made of hardened earth but were ordinarily built with stone in later periods.

In ancient Japan, most people were hunter-gatherers, fishermen, or farmers. They lived in simple wooden huts with hard earthen floors and thatched roofs. When widespread rice cultivation began around 300 B.C., houses raised on stilts became commonplace. Villagers additionally erected wooden

watchtowers and wooden fences as defensive measures. In later periods, commoners built homes in the *minka* style. These were wooden dwellings with two or three floors and peaked roofs with steep slopes extending practically to the ground. The steep roofs were necessary to prevent the accumulation of rain or snow during periods of heavy precipitation.

The arrival of Buddhism from China in the sixth century resulted in major changes, including building styles. Initially, the Japanese copied Chinese styles, but they gradually started imposing local influences on Buddhist temples. Large multistory palaces for Japan's ruling class also became routine then. From the twelfth century to the sixteenth, many other well-known aspects of Japanese architecture, including its famed gardens and teahouses, were developed. At the end of this period, a long civil war prompted the building of castles with huge central towers, numerous outbuildings, and strong stone walls with deep moats.

The Tokugawa Shogunate period that followed this civil war was a long era of stability lasting until the mid-nineteenth century. The new rulers of Japan moved the capital from Kyoto to Edo, which became modern-day Tokyo. The extensive construction of buildings in Edo and nearby regions required vast amounts of wood, which led to pervasive deforestation. That, in turn, resulted in the soil eroding in many places. Starting in 1666, laws dealing with forest management were enacted, so many restrictions were placed on using wood as a building material. This caused Japan's architectural growth to stagnate for several centuries. Despite the ban, wood was still favored over brick and stone because those two materials were vulnerable in Japan's earthquake-prone environment; however, wood and paper houses were equally susceptible to fire. In fact, fires plagued Japan's urban development for hundreds of years by sometimes rapidly destroying wide sections of cities.

When widespread contact with the West began in the 1860s, the Japanese were exposed to Western notions of architecture. As a result, in spite of fears of damage from earthquakes, builders began widely utilizing brick and stone, and Japan's architectural style transformed again. Eventually, the Japanese learned to create buildings capable of withstanding earthquakes and fires. Today, the skyscrapers dotting the skylines of Tokyo and other major cities are among the world's most robustly constructed buildings.

*Glossary

thatching: the stalks of plants that are used for roofing

outbuilding: a building set apart from a main building but still associated with it

Beginning

21 In paragraph 1, the author's description of Japanese architecture mentions which of the following?

　Ⓐ Some of the outside influences on it

　Ⓑ When it was first developed

　Ⓒ The most popular building materials in ancient times

　Ⓓ The types of homes the Japanese built the most

Paragraph 1 is marked with an arrow (➡).

Japanese Architecture

➡ Modern Japanese architecture employs steel, glass, cement, stone, and brick as building materials for immense structures reaching high into the sky. However, Japan has its own unique architectural style that developed throughout its past. From ancient times until the mid-nineteenth century, Japanese architecture underwent numerous transformations. The Japanese developed their own special architectural styles for simple farmers' huts, enormous temples, and powerful fortresses. Yet Japanese architecture did not develop in a vacuum but was instead influenced by several outside factors, among them being the spread of Buddhism, the fighting of a civil war, and the Western world once contact with it was established.

REVIEW

HELP

BACK

NEXT

HIDE TIME 00:54:00

More Available

22 The word "reconfigured" in the passage is closest in meaning to

(A) reversed

(B) replaced

(C) reapportioned

(D) rearranged

23 In paragraph 2, the author implies that Japan

(A) had so many wars that they influenced the country's architecture

(B) has regular floods that require special houses to be constructed

(C) has a large number of forested areas throughout the country

(D) completely changed its architectural style during every era

Paragraph 2 is marked with an arrow (➡).

24 According to paragraph 2, which of the following is NOT true about Japanese homes?

(A) They had roofs that were sloped on the sides and flat on the tops.

(B) A large number of them were constructed with wood in the past.

(C) Some of the walls in them were capable of being moved around.

(D) They were once built on poles raised above the ground.

Paragraph 2 is marked with an arrow (➡).

➡ Many factors in Japanese architecture were common during all ages. For instance, wood was the dominant building material in every period thanks to the ease with which it was attained. In addition, the Japanese used stone for foundations, thatching and clay tiles for roofs, and stiffened paper in wooden frames for interior walls and sliding screens. Roofs were large with sharp peaks and steep, sloping sides ending in curved eaves, and thick, square wooden posts supported the roofs. The interiors of buildings contained a central main room with smaller rooms branching off from it. Japanese structures in the past had movable paper interior walls, allowing them to be reconfigured if the need arose. Some exterior walls could be moved to permit access to gardens or verandas. In ancient times, many Japanese homes were built on raised stilts, ostensibly to keep out mice and other small creatures. In later periods, the stilts were abandoned, but the main floor was often raised above the level of the foundation. As for the foundations, they were initially made of hardened earth but were ordinarily built with stone in later periods.

*Glossary

thatching: the stalks of plants that are used for roofing

25 According to paragraph 3, why did homes in the *minka* style have sloped roofs?

Ⓐ Sloped roofs enabled people to gain easy access to the upper floors.

Ⓑ That prevented various types of precipitation from settling on the roofs.

Ⓒ That particular style was the most aesthetically pleasing to the Japanese.

Ⓓ The Japanese did not know how to make roofs that were flat or had other shapes.

Paragraph 3 is marked with an arrow (➡).

26 The word "prompted" in the passage is closest in meaning to

Ⓐ encouraged

Ⓑ initiated

Ⓒ obligated

Ⓓ proposed

➡ In ancient Japan, most people were hunter-gatherers, fishermen, or farmers. They lived in simple wooden huts with hard earthen floors and thatched roofs. When widespread rice cultivation began around 300 B.C., houses raised on stilts became commonplace. Villagers additionally erected wooden watchtowers and wooden fences as defensive measures. In later periods, commoners built homes in the *minka* style. These were wooden dwellings with two or three floors and peaked roofs with steep slopes extending practically to the ground. The steep roofs were necessary to prevent the accumulation of rain or snow during periods of heavy precipitation.

The arrival of Buddhism from China in the sixth century resulted in major changes, including building styles. Initially, the Japanese copied Chinese styles, but they gradually started imposing local influences on Buddhist temples. Large multistory palaces for Japan's ruling class also became routine then. From the twelfth century to the sixteenth, many other well-known aspects of Japanese architecture, including its famed gardens and teahouses, were developed. At the end of this period, a long civil war prompted the building of castles with huge central towers, numerous outbuildings, and strong stone walls with deep moats.

*Glossary

outbuilding: a building set apart from a main building but still associated with it

REVIEW

HELP

BACK

NEXT

HIDE TIME 00:54:00

End ▲

27 Why does the author mention "The Tokugawa Shogunate period"?

Ⓐ To compare its influence on Japanese architecture with the West's

Ⓑ To describe some of the changes that happened during it

Ⓒ To explain why Japan's capital was moved to another city

Ⓓ To detail a terrible fire that occurred in a city during that time

28 Which of the following can be inferred from paragraph 6 about "Western notions of architecture"?

Ⓐ They were influential at getting the Japanese to use brick and stone for construction.

Ⓑ They were frequently rejected by the Japanese as they were considered too radical.

Ⓒ They enabled the Japanese to construct buildings that would not collapse during earthquakes.

Ⓓ They led to more changes in Japanese architecture than the influence of China did.

Paragraph 6 is marked with an arrow (➡).

The Tokugawa Shogunate period that followed this civil war was a long era of stability lasting until the mid-nineteenth century. The new rulers of Japan moved the capital from Kyoto to Edo, which became modern-day Tokyo. The extensive construction of buildings in Edo and nearby regions required vast amounts of wood, which led to pervasive deforestation. That, in turn, resulted in the soil eroding in many places. Starting in 1666, laws dealing with forest management were enacted, so many restrictions were placed on using wood as a building material. This caused Japan's architectural growth to stagnate for several centuries. Despite the ban, wood was still favored over brick and stone because those two materials were vulnerable in Japan's earthquake-prone environment; however, wood and paper houses were equally susceptible to fire. In fact, fires plagued Japan's urban development for hundreds of years by sometimes rapidly destroying wide sections of cities.

➡ When widespread contact with the West began in the 1860s, the Japanese were exposed to Western notions of architecture. As a result, in spite of fears of damage from earthquakes, builders began widely utilizing brick and stone, and Japan's architectural style transformed again. Eventually, the Japanese learned to create buildings capable of withstanding earthquakes and fires. Today, the skyscrapers dotting the skylines of Tokyo and other major cities are among the world's most robustly constructed buildings.

29   Look at the four squares [■] that indicate where the following sentence could be added to the passage.

These both provided some measure of protection from bandits as well as organized attempts to attack residential areas.

Where would the sentence best fit?

Click on a square [■] to add the sentence to the passage.

In ancient Japan, most people were hunter-gatherers, fishermen, or farmers. They lived in simple wooden huts with hard earthen floors and thatched roofs. When widespread rice cultivation began around 300 B.C., houses raised on stilts became commonplace. ■ Villagers additionally erected wooden watchtowers and wooden fences as defensive measures. ■ In later periods, commoners built homes in the *minka* style. ■ These were wooden dwellings with two or three floors and peaked roofs with steep slopes extending practically to the ground. ■ The steep roofs were necessary to prevent the accumulation of rain or snow during periods of heavy precipitation.

30 Directions: An introductory sentence for a brief summary of the passage is provided below. Complete the summary by selecting the THREE answer choices that express the most important ideas of the passage. Some sentences do not belong because they express ideas that are not presented in the passage or are minor ideas in the passage. **This question is worth 2 points.**

Drag your answer choices to the spaces where they belong. To remove an answer choice, click on it. To review the passage, click on **VIEW TEXT**.

Throughout its history, Japanese architecture has remained the same in some aspects, but it has also undergone a great amount of change.

-
-
-

ANSWER CHOICES

1. A period in which there was a civil war in Japan got the Japanese to focus on constructing defensive buildings such as castles.

2. Early Japanese Buddhist temples had a Chinese influence, but later ones used Japanese styles.

3. Ideas about architecture from both China and the West caused Japanese architecture to transform in various ways.

4. Modern Japanese cities have many skyscrapers that can resist even powerful earthquakes that topple smaller buildings.

5. The roofs of many Japanese homes are sloped and extend from the top of the building all the way to the ground.

6. The Japanese have utilized wood for the construction of many of their buildings all throughout their history.

Actual Test

06

Reading Section Directions

This section measures your ability to understand academic passages in English. You will have **54 minutes** to read and answer questions about **3 passages**. A clock at the top of the screen will show you how much time is remaining.

Most questions are worth 1 point but the last question for each passage is worth more than 1 point. The directions for the last question indicate how many points you may receive.

Some passages include a word or phrase that is <u>underlined</u> in blue. Click on the word or phrase to see a definition or an explanation.

When you want to move to the next question, click on **NEXT**. You may skip questions and go back to them later. If you want to return to previous questions, click on **BACK**. You can click on **REVIEW** at any time, and the review screen will show you which questions you have answered and which you have not answered. From this review screen, you may go directly to any question you have already seen in the Reading section.

Click on **CONTINUE** to go on.

Training in Medieval Guilds

Centuries ago in medieval Europe, guilds were organizations whose members were highly skilled in one specific craft. There were guilds for carpenters, masons, blacksmiths, tailors, seamstresses, and bakers, among others. Guilds arose in the Middle Ages sometime during the twelfth century and soon dominated economic activity throughout Europe. They became so powerful that they often had monopolies on their particular skills, and laws were passed prohibiting non-guild members from practicing their trades. Therefore, to make a living at some trades, people were required to become guild members. Upon joining, they agreed to certain professional standards, including their pay rates and the quality of their work. However, before individuals could become guild members, they trained as apprentices and were required to attain certain levels of knowledge or skill.

Most people began their apprenticeships around the age of twelve although this varied depending upon the trade. Most apprentices were boys, but girls could become apprentice seamstresses, tailors, and bakers. The parents of an apprentice paid a master in a guild to take on their son or daughter and to train their child. Once accepted as an apprentice, the child lived in the master's home along with his family. The master provided the apprentice with shelter, food, and training, and, in return, the apprentice did everything that was asked, which initially meant the lowest and dirtiest tasks. Though laws varied from region to region, anyone who was an apprentice was not permitted to marry and had to remain in the master's home. Most apprenticeships lasted for seven years, after which time the master nearly always decided that the apprentice was skilled enough to be elevated to the rank of journeyman.

Once a person became a journeyman, this individual was considered skilled enough at his or her trade to be a paid worker but was not talented enough to be called a master. A journeyman was permitted to make money by practicing his or her trade but was not allowed to employ others or to open a shop. Most journeymen were employed by the masters with whom they did their apprenticeships. Others went on journeys and traveled to different towns and cities to learn new skills and to earn a living. Eventually, a journeyman would feel confident enough to begin preparing to become a master. To do this, the person had to produce a great work demonstrating his or her talents. When completed, the work was judged by the master craftsmen who belonged to the guild since only they could approve it and therefore give the journeyman the right to join the guild and to be called a master.

Unfortunately for journeymen, skill was not the only factor the masters took into consideration. They frequently failed journeymen simply to prevent there from being too many masters in a region. Additionally, most guilds required journeymen to pay a large sum of money before being permitted to become members. Many journeymen were thusly prevented from ever joining guilds, so they remained in their positions for the rest of their lives and typically worked for the very masters who refused to elevate them

to the highest rank. However, whenever a journeyman finally became a master, that person could open a shop, had the right to employ others, and was allowed to train apprentices. For members of the middle class, being a master in a guild was an important social step and was as high in society as they could legitimately hope to rise.

The medieval guild system was sometimes criticized for being too restrictive. It required people to commit their lives to a single skill set and to spend years of training in it only for them frequently to be rejected from their life's objective. Guilds also came to dominate many aspects of economic activity in medieval times, and their members jealously guarded their prerogatives and were suspicious of innovation. When industrialization began centuries later in the eighteenth century, the need for skilled craftsmen declined. Unskilled workers could do the same jobs as many guild masters on account of the machines they used. The guilds tried to halt these changes but failed, so most of them disappeared or eventually transformed into trade unions.

*Glossary

seamstress: a woman who sews clothes
apprenticeship: a set period of time in which one person learns a skill or trade from another

1 The word "prohibiting" in the passage is closest in meaning to

   Ⓐ criticizing

   Ⓑ forbidding

   Ⓒ warning

   Ⓓ arresting

2 According to paragraph 1, which of the following is true about guilds?

   Ⓐ The period of economic expansion in the Middle Ages was caused by them.

   Ⓑ Any person who wished to work in the Middle Ages needed permission from a guild.

   Ⓒ They obligated all of their members to follow certain regulations they had passed.

   Ⓓ The Romans had them, but they became much more popular during medieval times.

Paragraph 1 is marked with an arrow (➡).

Training in Medieval Guilds

➡ Centuries ago in medieval Europe, guilds were organizations whose members were highly skilled in one specific craft. There were guilds for carpenters, masons, blacksmiths, tailors, seamstresses, and bakers, among others. Guilds arose in the Middle Ages sometime during the twelfth century and soon dominated economic activity throughout Europe. They became so powerful that they often had monopolies on their particular skills, and laws were passed prohibiting non-guild members from practicing their trades. Therefore, to make a living at some trades, people were required to become guild members. Upon joining, they agreed to certain professional standards, including their pay rates and the quality of their work. However, before individuals could become guild members, they trained as apprentices and were required to attain certain levels of knowledge or skill.

*Glossary

seamstress: a woman who sews clothes

3   Which of the sentences below best expresses the essential information in the highlighted sentence in the passage? Incorrect answer choices change the meaning in important ways or leave out essential information.

The master provided the apprentice with shelter, food, and training, and, in return, the apprentice did everything that was asked, which initially meant the lowest and dirtiest tasks.

Ⓐ An apprentice did all of the jobs required of him or her while the master provided food and a home as well as knowledge.

Ⓑ The master housed, clothed, and trained the apprentice, who, in return, was expected to work as hard as possible.

Ⓒ Apprentices often came to dislike the difficult and dirty chores that they were assigned to do by their masters.

Ⓓ Even though masters provided their apprentices with everything they needed, some apprentices refused to do various hard tasks.

4   According to paragraph 2, which of the following is NOT true about apprentices?

Ⓐ They were restricted in the activities that they were permitted to do.

Ⓑ All of their needs were provided for by the masters with whom they apprenticed.

Ⓒ As they gained knowledge, they were permitted to do more complicated tasks.

Ⓓ The families of children had to pay a fee for them to be taken on as apprentices.

Paragraph 2 is marked with an arrow (➡).

➡ Most people began their apprenticeships around the age of twelve although this varied depending upon the trade. Most apprentices were boys, but girls could become apprentice seamstresses, tailors, and bakers. The parents of an apprentice paid a master in a guild to take on their son or daughter and to train their child. Once accepted as an apprentice, the child lived in the master's home along with his family. The master provided the apprentice with shelter, food, and training, and, in return, the apprentice did everything that was asked, which initially meant the lowest and dirtiest tasks. Though laws varied from region to region, anyone who was an apprentice was not permitted to marry and had to remain in the master's home. Most apprenticeships lasted for seven years, after which time the master nearly always decided that the apprentice was skilled enough to be elevated to the rank of journeyman.

*Glossary

apprenticeship: a set period of time in which one person learns a skill or trade from another

5   The word "it" in the passage refers to

   Ⓐ his or her trade

   Ⓑ a shop

   Ⓒ a great work

   Ⓓ the guild

6   According to paragraph 3, what were journeymen permitted to do?

   Ⓐ Become members of the local guilds in their trades

   Ⓑ Engage in activities that allowed them to be compensated

   Ⓒ Train younger people in the trade that they specialized in

   Ⓓ Open shops so that they could be hired by others

Paragraph 3 is marked with an arrow (➡).

➡ Once a person became a journeyman, this individual was considered skilled enough at his or her trade to be a paid worker but was not talented enough to be called a master. A journeyman was permitted to make money by practicing his or her trade but was not allowed to employ others or to open a shop. Most journeymen were employed by the masters with whom they did their apprenticeships. Others went on journeys and traveled to different towns and cities to learn new skills and to earn a living. Eventually, a journeyman would feel confident enough to begin preparing to become a master. To do this, the person had to produce a great work demonstrating his or her talents. When completed, the work was judged by the master craftsmen who belonged to the guild since only they could approve it and therefore give the journeyman the right to join the guild and to be called a master.

7　According to paragraph 4, many journeymen never became guild members because

- (A) there was not enough need in their communities for a larger number of masters
- (B) they failed sufficiently to impress the masters with their final projects
- (C) the masters conspired to keep the guild from having too many members
- (D) they refused to pay the entrance fee since they considered it to be too high

Paragraph 4 is marked with an arrow (➡).

8　The word "prerogatives" in the passage is closest in meaning to

- (A) inducements
- (B) privileges
- (C) regulations
- (D) possessions

➡ Unfortunately for journeymen, skill was not the only factor the masters took into consideration. They frequently failed journeymen simply to prevent there from being too many masters in a region. Additionally, most guilds required journeymen to pay a large sum of money before being permitted to become members. Many journeymen were thusly prevented from ever joining guilds, so they remained in their positions for the rest of their lives and typically worked for the very masters who refused to elevate them to the highest rank. However, whenever a journeyman finally became a master, that person could open a shop, had the right to employ others, and was allowed to train apprentices. For members of the middle class, being a master in a guild was an important social step and was as high in society as they could legitimately hope to rise.

The medieval guild system was sometimes criticized for being too restrictive. It required people to commit their lives to a single skill set and to spend years of training in it only for them frequently to be rejected from their life's objective. Guilds also came to dominate many aspects of economic activity in medieval times, and their members jealously guarded their prerogatives and were suspicious of innovation. When industrialization began centuries later in the eighteenth century, the need for skilled craftsmen declined. Unskilled workers could do the same jobs as many guild masters on account of the machines they used. The guilds tried to halt these changes but failed, so most of them disappeared or eventually transformed into trade unions.

9 Look at the four squares [■] that indicate where the following sentence could be added to the passage.

One result of this was that there were few inventions in the various trades that had guilds from medieval times until the Industrial Revolution.

Where would the sentence best fit?

Click on a square [■] to add the sentence to the passage.

The medieval guild system was sometimes criticized for being too restrictive. It required people to commit their lives to a single skill set and to spend years of training in it only for them frequently to be rejected from their life's objective. ■ Guilds also came to dominate many aspects of economic activity in medieval times, and their members jealously guarded their prerogatives and were suspicious of innovation. ■ When industrialization began centuries later in the eighteenth century, the need for skilled craftsmen declined. ■ Unskilled workers could do the same jobs as many guild masters on account of the machines they used. ■ The guilds tried to halt these changes but failed, so most of them disappeared or eventually transformed into trade unions.

10 **Directions:** An introductory sentence for a brief summary of the passage is provided below. Complete the summary by selecting the THREE answer choices that express the most important ideas of the passage. Some sentences do not belong because they express ideas that are not presented in the passage or are minor ideas in the passage. **This question is worth 2 points.**

Drag your answer choices to the spaces where they belong. To remove an answer choice, click on it. To review the passage, click on VIEW TEXT.

In order to become a guild master, an individual had to go through a long and difficult process of training.

-

-

-

ANSWER CHOICES

1 When industrialization started to happen, guilds began losing their power and thus eventually disappeared.

2 Most apprentices endured seven years of training in order to learn enough to become journeymen.

3 There were guilds for people with many different trades, and they dominated the economy of the Middle Ages.

4 The majority of people who became apprentices did so when they were children sometime around the age of twelve.

5 Journeymen continued learning either by being employed by masters or by traveling from place to place.

6 The final step to guild membership, which many people did not succeed at, was to make a work showing how advanced one's knowledge was.

Plant and Animal Distribution Limitations

There are plants and animals living around the world, yet not all of them are found everywhere. Alligators and palm trees do not appear in the Arctic whereas polar bears and redwood trees do not live in the Sahara Desert. While it is the nature of most species to expand as rapidly and as far as they can, many are restricted from moving to other regions. Some limiting factors involve geography, climate, soil composition, the availability of food and water, and obstacles caused by disasters as well as humans. Furthermore, the features enabling a plant or animal to prosper in one location may not be present in another. Every plant and animal occupies an environmental niche controlled by a variety of factors, and, once an organism is outside its comfort zone, if it cannot adapt quickly, it will fail to gain a foothold in a new region and, most likely, die.

One of the most vital factors controlling plant and animal distribution is geography. Land animals cannot cross wide oceans while aquatic animals cannot go onto land. Moreover, with few exceptions, aquatic animals cannot move from freshwater to saltwater environments, and vice versa. On land, mountains, deserts, rivers, and lakes create barriers numerous animals cannot cross. In the oceans, most species cannot dwell deep beneath the surface on account of the crushing force of water pressure. As for plants, they are less restricted by physical barriers than animals since their seeds may be carried vast distances by the wind or birds; however, when these seeds are deposited in new regions, they may not germinate and grow due to poor soil, a lack of water, or a climate unsuitable to them. Tropical plants, for instance, cannot survive in cold northern climates, and few plants are capable of growing in places with sandy soil. Over time, a plant or animal that moves to a new region may evolve and adapt to its new conditions, but it does not have the luxury of time in extremely harsh conditions. Deserts with high temperatures and few water sources, as well as the frigid Arctic and Antarctic, are unforgiving to species that fail to adapt quickly.

The availability of food is another limiting factor, primarily for animals. Predators—particularly mammals—require a constant supply of prey and often compete with other species of predators for limited food sources. This factor restricts predators from moving into regions where prey animals are not abundant. Other animals are particular about the food they consume. The Australian koala almost exclusively eats the leaves of the eucalyptus tree and would not survive in any ecosystem lacking them. While most plants get their nourishment from photosynthesis, if the soil lacks nutrients or is too acidic, they simply will not grow.

The final barriers to plant and animal distribution are obstacles created by natural disasters and human activity. Prolonged droughts can cause deserts to enlarge and therefore establish large barriers. Volcanic eruptions can form large wastelands in which few plants and animals can survive. Forest fires

also create dead zones that hinder plant and animal movement. Humans, by building new population centers and highways across known migration routes, can limit species to specific areas. Additionally, as humans clear tracts of land for agriculture, they move into regions that wild animals once dominated. Human polluting of the oceans is another problem since there are now dead zones, which have limited amounts of oxygen, in the oceans, and many coral reefs, which are home to myriad species of animals, have been damaged or destroyed, too.

Conversely, human activity has enabled many plants and animals to be more widely distributed than ever before. Corn, potatoes, and tomatoes were once found only in the Americas, but European explorers spread them so widely that they grow virtually everywhere today. Not all human distribution of plants and animals has been beneficial though as some invasive species have caused a great amount of damage both to the land and the native flora and fauna. One of the best-known examples happened in the nineteenth century when several dozen rabbits were introduced to Australia. They reproduced so quickly that, a few decades later, there were millions of rabbits causing problems around the country.

*Glossary

photosynthesis: the process through which plants create food for themselves and release oxygen into the atmosphere
flora and fauna: plant and animal life

11 The word "niche" in the passage is closest in meaning to

Ⓐ obligation

Ⓑ practice

Ⓒ role

Ⓓ slot

Plant and Animal Distribution Limitations

➡ There are plants and animals living around the world, yet not all of them are found everywhere. Alligators and palm trees do not appear in the Arctic whereas polar bears and redwood trees do not live in the Sahara Desert. While it is the nature of most species to expand as rapidly and as far as they can, many are restricted from moving to other regions. Some limiting factors involve geography, climate, soil composition, the availability of food and water, and obstacles caused by disasters as well as humans. Furthermore, the features enabling a plant or animal to prosper in one location may not be present in another. Every plant and animal occupies an environmental niche controlled by a variety of factors, and, once an organism is outside its comfort zone, if it cannot adapt quickly, it will fail to gain a foothold in a new region and, most likely, die.

More Available ▲

12 According to paragraph 2, which of the following is NOT true about plants?

Ⓐ Their seeds can be transported elsewhere by animals and natural forces.

Ⓑ Water is the most crucial element they need when they move to a new environment.

Ⓒ Ones that live in tropical environments may not grow well in colder places.

Ⓓ They may not germinate if they are deposited into unfitting soil.

Paragraph 2 is marked with an arrow (➡).

13 Which of the following can be inferred about the Arctic and Antarctic?

Ⓐ They have environments that are harsher than the world's hottest deserts.

Ⓑ The lowest temperatures on the Earth have been recorded in those regions.

Ⓒ Animals and plants moving to those regions typically fail to adapt and die.

Ⓓ Humans have more problems living in them than they do living in deserts.

➡ One of the most vital factors controlling plant and animal distribution is geography. Land animals cannot cross wide oceans while aquatic animals cannot go onto land. Moreover, with few exceptions, aquatic animals cannot move from freshwater to saltwater environments, and vice versa. On land, mountains, deserts, rivers, and lakes create barriers numerous animals cannot cross. In the oceans, most species cannot dwell deep beneath the surface on account of the crushing force of water pressure. As for plants, they are less restricted by physical barriers than animals since their seeds may be carried vast distances by the wind or birds; however, when these seeds are deposited in new regions, they may not germinate and grow due to poor soil, a lack of water, or a climate unsuitable to them. Tropical plants, for instance, cannot survive in cold northern climates, and few plants are capable of growing in places with sandy soil. Over time, a plant or animal that moves to a new region may evolve and adapt to its new conditions, but it does not have the luxury of time in extremely harsh conditions. Deserts with high temperatures and few water sources, as well as the frigid Arctic and Antarctic, are unforgiving to species that fail to adapt quickly.

▼

REVIEW

HELP

BACK

NEXT

HIDE TIME 00:54:00

More Available ▲

14 In paragraph 3, the author uses "The Australian koala" as an example of

Ⓐ the only animal in the world capable of consuming eucalyptus leaves

Ⓑ a mammal that can be found living in a variety of different ecosystems

Ⓒ a prey animal that must be careful to avoid being eaten by predators

Ⓓ an animal which is such a fussy eater that it is limited in where it can live

Paragraph 3 is marked with an arrow (➡).

15 The word "hinder" in the passage is closest in meaning to

Ⓐ impede

Ⓑ detour

Ⓒ resist

Ⓓ encroach

16 Select the TWO answer choices from paragraph 4 that identify how humans serve as barriers to plant and animal distribution. *To receive credit, you must select TWO answers.*

Ⓐ By burning large amounts of forested land

Ⓑ By creating places in oceans where there is excessive pollution

Ⓒ By constructing roads in places where animals migrate

Ⓓ By diverting water supplies so that large-scale farming may be done

Paragraph 4 is marked with an arrow (⇨).

➡ The availability of food is another limiting factor, primarily for animals. Predators—particularly mammals—require a constant supply of prey and often compete with other species of predators for limited food sources. This factor restricts predators from moving into regions where prey animals are not abundant. Other animals are particular about the food they consume. The Australian koala almost exclusively eats the leaves of the eucalyptus tree and would not survive in any ecosystem lacking them. While most plants get their nourishment from photosynthesis, if the soil lacks nutrients or is too acidic, they simply will not grow.

⇨ The final barriers to plant and animal distribution are obstacles created by natural disasters and human activity. Prolonged droughts can cause deserts to enlarge and therefore establish large barriers. Volcanic eruptions can form large wastelands in which few plants and animals can survive. Forest fires also create dead zones that hinder plant and animal movement. Humans, by building new population centers and highways across known migration routes, can limit species to specific areas. Additionally, as humans clear tracts of land for agriculture, they move into regions that wild animals once dominated. Human polluting of the oceans is another problem since there are now dead zones, which have limited amounts of oxygen, in the oceans, and many coral reefs, which are home to myriad species of animals, have been damaged or destroyed, too.

*Glossary

photosynthesis: the process through which plants create food for themselves and release oxygen into the atmosphere

17 According to paragraph 5, which of the following is true about invasive species?

- Ⓐ They only move to new regions because of human activity.
- Ⓑ They can create benefits for native flora and fauna.
- Ⓒ Most of them create problems like the rabbits in Australia did.
- Ⓓ They can have positive effects as well as negative ones.

Paragraph 5 is marked with an arrow (➡).

18 In paragraph 5, why does the author mention that some plants and animals have become more widely distributed?

- Ⓐ To claim that most animals that see increases in their populations can become nuisances
- Ⓑ To point out that the majority of the plants and animals on the Earth are seeing their populations rise
- Ⓒ To provide a contrast to the argument that humans are limiting plant and animal movement
- Ⓓ To cite some examples of how invasive species can cause problems to native plants and animals

Paragraph 5 is marked with an arrow (➡).

➡ Conversely, human activity has enabled many plants and animals to be more widely distributed than ever before. Corn, potatoes, and tomatoes were once found only in the Americas, but European explorers spread them so widely that they grow virtually everywhere today. Not all human distribution of plants and animals has been beneficial though as some invasive species have caused a great amount of damage both to the land and the native flora and fauna. One of the best-known examples happened in the nineteenth century when several dozen rabbits were introduced to Australia. They reproduced so quickly that, a few decades later, there were millions of rabbits causing problems around the country.

*Glossary

flora and fauna: plant and animal life

More Available ▲

19 Look at the four squares [■] that indicate where the following sentence could be added to the passage.

Likewise, the giant panda of China depends primarily upon a diet of bamboo and rarely ventures into areas where that plant does not grow.

Where would the sentence best fit?

Click on a square [■] to add the sentence to the passage.

The availability of food is another limiting factor, primarily for animals. Predators—particularly mammals—require a constant supply of prey and often compete with other species of predators for limited food sources. This factor restricts predators from moving into regions where prey animals are not abundant. **1** Other animals are particular about the food they consume. **2** The Australian koala almost exclusively eats the leaves of the eucalyptus tree and would not survive in any ecosystem lacking them. **3** While most plants get their nourishment from photosynthesis, if the soil lacks nutrients or is too acidic, they simply will not grow. **4**

*Glossary

photosynthesis: the process through which plants create food for themselves and release oxygen into the atmosphere

20 **Directions:** An introductory sentence for a brief summary of the passage is provided below. Complete the summary by selecting the THREE answer choices that express the most important ideas of the passage. Some sentences do not belong because they express ideas that are not presented in the passage or are minor ideas in the passage. **This question is worth 2 points.**

Drag your answer choices to the spaces where they belong. To remove an answer choice, click on it. To review the passage, click on **VIEW TEXT**.

There are a large number of reasons that the distribution of most plants and animals is limited.

-
-
-

ANSWER CHOICES

1 When rabbits were introduced to Australia, they quickly reproduced and became an invasive species there.

2 Natural obstacles such as mountains, rivers, and oceans frequently stop organisms from being widely distributed.

3 Both natural disasters and human activity can create various barriers that prevent plants and animals from moving elsewhere.

4 Some plants may not grow well in certain places because of environmental factors such as the soil quality, a lack of water, and an unsuitable climate.

5 It is possible for some aquatic animals to move from freshwater environments to saltwater ones.

6 Human activity in the oceans has caused coral reefs and other sensitive ecosystems to suffer a great amount of damage.

Shy and Outgoing Children

Not all children are the same. Besides obvious physical differences, children are different from one another in temperament. One of the biggest variances concerns how they react around others. While some children are outgoing and happy to play and be with other individuals, some children are quite shy and uncomfortable when in the company of others. Why this is so is one of the great questions in child psychology. Psychologists have not yet been able to determine whether a gene determines how shy or outgoing a child is, but they have devised two widely accepted theories. The first is that children are shy from birth and possess an innate sense of shyness, and the second is that children become shy due to the way they are brought up and the environment around them.

Studies on the long-term behavior of babies indicate that shyness is ingrained in them even before birth. In the studies, babies were exposed to a variety of outside stimuli, among them being unfamiliar lights, noises, objects, and people. At the two ends of the spectrum concerning their reactions were babies that remained calm and those that were highly reactive to the stimuli. Around forty percent of the babies had no reaction at all but merely observed the stimuli in a calm manner. In contrast, between fifteen and twenty percent had extreme reactions in which they waved their arms, thrashed about, screamed, cried, or engaged in some combination of those actions. The studies revealed that the sedate babies grew up to be quite outgoing whereas the babies that reacted in extreme manners became shyer as they grew older.

Why the babies had such differing reactions may have something to do with the chemical makeup of their brains. Scientists have learned that people who are shy have a very sensitive nervous system, which is affected by a chemical in the brain called monoamine oxidase. It acts as an inhibitor on impulsive actions and causes people with high levels of it to be shyer and more introverted and people with lower levels to be more outgoing and extroverted. Another region in the brain that affects shyness is the amygdala, which plays a role in causing fear. People with an overly active amygdala tend to inflate their fears and are therefore shyer in nature.

The second theory—that children are shy or outgoing based upon their environment and how they are raised—may also have some validity. It has long been observed that children who grow up in strict households with domineering parents tend to be much shyer than children whose parents behave in other ways. In addition, children with older siblings that are more dominant frequently exhibit more shyness than their elder brothers and sisters. There is very much anecdotal evidence that children who experience traumatic events early in their lives develop a greater fear of the outside world, and that causes them to become shy and introverted. Culture may also play a role in how children behave. Children who live in strict societies in which expressing themselves in an outgoing manner is frowned upon are nearly always

shyer than children raised in more gregarious societies.

In many cultures, there is a stigma attached to shy children in that they are regarded as having some sort of problem while outgoing children are considered normal. This has led to an emphasis in society on transforming shy children into more outgoing ones. However, actions meant to do that are not always for the best. Outgoing children have their own issues, and some engage in behavior that is too extroverted. Very outgoing children may exhibit behavioral problems associated with attention deficit hyperactivity disorder, also known as ADHD. Some outgoing children additionally become adults who are constantly seeking new thrills to such a point that they harm both themselves and others. In contrast, studies conducted on adult shyness show that up to forty percent of people may experience feelings of shyness yet are perfectly capable of functioning in society. A small percentage, however, are so overcome by shyness that they fear leaving their homes and must take medication that allows them to feel less anxious to participate in social activities.

*Glossary

temperament: mood; character; personality
stimulus: something that causes a response

PASSAGE 3

REVIEW

HELP

BACK

NEXT

HIDE TIME 00:54:00

Beginning

Shy and Outgoing Children

➡ Not all children are the same. Besides obvious physical differences, children are different from one another in temperament. One of the biggest variances concerns how they react around others. While some children are outgoing and happy to play and be with other individuals, some children are quite shy and uncomfortable when in the company of others. Why this is so is one of the great questions in child psychology. Psychologists have not yet been able to determine whether a gene determines how shy or outgoing a child is, but they have devised two widely accepted theories. The first is that children are shy from birth and possess an innate sense of shyness, and the second is that children become shy due to the way they are brought up and the environment around them.

⇨ Studies on the long-term behavior of babies indicate that shyness is ingrained in them even before birth. In the studies, babies were exposed to a variety of outside stimuli, among them being unfamiliar lights, noises, objects, and people. At the two ends of the spectrum concerning their reactions were babies that remained calm and those that were highly reactive to the stimuli. Around forty percent of the babies had no reaction at all but merely observed the stimuli in a calm manner. In contrast, between fifteen and twenty percent had extreme reactions in which they waved their arms, thrashed about, screamed, cried, or engaged in some combination of those actions. The studies revealed that the sedate babies grew up to be quite outgoing whereas the babies that reacted in extreme manners became shyer as they grew older.

21 The word "innate" in the passage is closest in meaning to

  Ⓐ immature

  Ⓑ undeveloped

  Ⓒ extraordinary

  Ⓓ instinctive

22 According to paragraph 1, psychologists believe some children may be shy because

  Ⓐ their parents actively attempt to make them less outgoing than others

  Ⓑ they are influenced by their friends and peers to act in that manner

  Ⓒ they prefer to be quieter and less outgoing than their peers

  Ⓓ the manner in which they are reared causes them to become shy

Paragraph 1 is marked with an arrow (➡).

23 In paragraph 2, the author's description of the studies carried out on babies mentions all of the following EXCEPT:

  Ⓐ what the extreme reactions of some babies to the stimuli were

  Ⓑ what percentage of babies failed to react to the outside stimuli

  Ⓒ which groups of psychologists carried out the experiments on babies

  Ⓓ what the characteristics of the calm babies were like after they aged

Paragraph 2 is marked with an arrow (⇨).

*Glossary

temperament: mood; character; personality
stimulus: something that causes a response

24 The author discusses "monoamine oxidase" in order to

Ⓐ explain how the body both produces and releases the chemical

Ⓑ describe how it can cause people to behave in an introverted manner

Ⓒ point out that it is typically released in the amygdala in the brain

Ⓓ contrast its effects on the human body with those of another chemical

25 According to paragraph 3, which of the following is true about the amygdala?

Ⓐ It can cause people to become more frightened.

Ⓑ It is a type of chemical produced by the brain.

Ⓒ It is the largest part of most people's brains.

Ⓓ It can cause people to become more outgoing.

Paragraph 3 is marked with an arrow (➡).

➡ Why the babies had such differing reactions may have something to do with the chemical makeup of their brains. Scientists have learned that people who are shy have a very sensitive nervous system, which is affected by a chemical in the brain called monoamine oxidase. It acts as an inhibitor on impulsive actions and causes people with high levels of it to be shyer and more introverted and people with lower levels to be more outgoing and extroverted. Another region in the brain that affects shyness is the amygdala, which plays a role in causing fear. People with an overly active amygdala tend to inflate their fears and are therefore shyer in nature.

Q
REVIEW
?
HELP
‹
BACK
›
NEXT

HIDE TIME 00:54:00

More Available ▲

26 Which of the sentences below best expresses the essential information in the highlighted sentence in the passage? *Incorrect* answer choices change the meaning in important ways or leave out essential information.

There is very much anecdotal evidence that children who experience traumatic events early in their lives develop a greater fear of the outside world, and that causes them to become shy and introverted.

Ⓐ Instances where children become shy and afraid of outside stimuli due to upsetting events in their lives have been recorded.

Ⓑ It is believed that children who are shyer and more introverted than others are prone to having disturbing events happen to them.

Ⓒ When something traumatic happens to a child, he or she may sometimes withdraw from partaking in a normal social life.

Ⓓ Children who are both shy and introverted like to tell stories about the traumatic events that happened in their lives.

27 The word "gregarious" in the passage is closest in meaning to

Ⓐ lighthearted

Ⓑ law-abiding

Ⓒ extroverted

Ⓓ relaxed

The second theory—that children are shy or outgoing based upon their environment and how they are raised—may also have some validity. It has long been observed that children who grow up in strict households with domineering parents tend to be much shyer than children whose parents behave in other ways. In addition, children with older siblings that are more dominant frequently exhibit more shyness than their elder brothers and sisters. There is very much anecdotal evidence that children who experience traumatic events early in their lives develop a greater fear of the outside world, and that causes them to become shy and introverted. Culture may also play a role in how children behave. Children who live in strict societies in which expressing themselves in an outgoing manner is frowned upon are nearly always shyer than children raised in more gregarious societies.

28 In paragraph 5, the author implies that shy children

Ⓐ have problems adjusting their behavior so that they become outgoing

Ⓑ are unable to assume positions of leadership after they grow older

Ⓒ are often diagnosed by doctors as having behavioral problems

Ⓓ are less preferred than outgoing children in a large number of cultures

Paragraph 5 is marked with an arrow (➡).

➡ In many cultures, there is a stigma attached to shy children in that they are regarded as having some sort of problem while outgoing children are considered normal. This has led to an emphasis in society on transforming shy children into more outgoing ones. However, actions meant to do that are not always for the best. Outgoing children have their own issues, and some engage in behavior that is too extroverted. Very outgoing children may exhibit behavioral problems associated with attention deficit hyperactivity disorder, also known as ADHD. Some outgoing children additionally become adults who are constantly seeking new thrills to such a point that they harm both themselves and others. In contrast, studies conducted on adult shyness show that up to forty percent of people may experience feelings of shyness yet are perfectly capable of functioning in society. A small percentage, however, are so overcome by shyness that they fear leaving their homes and must take medication that allows them to feel less anxious to participate in social activities.

29 Look at the four squares [■] that indicate where the following sentence could be added to the passage.

These problems which they cause can be either physical or mental in nature.

Where would the sentence best fit?

Click on a square [■] to add the sentence to the passage.

In many cultures, there is a stigma attached to shy children in that they are regarded as having some sort of problem while outgoing children are considered normal. This has led to an emphasis in society on transforming shy children into more outgoing ones. However, actions meant to do that are not always for the best. Outgoing children have their own issues, and some engage in behavior that is too extroverted. Very outgoing children may exhibit behavioral problems associated with attention deficit hyperactivity disorder, also known as ADHD. **1** Some outgoing children additionally become adults who are constantly seeking new thrills to such a point that they harm both themselves and others. **2** In contrast, studies conducted on adult shyness show that up to forty percent of people may experience feelings of shyness yet are perfectly capable of functioning in society. **3** A small percentage, however, are so overcome by shyness that they fear leaving their homes and must take medication that allows them to feel less anxious to participate in social activities. **4**

30 **Directions:** Select the appropriate statements from the answer choices and match them to the personality to which they relate. TWO of the answer choices will NOT be used. **This question is worth 3 points.**

Drag your answer choices to the spaces where they belong. To remove an answer choice, click on it. To review the passage, click on VIEW TEXT.

ANSWER CHOICES

1 Often remain calm as babies when exposed to stimuli

2 May become that way since they grow up in strict cultures

3 Frequently become leaders in society as adults

4 Can suffer from behavioral issues such as ADHD

5 May react extremely to stimuli when they are babies

6 Can have an amygdala that is too active

7 May have teachers that give them few rules to follow

PERSONALITY

Shy (Select 3)

-
-
-

Outgoing (Select 2)

-
-

Actual Test

07

Reading Section Directions

This section measures your ability to understand academic passages in English. You will have **54 minutes** to read and answer questions about **3 passages**. A clock at the top of the screen will show you how much time is remaining.

Most questions are worth 1 point but the last question for each passage is worth more than 1 point. The directions for the last question indicate how many points you may receive.

Some passages include a word or phrase that is underlined in blue. Click on the word or phrase to see a definition or an explanation.

When you want to move to the next question, click on **NEXT**. You may skip questions and go back to them later. If you want to return to previous questions, click on **BACK**. You can click on **REVIEW** at any time, and the review screen will show you which questions you have answered and which you have not answered. From this review screen, you may go directly to any question you have already seen in the Reading section.

Click on **CONTINUE** to go on.

Ancient Nile River Settlements

The Nile River Valley in Africa was the location of one of mankind's earliest civilizations as evidence of permanent settlements there dates back as far as 7,000 years. Nomadic hunter-gatherers were first attracted to the Nile River Valley because of its wealth of wildlife and vegetation. Over time, these nomads' descendants settled down once they learned the art of agriculture. The fertile soil in the river valley and the annual replenishment of nutrients during the flood season were incentives as was the fact that the inhospitable nearby desert lands provided few alternatives. The Nile River was additionally a source of fresh water, served as an easy means of transportation, and provided its inhabitants with protection since marauding tribes could not easily cross the surrounding deserts to attack them.

Humans hailing from lands south, west, and east of the Nile River Valley found their way there tens of thousands of years ago. They may have initially ventured there accidentally, or perhaps they were in search of places with water and game. What they discovered was a fertile valley with fresh water and abundant food. Fish thrived in the Nile River, and fowl nested on its shores; they, in turn, attracted larger animals, which provided numerous sources of food for the hunter-gatherers. When the Nile River flooded every year, it left behind a narrow strip of nutrient-rich soil in which berry plants and fruit trees grew exceptionally well. Eventually, the nomads learned how to farm, so they established permanent settlements in the region around 5500 B.C.

To construct settlements that would not be damaged or washed away by the annual floods, these people learned to build their villages and towns above the Nile River's flood levels. As the riverbed eroded and sediment was deposited alongside its shores, a wide number of areas developed above the level of the Nile's floodplain. The Nile River had also changed its course over its long history, and, in places where it had meandered, there were built-up regions of deposited sediment and gravel situated in the middle of the floodplain. Finally, some small islands in the river and its delta were high enough to keep from being flooded. The inhabitants of the Nile River Valley utilized all three locations to construct their homes and other buildings.

Like today, in the past, the Nile River Valley had few large trees to provide wood for buildings. Resultantly, early Egyptians built simple huts from woven papyrus reeds. Many years later, they realized that the mud left behind by the annual floods could be combined with straw to make bricks. The bricks were made in molds to give them a common shape, which made them easier to stack and to join. Most buildings constructed had floors of packed earth and walls of bricks and were topped by flat roofs with a few imported wooded beams to provide support. While most Egyptians lived in rudimentary dwellings like that since they could not afford to be extravagant, well-off families normally built homes with two or more layers of strong bricks or carved stones. Their homes were well built, but those of poorer individuals

crumbled after a few years and had to undergo major repairs or be entirely rebuilt.

Most domiciles that were built had two floors; the bottom one was used to store grain, and the top one was the family's living space. There was typically a papyrus reed canopy to provide shade, and the reed coverings on windows and doors kept fleas, dust, and sand out. Exterior doors were often raised above ground level to prevent sand from blowing in. As Egypt became a richer land, some wealthy families arose. They built massive homes with several floors and a few dozen rooms that were often surrounded by a central courtyard. Tiled floors and whitewashed exteriors were common, and some even had private wells. A few homes had indoor plumbing, but most people dug pits for their sewage or merely discarded it into the Nile River. Furniture was rare in Egyptian homes as most Egyptians had mats for sleeping and sitting on; however, a few wealthy families had furniture, but anything made of wood was expensive since it had to be imported to the Nile River Valley.

*Glossary

game: wild animals, fish, and birds that people hunt for food

papyrus: a tall aquatic plant that grows in Northern Africa and Southern Europe

Beginning

Ancient Nile River Settlements

➡ The Nile River Valley in Africa was the location of one of mankind's earliest civilizations as evidence of permanent settlements there dates back as far as 7,000 years. Nomadic hunter-gatherers were first attracted to the Nile River Valley because of its wealth of wildlife and vegetation. Over time, these nomads' descendants settled down once they learned the art of agriculture. The fertile soil in the river valley and the annual replenishment of nutrients during the flood season were incentives as was the fact that the inhospitable nearby desert lands provided few alternatives. The Nile River was additionally a source of fresh water, served as an easy means of transportation, and provided its inhabitants with some measure of protection since marauding tribes could not easily cross the surrounding deserts to attack them.

⇨ Humans hailing from lands south, west, and east of the Nile River Valley found their way there tens of thousands of years ago. They may have initially ventured there accidentally, or perhaps they were in search of places with water and game. What they discovered was a fertile valley with fresh water and abundant food. Fish thrived in the Nile River, and fowl nested on its shores; they, in turn, attracted larger animals, which provided numerous sources of food for the hunter-gatherers. When the Nile River flooded every year, it left behind a narrow strip of nutrient-rich soil in which berry plants and fruit trees grew exceptionally well. Eventually, the nomads learned how to farm, so they established permanent settlements in the region around 5500 B.C.

1 The word "marauding" in the passage is closest in meaning to

Ⓐ wandering

Ⓑ warlike

Ⓒ hostile

Ⓓ raiding

2 According to paragraph 1, which of the following is NOT true about the advantages of living in the Nile River Valley?

Ⓐ A wide variety of grains grew well in the region's fertile soil.

Ⓑ The denizens had access to a supply of water they could drink.

Ⓒ The area was difficult for invaders to gain easy access to.

Ⓓ The people living there could sail goods up and down the Nile River.

Paragraph 1 is marked with an arrow (➡).

3 According to paragraph 2, the inhabitants of the Nile River Valley began to make permanent settlements because

Ⓐ the flooding of the Nile made roaming the land difficult

Ⓑ they learned how to cultivate the land

Ⓒ the animals in the region never migrated

Ⓓ their homes provided them with defensive fortifications

Paragraph 2 is marked with an arrow (⇨).

*Glossary

game: wild animals, fish, and birds that people hunt for food

4 Which of the sentences below best expresses the essential information in the highlighted sentence in the passage? Incorrect answer choices change the meaning in important ways or leave out essential information.

The Nile River had also changed its course over its long history, and, in places where it had meandered, there were built-up regions of deposited sediment and gravel situated in the middle of the floodplain.

(A) As the Nile River flowed to the sea, it constantly changed its course, so it left sediment and gravel in places all around the desert.

(B) If too much sediment and gravel was gathered in one place, the Nile River changed its course because the land was too high for it to flow through.

(C) When the Nile River began flowing through different areas, it left sections of land in its floodplain that were higher in altitude than other places.

(D) Deposits of sediment and gravel in the floodplain of the Nile River Valley prove that the river changed its course numerous times in the past.

To construct settlements that would not be damaged or washed away by the annual floods, these people learned to build their villages and towns above the Nile River's flood levels. As the riverbed eroded and sediment was deposited alongside its shores, a wide number of areas developed above the level of the Nile's floodplain. The Nile River had also changed its course over its long history, and, in places where it had meandered, there were built-up regions of deposited sediment and gravel situated in the middle of the floodplain. Finally, some small islands in the river and its delta were high enough to keep from being flooded. The inhabitants of the Nile River Valley utilized all three locations to construct their homes and other buildings.

5 In paragraph 4, the author uses "bricks" as an example of

   Ⓐ a building material that Egyptians learned to make in later times

   Ⓑ the most effective material used to make buildings in ancient Egypt

   Ⓒ the first type of building material used by the Egyptians

   Ⓓ a building material favored mostly by wealthy ancient Egyptians

   Paragraph 4 is marked with an arrow (➡).

6 The word "rudimentary" in the passage is closest in meaning to

   Ⓐ simple

   Ⓑ tiny

   Ⓒ homemade

   Ⓓ aboveground

7 In paragraph 4, which of the following can be inferred about the homes of poor individuals?

   Ⓐ They were constructed by many people working together.

   Ⓑ They were of relatively low quality so were not long lasting.

   Ⓒ They often collapsed on their inhabitants due to their poor craftsmanship.

   Ⓓ They were built solely of mud and papyrus reeds.

   Paragraph 4 is marked with an arrow (➡).

➡ Like today, in the past, the Nile River Valley had few large trees to provide wood for buildings. Resultantly, early Egyptians built simple huts from woven papyrus reeds. Many years later, they realized that the mud left behind by the annual floods could be combined with straw to make bricks. The bricks were made in molds to give them a common shape, which made them easier to stack and to join. Most buildings constructed had floors of packed earth and walls of bricks and were topped by flat roofs with a few imported wooded beams to provide support. While most Egyptians lived in rudimentary dwellings like that since they could not afford to be extravagant, well-off families normally built homes with two or more layers of strong bricks or carved stones. Their homes were well built, but those of poorer individuals crumbled after a few years and had to undergo major repairs or be entirely rebuilt.

*Glossary

papyrus: a tall aquatic plant that grows in Northern Africa and Southern Europe

End ▲

8   According to paragraph 5, which of the following is true about Egyptian furniture?

(A) It was always imported to the Nile River Valley.

(B) It could be made with wood, mud, or stone.

(C) It was seldom used by the majority of Egyptians.

(D) It was often ornately designed and well-built.

Paragraph 5 is marked with an arrow (➡).

➡ Most domiciles that were built had two floors; the bottom one was used to store grain, and the top one was the family's living space. There was typically a papyrus reed canopy to provide shade, and the reed coverings on windows and doors kept fleas, dust, and sand out. Exterior doors were often raised above ground level to prevent sand from blowing in. As Egypt became a richer land, some wealthy families arose. They built massive homes with several floors and a few dozen rooms that were often surrounded by a central courtyard. Tiled floors and whitewashed exteriors were common, and some even had private wells. A few homes had indoor plumbing, but most people dug pits for their sewage or merely discarded it into the Nile River. Furniture was rare in Egyptian homes as most Egyptians had mats for sleeping and sitting on; however, a few wealthy families had furniture, but anything made of wood was expensive since it had to be imported to the Nile River Valley.

9 Look at the four squares [■] that indicate where the following sentence could be added to the passage.

This arrangement helped people avoid encounters with dangerous animals such as snakes and scorpions while they were sleeping.

Where would the sentence best fit?

Click on a square [■] to add the sentence to the passage.

Most domiciles that were built had two floors; the bottom one was used to store grain, and the top one was the family's living space. ■ There was typically a papyrus reed canopy to provide shade, and the reed coverings on windows and doors kept fleas, dust, and sand out. ■ Exterior doors were often raised above ground level to prevent sand from blowing in. ■ As Egypt became a richer land, some wealthy families arose. ■ They built massive homes with several floors and a few dozen rooms that were often surrounded by a central courtyard. Tiled floors and whitewashed exteriors were common, and some even had private wells. A few homes had indoor plumbing, but most people dug pits for their sewage or merely discarded it into the Nile River. Furniture was rare in Egyptian homes as most Egyptians had mats for sleeping and sitting on; however, a few wealthy families had furniture, but anything made of wood was expensive since it had to be imported to the Nile River Valley.

10 Directions: An introductory sentence for a brief summary of the passage is provided below. Complete the summary by selecting the THREE answer choices that express the most important ideas of the passage. Some sentences do not belong because they express ideas that are not presented in the passage or are minor ideas in the passage. **This question is worth 2 points.**

Drag your answer choices to the spaces where they belong. To remove an answer choice, click on it. To review the passage, click on **VIEW TEXT**.

Once the ancient Egyptians began to establish permanent settlements in the Nile River Valley, they built them in various places and constructed homes of differing quality.

-
-
-

ANSWER CHOICES

1 Some of the homes of rich individuals had many rooms, access to water, and indoor plumbing for their residents.

2 When the Nile River caused the land to be higher in elevation in some places, people made settlements there to avoid flooding.

3 The homes in the Nile River Valley were made of papyrus reeds, mud, bricks, and other materials and could be quite small or very large.

4 The first people to live in the Nile River Valley were nomadic hunter-gatherers who wandered there from other places in Africa.

5 The Nile River flooded every year, and its floodwaters brought nutrients that made the land beside the river very fertile.

6 The ecosystem of the Nile River Valley had many kinds of animals, which people hunted for food.

The Inner Earth

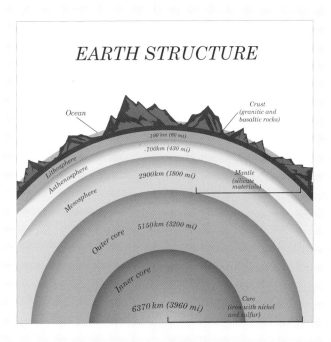

The Earth is not a single solid piece of rock but instead consists of several layers, the main ones of which are the crust, mantle, outer core, and inner core. While scientists have thus far not been able to penetrate the planet's deepest parts, they understand its structure thanks to a variety of observations and experiments they have performed. These include studying rocks brought to the surface by volcanic eruptions and other geological activity, examining the planet's gravitational and magnetic fields, estimating the Earth's density, volume, and mass, and studying seismic activity during earthquakes. Scientists can additionally understand the geological processes occurring deep within the Earth by conducting experiments with pressure and heat on rocks.

At the very center of the Earth is the inner core, which is estimated to be approximately 2,400 kilometers in diameter. It consists of a solid ball of iron that also contains the elements nickel and sulfur. The inner core is thought to have formed at the same time the Earth did 4.5 billion years ago. As the Earth cooled, the heavier elements sank to the center of the Earth while the lighter elements—mostly silicates— remained closer to the surface. The inner core is extremely hot as geologists believe the temperatures there range from 5,000 to 7,000 degrees Celsius. Despite this intense heat, the core does not melt due to the enormous amount of pressure being exerted on it.

Surrounding the inner core is the 2,300-kilometer-thick outer core, which is composed mostly of liquid iron but, like the inner core, contains substantial amounts of nickel and sulfur. The temperatures in it range

between 4,000 and 5,000 degrees Celsius, making it cooler than the inner core. Nevertheless, the pressure there is not so great as to prevent melting, and it gives the outer core its viscosity, which allows the liquid metals in it to flow. The Earth's magnetic field is created by the outer core, and the flowing metals there contribute to its strength.

Above the outer core is the mantle, the largest and deepest layer of the Earth's inner structure. The mantle is believed to be around 2,900 kilometers thick and contains the greatest amount of the planet's volume. It consists of molten rock, mainly silicates high in concentrations of magnesium and iron, which is slowly flowing. This liquid rock rises and falls within the mantle as it cools and then becomes hotter. Like the core, the mantle is comprised of two layers: the upper mantle and lower mantle. The boundary between the upper and lower mantles is about 750 kilometers beneath the surface of the Earth and consists of a zone of transition in which the temperature and viscosity of the molten rock are notably different. The lower mantle has temperatures around 4,000 degrees Celsius whereas the temperature in the upper mantle ranges between 500 and 900 degrees Celsius. The lower mantle, lying next to the outer core, is under a great amount of pressure, so the melted rocks in it flow more slowly than those in the upper mantle.

At the topmost part of the upper mantle is a region known as the asthenosphere, which is roughly eighty to 200 kilometers beneath the surface of the Earth. It is thought that the large tectonic plates comprising the Earth's crust float on the asthenosphere. Temperature changes within the asthenosphere cause convection currents in this layer. These make the molten rock in the asthenosphere move, which, in turn, causes the tectonic plates to move. The movement of the plates instigates much of the geological activity—primarily earthquakes and volcanic eruptions—that the planet's surface experiences.

By studying seismic activity, geologists have been able to determine where the crust ends and the mantle begins. The boundary between the two is known as the Moho Discontinuity. It fluctuates in depth around the planet, but it has an average depth of thirty-two kilometers beneath the surface. It was discovered because seismic waves from earthquakes changed speed when they hit the mantle, which is much denser than the crust. Geologists hope to be able to study seismic waves and other factors in the future to help them learn more about the regions far beneath the planet's surface.

*Glossary

seismic: relating to earthquakes or the vibrating of the Earth
silicate: any chemical that contains silicon

11 Which of the sentences below best expresses the essential information in the highlighted sentence in the passage? Incorrect answer choices change the meaning in important ways or leave out essential information.

While scientists have thus far not been able to penetrate the planet's deepest parts, they understand its structure thanks to a variety of observations and experiments they have performed.

Ⓐ Scientists believe that they will learn a great deal about the Earth as soon as they are able to get to its deepest layers.

Ⓑ Despite not physically being able to visit the inner planet, scientists have used various methods to learn what it is like.

Ⓒ There are many experiments that scientists have conducted to learn about how big the layers of the Earth are.

Ⓓ By observing and conducting experiments, scientists think they will be able to reach the inner layers of the Earth someday.

12 In paragraph 1, the author's description of the layers of the Earth mentions all of the following EXCEPT:

Ⓐ how scientists have managed to get information about them

Ⓑ what the names of the primary layers of the planet are

Ⓒ what types of experiments scientists conduct on them

Ⓓ how large the layers are in comparison with one another

Paragraph 1 is marked with an arrow (➡).

The Inner Earth

➡ The Earth is not a single solid piece of rock but instead consists of several layers, the main ones of which are the crust, mantle, outer core, and inner core. While scientists have thus far not been able to penetrate the planet's deepest parts, they understand its structure thanks to a variety of observations and experiments they have performed. These include studying rocks brought to the surface by volcanic eruptions and other geological activity, examining the planet's gravitational and magnetic fields, estimating the Earth's density, volume, and mass, and studying seismic activity during earthquakes. Scientists can additionally understand the geological processes occurring deep within the Earth by conducting experiments with pressure and heat on rocks.

*Glossary

seismic: relating to earthquakes or the vibrating of the Earth

▼

13 In paragraph 2, the author implies that iron

   Ⓐ is one of the heavier elements

   Ⓑ has a boiling point of 5,000 degrees
       Celsius

   Ⓒ is found in its liquid form in the inner core

   Ⓓ can combine with nickel to create various
       compounds

Paragraph 2 is marked with an arrow (➡).

14 The word "substantial" in the passage is
    closest in meaning to

   Ⓐ considerable

   Ⓑ varying

   Ⓒ measurable

   Ⓓ suspected

➡ At the very center of the Earth is the inner core, which is estimated to be approximately 2,400 kilometers in diameter. It consists of a solid ball of iron that also contains the elements nickel and sulfur. The inner core is thought to have formed at the same time the Earth did 4.5 billion years ago. As the Earth cooled, the heavier elements sank to the center of the Earth while the lighter elements— mostly silicates—remained closer to the surface. The inner core is extremely hot as geologists believe the temperatures there range from 5,000 to 7,000 degrees Celsius. Despite this intense heat, the core does not melt due to the enormous amount of pressure being exerted on it.

Surrounding the inner core is the 2,300-kilometer-thick outer core, which is composed mostly of liquid iron but, like the inner core, contains substantial amounts of nickel and sulfur. The temperatures in it range between 4,000 and 5,000 degrees Celsius, making it cooler than the inner core. Nevertheless, the pressure there is not so great as to prevent melting, and it gives the outer core its viscosity, which allows the liquid metals in it to flow. The Earth's magnetic field is created by the outer core, and the flowing metals there contribute to its strength.

*Glossary

silicate: any chemical that contains silicon

More Available ▲

15 According to paragraph 4, how is the lower mantle different from the upper mantle?

Ⓐ It has a volume that is less than that of the upper mantle.

Ⓑ It has temperatures that are hotter than those in the upper mantle.

Ⓒ It is made mostly of iron whereas the upper mantle has mainly silicates.

Ⓓ It is located closer to the surface of the planet than the upper mantle.

Paragraph 4 is marked with an arrow (➡).

16 The word "instigates" in the passage is closest in meaning to

Ⓐ formulates

Ⓑ predicates

Ⓒ reduces

Ⓓ causes

17 According to paragraph 5, the tectonic plates on the Earth move because of

Ⓐ the movement of molten rock within the asthenosphere

Ⓑ forces within the outer core and the mantle that cause them to do so

Ⓒ convection currents that move through all of the Earth's layers

Ⓓ the high temperatures that are found in the crust and the mantle

Paragraph 5 is marked with an arrow (⇨).

➡ Above the outer core is the mantle, the largest and deepest layer of the Earth's inner structure. The mantle is believed to be around 2,900 kilometers thick and contains the greatest amount of the planet's volume. It consists of molten rock, mainly silicates high in concentrations of magnesium and iron, which is slowly flowing. This liquid rock rises and falls within the mantle as it cools and then becomes hotter. Like the core, the mantle is comprised of two layers: the upper mantle and lower mantle. The boundary between the upper and lower mantles is about 750 kilometers beneath the surface of the Earth and consists of a zone of transition in which the temperature and viscosity of the molten rock are notably different. The lower mantle has temperatures around 4,000 degrees Celsius whereas the temperature in the upper mantle ranges between 500 and 900 degrees Celsius. The lower mantle, lying next to the outer core, is under a great amount of pressure, so the melted rocks in it flow more slowly than those in the upper mantle.

⇨ At the topmost part of the upper mantle is a region known as the asthenosphere, which is roughly eighty to 200 kilometers beneath the surface of the Earth. It is thought that the large tectonic plates comprising the Earth's crust float on the asthenosphere. Temperature changes within the asthenosphere cause convection currents in this layer. These make the molten rock in the asthenosphere move, which, in turn, causes the tectonic plates to move. The movement of the plates instigates much of the geological activity—primarily earthquakes and volcanic eruptions—that the planet's surface experiences.

18 The author discusses "the Moho Discontinuity" in paragraph 6 in order to

  Ⓐ point out where the boundary between the crust and the mantle is located

  Ⓑ provide some details about the geologist who discovered it

  Ⓒ claim that very little has been learned about it

  Ⓓ compare its effects on the crust with those of the asthenosphere's

Paragraph 6 is marked with an arrow (➡).

➡ By studying seismic activity, geologists have been able to determine where the crust ends and the mantle begins. The boundary between the two is known as the Moho Discontinuity. It fluctuates in depth around the planet, but it has an average depth of thirty-two kilometers beneath the surface. It was discovered because seismic waves from earthquakes changed speed when they hit the mantle, which is much denser than the crust. Geologists hope to be able to study seismic waves and other factors in the future to help them learn more about the regions far beneath the planet's surface.

More Available ▲

19 Look at the four squares [■] that indicate where the following sentence could be added to the passage.

In addition, geologists speculate that there are trace amounts of silicon and oxygen there.

Where would the sentence best fit?

Click on a square [■] to add the sentence to the passage.

Surrounding the inner core is the 2,300-kilometer-thick outer core, which is composed mostly of liquid iron but, like the inner core, contains substantial amounts of nickel and sulfur. **1** The temperatures in it range between 4,000 and 5,000 degrees Celsius, making it cooler than the inner core. **2** Nevertheless, the pressure there is not so great as to prevent melting, and it gives the outer core its viscosity, which allows the liquid metals in it to flow. **3** The Earth's magnetic field is created by the outer core, and the flowing metals there contribute to its strength. **4**

20 **Directions:** Select the appropriate statements from the answer choices and match them to the layer of the Earth to which they relate. TWO of the answer choices will NOT be used. **This question is worth 4 points.**

Drag your answer choices to the spaces where they belong. To remove an answer choice, click on it. To review the passage, click on VIEW TEXT.

ANSWER CHOICES

1. Is responsible for the creation of the planet's magnetic field

2. Has rocks that ascend and descend depending upon how much they are heated

3. Contains both silicates as well as iron and magnesium

4. Is comprised entirely of tectonic plates that slowly change positions

5. Is the second largest of the Earth's layers according to diameter

6. Has certain quantities of the elements nickel and sulfur in their liquid forms

7. Is solid on account of the great amount of pressure within it

8. Includes large amounts of earth that are found above the Moho Discontinuity

9. Causes the movement of the tectonic plates of the crust

LAYER OF THE EARTH

Inner Core (Select 2)

-
-

Outer Core (Select 2)

-
-

Mantle (Select 3)

-
-
-

The Hanseatic League

On the coasts of the North and Baltic seas, a loose confederation of cities called the Hanseatic League arose in the thirteenth century. The league's major purposes were to secure trade routes and to create a trade monopoly. At its height, around 170 cities, the majority of which were Germanic, belonged to the league, and its members agreed to established rules and regulations governing trade. Eventually, its membership stretched from the Netherlands to Estonia, and there were merchant enclaves in places as far apart as London, England, and Novgorod, Russia. In its glory days, the Hanseatic League was wealthy and powerful, had its own military force, and controlled much of the Northern European economy. The league's eventual decline was a direct result of the rise of the nation-state in the 1500s and the control monarchs began exercising over aspects of trade within their realms.

The motivation to form a merchant league arose from the lack of security most merchants experienced in the Middle Ages, a time before nation-states and permanent armies and navies were the norm. On land and sea, merchants and their wares were subject to numerous risks from brigands. In the Middle Ages, Germanic merchants started forming guilds, called *hansa*, and armed men to protect their cities and trade routes. This gave rise to a sense of independence among the residents of cities. By the 1100s, many coastal cities along the North and Baltic seas were ruled by merchant guilds, so forming a confederation of these cities with the main interest being trade was the logical next step.

The Hanseatic League originated around 1240 in the city of Lubeck, located on the Baltic Sea east of the Denmark peninsula. Lubeck was ideally suited to deal in the Baltic Sea fish trade, yet, having no ready access to salt, it lacked the means to preserve fish. Near Kiel were salt mines, which could easily be attained from Hamburg. The merchant guilds of Hamburg and Lubeck formed a secure "salt road" between their cities by providing guards for salt wagons going to Lubeck and for salted fish and other goods heading for Hamburg. Salted fish was a major trade item in Christian Europe as nearly everyone ate fish on Fridays, so Lubeck and Hamburg prospered from this trade. Lubeck, however, reaped more benefits and soon became the dominant city in the region since it served as a major entry port for seaborne trade for items heading east and west.

Soon afterward, other cities realized the benefits of establishing protected trade routes. Over the next several decades, more cities united in a loose organization that, by the mid-1300s, was being called the Hanseatic League, or Hansa, with Lubeck its leading city. The merchant guilds and their cities became so rich and powerful that the league and its member cities actually went to war with Denmark over trade rights in the 1360s. By 1370, the Hanseatic League emerged victorious and forced the Danish monarchy to give fifteen percent of its trade profits to the league. This was when the league was at its peak. In fact, its power made the European nobility jealous despite the fact that the league frequently loaned money to monarchs

to fight wars, like it did for the English during the Hundred Years' War. Nevertheless, as noblemen and kings gained power, they began lashing out at the league and slowly stripped it of its wealth and privileges.

The rise of Sweden as a Baltic power in the 1400s further weakened the league. Additionally, in the late 1400s, the discovery of the New World led to the rise of Spain, Portugal, England, and France as great powers, so there was a shift in economic power from Northern Europe to countries close to the Atlantic Ocean in the western and southern parts of Europe. The Hanseatic League somewhat contributed to this as its development of large merchant sailing ships allowed nations to sail the world's oceans to find new markets and resources. The league also lost power since it was never anything more than a loose confederation whose members had conflicting interests and loyalties. While its member cities themselves survived, by the 1600s, the Hanseatic League was no longer the dominant economic power in Northern Europe.

*Glossary

confederation: an allied group
brigand: a thief; a pirate

Beginning

21 According to paragraph 1, which of the following is true about the Hanseatic League?

Ⓐ The league was a major influence in Europe for more than 170 years.

Ⓑ It had a significant influence on the economy of the entire European continent.

Ⓒ Kings in Europe were responsible for the defeat of the league in battle.

Ⓓ Its member cities agreed that they should all follow the same rules.

Paragraph 1 is marked with an arrow (➡).

The Hanseatic League

➡ On the coasts of the North and Baltic seas, a loose confederation of cities called the Hanseatic League arose in the thirteenth century. The league's major purposes were to secure trade routes and to create a trade monopoly. At its height, around 170 cities, the majority of which were Germanic, belonged to the league, and its members agreed to established rules and regulations governing trade. Eventually, its membership stretched from the Netherlands to Estonia, and there were merchant enclaves in places as far apart as London, England, and Novgorod, Russia. In its glory days, the Hanseatic League was wealthy and powerful, had its own military force, and controlled much of the Northern European economy. The league's eventual decline was a direct result of the rise of the nation-state in the 1500s and the control monarchs began exercising over aspects of trade within their realms.

*Glossary

confederation: an allied group

22 Which of the sentences below best expresses the essential information in the highlighted sentence in the passage? Incorrect answer choices change the meaning in important ways or leave out essential information.

By the 1100s, many coastal cities along the North and Baltic seas were ruled by merchant guilds, so forming a confederation of these cities with the main interest being trade was the logical next step.

(A) During the 1100s, merchants in several cities on the North and Baltic seas met to establish guilds that would control various aspects of trade between them.

(B) Groups of merchants controlled many cities along the North Sea and Baltic Sea in the twelfth century, so it was natural for them to ally on the basis of trade.

(C) Since merchant guilds were interested in trade, the guilds in some cities on the North Sea and Baltic Sea decided to make an alliance during the twelfth century.

(D) The cities that were located on the coasts of the North and Baltic seas started to form merchant guilds to regulate trade between them during the 1100s.

23 According to paragraph 2, merchants wanted to form a league because

(A) it would help them regulate standards between cities

(B) they thought it would let them trade in more countries

(C) they felt it would improve the influence of the cities they lived in

(D) it would provide security for them and their trade goods

Paragraph 2 is marked with an arrow (➡).

➡ The motivation to form a merchant league arose from the lack of security most merchants experienced in the Middle Ages, a time before nation-states and permanent armies and navies were the norm. On land and sea, merchants and their wares were subject to numerous risks from brigands. In the Middle Ages, Germanic merchants started forming guilds, called *hansa*, and armed men to protect their cities and trade routes. This gave rise to a sense of independence among the residents of cities. By the 1100s, many coastal cities along the North and Baltic seas were ruled by merchant guilds, so forming a confederation of these cities with the main interest being trade was the logical next step.

*Glossary

brigand: a thief; a pirate

178

REVIEW

HELP

BACK

NEXT

HIDE TIME 00:54:00

More Available

24 The author discusses "the city of Lubeck" in paragraph 3 in order to

  (A) detail its role in the founding of the Hanseatic League

  (B) describe the type of trade that its merchants specialized in

  (C) point out how rich it became thanks to its merchants

  (D) focus on the trade it did with Hamburg and Kiel

Paragraph 3 is marked with an arrow (➡).

25 The word "reaped" in the passage is closest in meaning to

  (A) purchased

  (B) cultivated

  (C) secured

  (D) negotiated

26 In stating that noblemen and kings began "lashing out" at the league, the author means that the noblemen and kings

  (A) rehabilitated the league

  (B) banned the league

  (C) fined the league

  (D) assailed the league

27 Which of the following can be inferred from paragraph 4 about the Hanseatic League?

  (A) It had some armed soldiers that it employed.

  (B) None of its member cities was located in Denmark.

  (C) It was the wealthiest organization in Europe at one time.

  (D) Some of its member cities were taken over by monarchs.

Paragraph 4 is marked with an arrow (⇨).

➡ The Hanseatic League originated around 1240 in the city of Lubeck, located on the Baltic Sea east of the Denmark peninsula. Lubeck was ideally suited to deal in the Baltic Sea fish trade, yet, having no ready access to salt, it lacked the means to preserve fish. Near Kiel were salt mines, which could easily be attained from Hamburg. The merchant guilds of Hamburg and Lubeck formed a secure "salt road" between their cities by providing guards for salt wagons going to Lubeck and for salted fish and other goods heading for Hamburg. Salted fish was a major trade item in Christian Europe as nearly everyone ate fish on Fridays, so Lubeck and Hamburg prospered from this trade. Lubeck, however, reaped more benefits and soon became the dominant city in the region since it served as a major entry port for seaborne trade for items heading east and west.

⇨ Soon afterward, other cities realized the benefits of establishing protected trade routes. Over the next several decades, more cities united in a loose organization that, by the mid-1300s, was being called the Hanseatic League, or Hansa, with Lubeck its leading city. The merchant guilds and their cities became so rich and powerful that the league and its member cities actually went to war with Denmark over trade rights in the 1360s. By 1370, the Hanseatic League emerged victorious and forced the Danish monarchy to give fifteen percent of its trade profits to the league. This was when the league was at its peak. In fact, its power made the European nobility jealous despite the fact that the league frequently loaned money to monarchs to fight wars, like it did for the English during the Hundred Years' War. Nevertheless, as noblemen and kings gained power, they began lashing out at the league and slowly stripped it of its wealth and privileges.

End ▲

28 According to paragraph 5, the author's description of why the Hanseatic League lost power mentions all of the following EXCEPT:

(A) The cities that belonged to the league did not always act in concert with one another.

(B) Denmark gained power in the area around the Baltic Sea.

(C) New ships that could sail far distances were developed by the league.

(D) Countries located in other parts of Europe gained power in the 1500s.

Paragraph 5 is marked with an arrow (➡).

➡ The rise of Sweden as a Baltic power in the 1400s further weakened the league. Additionally, in the late 1400s, the discovery of the New World led to the rise of Spain, Portugal, England, and France as great powers, so there was a shift in economic power from Northern Europe to countries close to the Atlantic Ocean in the western and southern parts of Europe. The Hanseatic League somewhat contributed to this as its development of large merchant sailing ships allowed nations to sail the world's oceans to find new markets and resources. The league also lost power since it was never anything more than a loose confederation whose members had conflicting interests and loyalties. While its member cities themselves survived, by the 1600s, the Hanseatic League was no longer the dominant economic power in Northern Europe.

29 Look at the four squares [■] that indicate where the following sentence could be added to the passage.

After all, with fewer merchants being waylaid on the roads, the citizens of various cities were becoming much more prosperous.

Where would the sentence best fit?

Click on a square [■] to add the sentence to the passage.

Soon afterward, other cities realized the benefits of establishing protected trade routes. **1** Over the next several decades, more cities united in a loose organization that, by the mid-1300s, was being called the Hanseatic League, or Hansa, with Lubeck its leading city. **2** The merchant guilds and their cities became so rich and powerful that the league and its member cities actually went to war with Denmark over trade rights in the 1360s. **3** By 1370, the Hanseatic League emerged victorious and forced the Danish monarchy to give fifteen percent of its trade profits to the league. **4** This was when the league was at its peak. In fact, its power made the European nobility jealous despite the fact that the league frequently loaned money to monarchs to fight wars, like it did for the English during the Hundred Years' War. Nevertheless, as noblemen and kings gained power, they began lashing out at the league and slowly stripped it of its wealth and privileges.

30 **Directions:** An introductory sentence for a brief summary of the passage is provided below. Complete the summary by selecting the THREE answer choices that express the most important ideas of the passage. Some sentences do not belong because they express ideas that are not presented in the passage or are minor ideas in the passage. **This question is worth 2 points.**

> Drag your answer choices to the spaces where they belong. To remove an answer choice, click on it. To review the passage, click on **VIEW TEXT**.

The Hanseatic League was the dominant economic power in the Baltic and North Sea regions for a couple of centuries until several factors led to a decline in its influence.

-
-
-

ANSWER CHOICES

☐1 The cities of Lubeck and Hamburg were primarily responsible for the forming of the league in the thirteenth century.

☐2 A power shift to countries near the Atlantic Ocean in the 1500s helped the league lose some of its economic power.

☐3 Many of the Germanic cities that joined the league were independent and were therefore not ruled by kings or princes.

☐4 Roughly 170 cities belonged to the league at one point, and they were of varying sizes and wealth.

☐5 Because the league provided security for member cities, the trade routes between them became safer, so the cities gained a great deal of wealth.

☐6 The league became so powerful that members of the royalty took measures to cause its influence in Europe to decline.

Actual Test

08

Reading Section Directions

This section measures your ability to understand academic passages in English. You will have **54 minutes** to read and answer questions about **3 passages**. A clock at the top of the screen will show you how much time is remaining.

Most questions are worth 1 point but the last question for each passage is worth more than 1 point. The directions for the last question indicate how many points you may receive.

Some passages include a word or phrase that is underlined in blue. Click on the word or phrase to see a definition or an explanation.

When you want to move to the next question, click on **NEXT**. You may skip questions and go back to them later. If you want to return to previous questions, click on **BACK**. You can click on **REVIEW** at any time, and the review screen will show you which questions you have answered and which you have not answered. From this review screen, you may go directly to any question you have already seen in the Reading section.

Click on **CONTINUE** to go on.

Animal Eyes

An impala's eyes

The great majority of species in the animal kingdom have eyes that function much like those of humans, where light enters and forms electric signals which the brain interprets as images. However, understanding how animals interpret those signals is problematic since scientists do not fully understand how animals' brains function. Nevertheless, it is known that some animals have specialized eyes that provide them with advantages. Eagles and other birds of prey, for example, can focus on tiny distant objects, which benefits them while hunting. For other animals, their eye positioning is advantageous. There are two primary eye positions: eyes on the front of the head and one eye on either side of the head. These are known respectively as binocular vision and monocular vision.

An animal with binocular vision has its eyes placed close together on the front of its head. Most animals with binocular vision are predators such as lions, tigers, and wolves. With their eyes set closely together in front, these animals have intersecting fields of vision, thereby allowing them to judge depth. The manner in which the brain interprets the images seen by each eye in a slightly different position allows for depth perception. Many predators with binocular vision are ambush hunters that typically wait in silence until the prey animal they are targeting is close enough to attack. For them, a sense of depth is vital to ensure a successful attack.

There are disadvantages to binocular vision though, the primary one of which is the lack of a wide field of vision. Most animals with binocular vision cannot see an area covering more than 180 degrees. This leaves them susceptible to another predator that may be tracking them from behind. As a result, many predators have developed heightened senses of smell and hearing to permit them to know when danger is approaching. Additionally, numerous animals, including those in the feline family, have superior night vision, which gives them advantages when hunting and when avoiding being hunted. Some

predators lack binocular vision though. For instance, the majority of sharks are predators, yet the eyes of a shark are on each side of its head. For sharks, eyes are secondary when it comes to finding prey because they have other highly attuned senses, particularly smell, that they utilize when hunting.

As for animals with monocular vision, they tend to be those that are hunted and include deer, rabbits, warthogs, and numerous other herbivores. Each of these animals has eyes located on the sides of its head. Each eye views a separate image, and neither overlaps with the other. The advantage of this eye positioning is that animals are provided with a wide field of vision—nearly 360 degrees for some species. This is far greater than the 180-degree field of vision of those animals with binocular vision. The eyes of prey animals evolved to the side position in order for them to have sufficient warning of nearby predators. Having eyes on the sides of the head reduces an animal's ability to perceive depth, yet creatures with monocular vision can attain a slight degree of depth perception by comparing a moving object with more distant stationary background objects.

Another advantage some prey animals have is eyes with horizontally slit pupils. Scientific studies have shown that animals with these have a much better field of vision. While grazing in open fields, the eyes of these prey animals shift positions so that when their heads dip as they feed on plant matter, their pupils remain in a horizontal position. This increases their chances of spotting an attacking predator and making a successful escape.

It is strongly believed by biologists that the development of the eye positions of both predators and prey animals is closely linked. With predators able to spot prey from far distances and then focus on them, prey animals had to evolve eyes that could detect danger before it was too late. In turn, as prey animals developed methods of avoiding attacks, predators came up with different styles of hunting. Some evolved into ambush hunters whereas others, such as lions, learned to use natural cover such as tall grasses to get near grazing prey animals in a stealthy manner.

*Glossary

feline family: all species of cats, including lions, tigers, leopards, and housecats
herbivore: an animal that only eats vegetation and consumes no meat

1 The word "them" in the passage refers to

Ⓐ animals' brains

Ⓑ some animals

Ⓒ specialized eyes

Ⓓ advantages

2 The word "judge" in the passage is closest in meaning to

Ⓐ attain

Ⓑ alternate

Ⓒ determine

Ⓓ obscure

3 According to paragraph 2, which of the following is true about ambush hunters?

Ⓐ They rely upon their depth perception to hunt prey animals successfully.

Ⓑ They prefer to attack animals from behind while hiding in tall grass.

Ⓒ They utilize their great speed to run down any animals that they attack.

Ⓓ They suffer in their ability to hunt whenever one of their eyes gets damaged.

Paragraph 2 is marked with an arrow (➡).

Animal Eyes

The great majority of species in the animal kingdom have eyes that function much like those of humans, where light enters and forms electric signals which the brain interprets as images. However, understanding how animals interpret those signals is problematic since scientists do not fully understand how animals' brains function. Nevertheless, it is known that some animals have specialized eyes that provide them with advantages. Eagles and other birds of prey, for example, can focus on tiny distant objects, which benefits them while hunting. For other animals, their eye positioning is advantageous. There are two primary eye positions: eyes on the front of the head and one eye on either side of the head. These are known respectively as binocular vision and monocular vision.

➡ An animal with binocular vision has its eyes placed close together on the front of its head. Most animals with binocular vision are predators such as lions, tigers, and wolves. With their eyes set closely together in front, these animals have intersecting fields of vision, thereby allowing them to judge depth. The manner in which the brain interprets the images seen by each eye in a slightly different position allows for depth perception. Many predators with binocular vision are ambush hunters that typically wait in silence until the prey animal they are targeting is close enough to attack. For them, a sense of depth is vital to ensure a successful attack.

More Available

4   The phrase "susceptible to" in the passage is closest in meaning to

(A) open to

(B) frightened by

(C) aware of

(D) weaker than

5   In paragraph 3, why does the author mention "heightened senses of smell and hearing"?

(A) To explain the process that animals use to improve some of their senses

(B) To show what some animals utilize to detect various unsafe situations

(C) To claim that they are more important than sight for most predators

(D) To mention what prey animals use in order to avoid attacks by predators

Paragraph 3 is marked with an arrow (➡).

➡ There are disadvantages to binocular vision though, the primary one of which is the lack of a wide field of vision. Most animals with binocular vision cannot see an area covering more than 180 degrees. This leaves them susceptible to another predator that may be tracking them from behind. As a result, many predators have developed heightened senses of smell and hearing to permit them to know when danger is approaching. Additionally, numerous animals, including those in the feline family, have superior night vision, which gives them advantages when hunting and when avoiding being hunted. Some predators lack binocular vision though. For instance, the majority of sharks are predators, yet the eyes of a shark are on each side of its head. For sharks, eyes are secondary when it comes to finding prey because they have other highly attuned senses, particularly smell, that they utilize when hunting.

*Glossary

feline family: all species of cats, including lions, tigers, leopards, and housecats

REVIEW

HELP

BACK

NEXT

HIDE TIME 00:54:00

More Available

6   Which of the following can be inferred from paragraph 4 about animals with monocular vision?

Ⓐ Many of them utilize their vision to hunt grazing animals such as deer and warthogs.

Ⓑ They once ate meat but became herbivores over time due to their inability to hunt.

Ⓒ They tend to eat in groups and post guards to alert others of approaching predators.

Ⓓ Some of them can see nearly everything in front of and behind them at the same time.

Paragraph 4 is marked with an arrow (➡).

7   According to paragraph 4, animals with monocular vision can obtain depth perception by

Ⓐ focusing a single eye on two objects distant from each other

Ⓑ viewing moving and nonmoving objects at the same time

Ⓒ using their 180-degree field of vision to observe objects around them

Ⓓ creating images that stack up on one another in a single eye

Paragraph 4 is marked with an arrow (➡).

➡ As for animals with monocular vision, they tend to be those that are hunted and include deer, rabbits, warthogs, and numerous other herbivores. Each of these animals has eyes located on the sides of its head. Each eye views a separate image, and neither overlaps with the other. The advantage of this eye positioning is that animals are provided with a wide field of vision—nearly 360 degrees for some species. This is far greater than the 180-degree field of vision of those animals with binocular vision. The eyes of prey animals evolved to the side position in order for them to have sufficient warning of nearby predators. Having eyes on the sides of the head reduces an animal's ability to perceive depth, yet creatures with monocular vision can attain a slight degree of depth perception by comparing a moving object with more distant stationary background objects.

*Glossary

herbivore: an animal that only eats vegetation and consumes no meat

End ▲

8 According to paragraph 6, why did some predators become ambush hunters?

  (A) They were utilizing their unique body types to hunt in the best possible way.

  (B) They were using their monocular vision to learn to hunt better.

  (C) They were unable to approach prey animals stealthily when hunting.

  (D) They were responding to defense methods devised by prey animals.

Paragraph 6 is marked with an arrow (➡).

9 Look at the four squares [■] that indicate where the following sentence could be added to the passage.

This enables them to be able to observe what is happening around them even though they may appear to be unobservant to nearby predators.

Where would the sentence best fit?

Click on a square [■] to add the sentence to the passage.

Another advantage some prey animals have is eyes with horizontally slit pupils. **1** Scientific studies have shown that animals with these have a much better field of vision. **2** While grazing in open fields, the eyes of these prey animals shift positions so that when their heads dip as they feed on plant matter, their pupils remain in a horizontal position. **3** This increases their chances of spotting an attacking predator and making a successful escape. **4**

➡ It is strongly believed by biologists that the development of the eye positions of both predators and prey animals is closely linked. With predators able to spot prey from far distances and then focus on them, prey animals had to evolve eyes that could detect danger before it was too late. In turn, as prey animals developed methods of avoiding attacks, predators came up with different styles of hunting. Some evolved into ambush hunters whereas others, such as lions, learned to use natural cover such as tall grasses to get near grazing prey animals in a stealthy manner.

10 **Directions:** Select the appropriate statements from the answer choices and match them to the type of vision to which they relate. TWO of the answer choices will NOT be used. **This question is worth 3 points.**

Drag your answer choices to the spaces where they belong. To remove an answer choice, click on it. To review the passage, click on VIEW TEXT.

ANSWER CHOICES

TYPE OF VISION

1 Requires that the eyes of an animal be placed on the front of its head

2 Enables some animals to lie in wait for others before attacking them

3 Is the type of vision most commonly had by prey animals

4 Has helped sharks become outstanding marine hunters

5 Permits only a limited amount of depth perception for animals

6 Lets animals keep their eyes in a horizontal position while grazing

7 Prevents animals from being able to see positions behind them well

Binocular (Select 3)

-
-
-

Monocular (Select 2)

-
-

Ming Vases

A Ming Dynasty porcelain vase with a dragon © ben bryant

The Ming Dynasty, which was established by Zhu Yuan Zhang, ruled China from 1368 to 1644. It is notable for several major achievements, including throwing off the yoke of Mongol rule, setting the southern borders of China, moving the imperial capital to Beijing, and adopting the Mandarin dialect as the official language of the court and governmental administration. However, at present, what most people remember the Ming Dynasty for is the talent of its ceramic makers, who made pottery, particularly vases, which can fetch millions of dollars at auctions.

Prior to the advent of the Ming Dynasty, the Chinese had been making pottery for centuries, primarily for utilitarian purposes but also for decoration. The country was fortunate to have an abundance of deposits of fine clays that could easily be transformed into pottery. Most early Chinese pottery was celadon; it was green because the high iron content in the clay made the finish turn that color when fired. Later, the Chinese discovered deposits of fine white clay, called kaolin, near the city of Jingdezhen in southeastern China. This led to the creation of porcelain ceramics.

Over time, Chinese artisans perfected the art of putting fine designs on ceramics. Many were of animals, such as birds, and flowers while designs of mythical beasts such as dragons were also common. Of note was a preference for white ceramic vases with blue patterns on the glazed finish. At first, the Chinese had difficulty with the color blue because the mineral cobalt, which was used to make blue dyes, tended to bleed when fired in kilns; however, by adding manganese to the cobalt dyes, this problem was overcome. Blue was not the only color utilized as red, green, yellow, and orange colors were also favored, but blue-white vases and other similar ceramics are more highly prized for their beauty in modern times.

This style for vases was not novel to China when the Ming Dynasty was established, but by the early

fifteenth century, Ming vase makers had attained new heights of skill and design. New recipes for mixing kaolin enabled them to create thinner yet stronger vases. New glazes were more translucent, permitting a glossier finish. A wider variety of shapes of vases and other ceramics appeared during this period, which was a testament to the skill of the craftsmen and their imaginations. Ming rulers began ordering vast quantities of ceramics for their own use and for commercial purposes. One record shows that during the reign of Emperor Xuande in 1433, he ordered more than 400,000 pieces from imperial ceramic makers.

Such a large order was not merely for domestic use as China had extensive trade networks reaching as far as Africa and Europe during the Ming Dynasty. Huge trading fleets sailed the South Pacific and Indian oceans while extensive caravans traveled overland on the Silk Road to reach the Middle East. Most of the cobalt used in Chinese ceramics came from Iran. Large numbers of Ming ceramics, including vases, reached Arabian and European markets. This trade is speculated as being one reason so many Ming Dynasty ceramics have survived to modern times. However, when shopping for Ming products, buyers must be conscious of fakes. A true Ming vase has a reign mark on its bottom. This is a series of four or six Chinese characters indicating which era the ceramic product came from. In six-character reign marks, the first two characters name the dynasty, the next two name the reigning emperor, and the last two always read "made for" in Chinese. In four-character reign marks, the dynasty name is omitted.

A well-designed reign mark should indicate that the ceramic is an authentic work from the Ming Dynasty. However, to complicate matters, for many centuries after the dynasty ended, Chinese artists marked their ceramics with the names of Ming emperors to bestow honor upon them. Today, only experts can verify whether objects were made during the Ming Dynasty or in periods afterward. The prices of Ming ceramics, including vases, vary but are typically expensive, and authentic Ming pieces in pristine condition sell for millions of dollars. This was the case for one blue and white Ming vase that was recently sold for the price of 6.2 million dollars.

*Glossary

celadon: a type of ceramic made in China that has a pale green color
kiln: a furnace in which ceramics are baked

Ming Vases

➡ The Ming Dynasty, which was established by Zhu Yuan Zhang, ruled China from 1368 to 1644. It is notable for several major achievements, including throwing off the yoke of Mongol rule, setting the southern borders of China, moving the imperial capital to Beijing, and adopting the Mandarin dialect as the official language of the court and governmental administration. However, at present, what most people remember the Ming Dynasty for is the talent of its ceramic makers, who made pottery, particularly vases, which can fetch millions of dollars at auctions.

⇨ Prior to the advent of the Ming Dynasty, the Chinese had been making pottery for centuries, primarily for utilitarian purposes but also for decoration. The country was fortunate to have an abundance of deposits of fine clays that could easily be transformed into pottery. Most early Chinese pottery was celadon; it was green because the high iron content in the clay made the finish turn that color when fired. Later, the Chinese discovered deposits of fine white clay, called kaolin, near the city of Jingdezhen in southeastern China. This led to the creation of porcelain ceramics.

11 According to paragraphs 1 and 2, which of the following is NOT true about the Ming Dynasty?

Ⓐ Lines between it and other lands to the south were settled during it.

Ⓑ The location of the capital of China was moved at some time during it.

Ⓒ Its first ruler assumed the throne in the fourteenth century.

Ⓓ It was the time when the Chinese first began to make ceramic vases.

Paragraphs 1 and 2 are marked with arrows (➡) and (⇨).

12 The word "utilitarian" in the passage is closest in meaning to

Ⓐ ornamental

Ⓑ specific

Ⓒ practical

Ⓓ official

13 Which of the following can be inferred from paragraph 2 about porcelain?

Ⓐ It can be made when it contains the clay called kaolin.

Ⓑ The most famous place that made it is Jingdezhen, China.

Ⓒ Most people consider it to be more valuable than celadon.

Ⓓ It comes in a variety of colors, including both white and green.

Paragraph 2 is marked with an arrow (⇨).

*Glossary

celadon: a type of ceramic made in China that has a pale green color

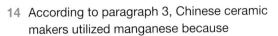

14 According to paragraph 3, Chinese ceramic makers utilized manganese because

Ⓐ they were able to use it to create dyes in a wide variety of colors

Ⓑ they lacked enough cobalt to make a sufficient amount of blue dye

Ⓒ it increased the strength of the clay that they mixed it with

Ⓓ it enabled them to make a dye that could be easily applied to pottery

Paragraph 3 is marked with an arrow (➡).

15 The word "translucent" in the passage is closest in meaning to

Ⓐ opaque

Ⓑ smooth

Ⓒ radiant

Ⓓ unique

16 In paragraph 4, the author uses "Emperor Xuande" as an example of

Ⓐ the emperor who, more than anyone else, spread Ming vases to places around the world

Ⓑ a person responsible for the creation of enormous numbers of Ming ceramics

Ⓒ an individual who sponsored the training of ceramic makers during the Ming Dynasty

Ⓓ the ruler who began the policy of ordering Chinese ceramics for personal use

Paragraph 4 is marked with an arrow (⇨).

➡ Over time, Chinese artisans perfected the art of putting fine designs on ceramics. Many were of animals, such as birds, and flowers while designs of mythical beasts such as dragons were also common. Of note was a preference for white ceramic vases with blue patterns on the glazed finish. At first, the Chinese had difficulty with the color blue because the mineral cobalt, which was used to make blue dyes, tended to bleed when fired in kilns; however, by adding manganese to the cobalt dyes, this problem was overcome. Blue was not the only color utilized as red, green, yellow, and orange colors were also favored, but blue-white vases and other similar ceramics are more highly prized for their beauty in modern times.

⇨ This style for vases was not novel to China when the Ming Dynasty was established, but by the early fifteenth century, Ming vase makers had attained new heights of skill and design. New recipes for mixing kaolin enabled them to create thinner yet stronger vases. New glazes were more translucent, permitting a glossier finish. A wider variety of shapes of vases and other ceramics appeared during this period, which was a testament to the skill of the craftsmen and their imaginations. Ming rulers began ordering vast quantities of ceramics for their own use and for commercial purposes. One record shows that during the reign of Emperor Xuande in 1433, he ordered more than 400,000 pieces from imperial ceramic makers.

*Glossary

kiln: a furnace in which ceramics are baked

17 Select the TWO answer choices from paragraph 4 that identify how Ming vase makers improved the quality of their ceramics. *To receive credit, you must select TWO answers.*

Ⓐ They made vases which were able to use a blue dye made from cobalt.

Ⓑ They created unique designs that included animals and flowers.

Ⓒ They made vases that looked very shiny when they were completed.

Ⓓ They created ceramics that were not as thick as others but were stronger.

Paragraph 4 is marked with an arrow (➡).

18 In paragraph 5, the author implies that Chinese ceramics

Ⓐ were rejected as fakes when six-character reign marks were missing

Ⓑ were so profitable that Chinese merchants sold them in Africa

Ⓒ frequently relied upon materials that were imported from other lands

Ⓓ were the most desired items that were trade on the Silk Road

Paragraph 5 is marked with an arrow (⇨).

➡ This style for vases was not novel to China when the Ming Dynasty was established, but by the early fifteenth century, Ming vase makers had attained new heights of skill and design. New recipes for mixing kaolin enabled them to create thinner yet stronger vases. New glazes were more translucent, permitting a glossier finish. A wider variety of shapes of vases and other ceramics appeared during this period, which was a testament to the skill of the craftsmen and their imaginations. Ming rulers began ordering vast quantities of ceramics for their own use and for commercial purposes. One record shows that during the reign of Emperor Xuande in 1433, he ordered more than 400,000 pieces from imperial ceramic makers.

⇨ Such a large order was not merely for domestic use as China had extensive trade networks reaching as far as Africa and Europe during the Ming Dynasty. Huge trading fleets sailed the South Pacific and Indian oceans while extensive caravans traveled overland on the Silk Road to reach the Middle East. Most of the cobalt used in Chinese ceramics came from Iran. Large numbers of Ming ceramics, including vases, reached Arabian and European markets. This trade is speculated as being one reason so many Ming Dynasty ceramics have survived to modern times. However, when shopping for Ming products, buyers must be conscious of fakes. A true Ming vase has a reign mark on its bottom. This is a series of four or six Chinese characters indicating which era the ceramic product came from. In six-character reign marks, the first two characters name the dynasty, the next two name the reigning emperor, and the last two always read "made for" in Chinese. In four-character reign marks, the dynasty name is omitted.

End ▲

19 Look at the four squares [■] that indicate where the following sentence could be added to the passage.

This has made it virtually impossible for regular people to determine the authenticity of a ceramic that is said to have been made during the Ming Dynasty.

Where would the sentence best fit?

Click on a square [■] to add the sentence to the passage.

    A well-designed reign mark should indicate that the ceramic is an authentic work from the Ming Dynasty. **1** However, to complicate matters, for many centuries after the dynasty ended, Chinese artists marked their ceramics with the names of Ming emperors to bestow honor upon them. **2** Today, only experts can verify whether objects were made during the Ming Dynasty or in periods afterward. **3** The prices of Ming ceramics, including vases, vary but are typically expensive, and authentic Ming pieces in pristine condition sell for millions of dollars. **4** This was the case for one blue and white Ming vase that was recently sold for the price of 6.2 million dollars.

20 **Directions:** An introductory sentence for a brief summary of the passage is provided below. Complete the summary by selecting the THREE answer choices that express the most important ideas of the passage. Some sentences do not belong because they express ideas that are not presented in the passage or are minor ideas in the passage. **This question is worth 2 points.**

Drag your answer choices to the spaces where they belong. To remove an answer choice, click on it. To review the passage, click on **VIEW TEXT**.

Ceramics, especially vases, that were made during the Ming Dynasty were of high quality and thus are considered valuable today.

-

-

-

ANSWER CHOICES

1 It is difficult for people who are not professionally trained to determine whether or not a vase is from the Ming Dynasty.

2 The Chinese learned how to mix cobalt and other ingredients to create a blue dye that was used on their ceramics.

3 Thanks to the talent of Ming artisans, some vases from centuries ago can sell for millions of dollars at auctions.

4 Ming ceramics were so well made that they were traded internationally in places such as Africa, the Middle East, and Europe.

5 Kaolin was just one type of clay that Chinese artisans used to make pottery in many different colors.

6 Most people know about the reign marks that were used by artisans to honor various Ming emperors.

The Origins of Animal Flight

Many animals, including insects, birds, and some mammals, are capable of flying. The ability to achieve flight requires a specialized body structure involving having a low total body mass plus flappable wings with a large surface area and a rigid structure. While biologists generally agree that insects were the first animals to achieve flight, there is an ongoing debate amongst scientists regarding why animals started flying in the first place. Furthermore, the question about whether animals learned to fly from the ground up or from elevated places such as trees remains unsettled. Unfortunately, the search for answers is complicated by the relative lack of remains of flying animals in the fossil record in comparison with larger and heavier animals such as dinosaurs.

Insects managed to fly before other creatures perhaps as many as 320 million years ago, which is when the fossil record shows they developed wings. There are three main theories about the origins of insect flight. One proclaims they learned to fly by skimming across the surface of water. Many insects lived in water and had gills which they utilized to breathe underwater. Movable gill plates may have acted as early prototypes for wings. A second theory is that insects used their jumping skills to develop into fliers. Many creatures have a startle response that, when confronted by predators, enables them to leap high into the air and far away. Over time, some insects' small dorsal projections might have evolved into winglets and then into full-grown wings. Leaping thus became flying. The third hypothesis is that insects with dorsal projections and later, wings, leaped from high places and either glided or were picked up by winds and dispersed. From this movement, they learned to fly.

This debate has carried over to the evolution of bird flight. Many experts subscribe to the tree-down theory of bird flight. Early protobirds began their lives on the ground but gradually moved higher to acquire food and to avoid predators. Perhaps they moved upward to avoid predators at first and then returned to the ground each day when the time of danger had passed. In this way, some birds might have developed the ability to glide down to the ground, a faster method than climbing. Over time, they evolved to have flapping wings, permitting them more easily to escape from predators by flying to higher locations. Eventually, many bird species made high locations their homes, built nests in them, laid eggs, and raised their young there.

There are, of course, exceptions. They include flightless birds such as the heavy emu and ostrich and the water-loving penguin. A classic example of what can happen to birds that never evolved to fly is the dodo bird of Mauritius Island, which lived in isolation with no natural predators, never became capable of flight, and built nests on the ground. When humans arrived on the island and brought various predatory animals, the dodo became easy prey and rapidly went extinct.

Despite the popularity of the tree-down theory, some biologists argue that birds initially achieved flight

from the ground by running and by flapping their wings to overcome the effects of gravity. They rightly point out that most birds today can achieve takeoff through these actions. However, their opponents argue that modern birds required millions of years to evolve to this stage and that early birds could not achieve ground takeoff. To do so, early birds would have required the ability to overcome the force of gravity by using all their strength to run and to flap their wings.

The fossil record, bereft as it is of many bird fossils, appears to indicate that early bird wings and bodies had not evolved enough to achieve ground takeoff. It also seems logical that by utilizing the power of gravity from a high position to attain flight rather than fighting against it, birds would have conserved energy, one of the cardinal rules of animal survival. In conclusion, the most likely scenario for the evolution of bird flight is that they began climbing to high places to avoid predators or to obtain food, became able to glide, and as their bodies transformed, learned the art of controlled and extended flight.

*Glossary

dorsal projection: a body part that comes out from the back
protobird: an ancient extinct animal that is a link between reptiles and birds

REVIEW

HELP

BACK

NEXT

HIDE TIME 00:54:00

Beginning ▲

21 Which of the sentences below best expresses the essential information in the highlighted sentence in the passage? Incorrect answer choices change the meaning in important ways or leave out essential information.

The ability to achieve flight requires a specialized body structure involving having a low total body mass plus flappable wings with a large surface area and a rigid structure.

Ⓐ Animals that have long, flappable wings can use their specialized bodies to make short flights at times.

Ⓑ The only animals that are capable of achieving flight have wings which they can extend and then flap.

Ⓒ When animals evolve specialized bodies that have wings, they can then teach themselves how to fly.

Ⓓ To fly, animals need special bodies that are low in weight and have strong, large wings they can flap.

The Origins of Animal Flight

Many animals, including insects, birds, and some mammals, are capable of flying. The ability to achieve flight requires a specialized body structure involving having a low total body mass plus flappable wings with a large surface area and a rigid structure. While biologists generally agree that insects were the first animals to achieve flight, there is an ongoing debate amongst scientists regarding why animals started flying in the first place. Furthermore, the question about whether animals learned to fly from the ground up or from elevated places such as trees remains unsettled. Unfortunately, the search for answers is complicated by the relative lack of remains of flying animals in the fossil record in comparison with larger and heavier animals such as dinosaurs.

More Available

22 The word "prototypes" in the passage is closest in meaning to

ⓐ models

ⓑ limbs

ⓒ simulations

ⓓ developments

23 According to paragraph 2, which of the following is NOT true about insects?

ⓐ They first arose as underwater creatures with gills and moved to land millions of years ago.

ⓑ There are several theories that attempt to explain how they first started flying.

ⓒ Some of them might have achieved flight as a result of attempts to escape from predators.

ⓓ They learned how to fly millions of years ago before any other animals did.

Paragraph 2 is marked with an arrow (➡).

➡ Insects managed to fly before other creatures perhaps as many as 320 million years ago, which is when the fossil record shows they developed wings. There are three main theories about the origins of insect flight. One proclaims they learned to fly by skimming across the surface of water. Many insects lived in water and had gills which they utilized to breathe underwater. Movable gill plates may have acted as early prototypes for wings. A second theory is that insects used their jumping skills to develop into fliers. Many creatures have a startle response that, when confronted by predators, enables them to leap high into the air and far away. Over time, some insects' small dorsal projections might have evolved into winglets and then into full-grown wings. Leaping thus became flying. The third hypothesis is that insects with dorsal projections and later, wings, leaped from high places and either glided or were picked up by winds and dispersed. From this movement, they learned to fly.

*Glossary

dorsal projection: a body part that comes out from the back

24 According to paragraph 3, which of the following is true about protobirds?

Ⓐ Fossils of them with rudimentary wings have been unearthed around the world.

Ⓑ Many of them were predators that moved to trees in search of food.

Ⓒ They learned how to glide from tree to tree to escape from creatures on the ground.

Ⓓ It is believed that they first lived on the ground and then moved up into trees.

Paragraph 3 is marked with an arrow (➡).

25 The author discusses "the dodo bird" in paragraph 4 in order to

Ⓐ show what is likely to happen to species of birds that are unable to fly at all

Ⓑ compare what happened to it with how a lack of flight has affected the penguin

Ⓒ point out that some birds which cannot fly are still able to thrive in their environments

Ⓓ explain why it, along with the emu, ostrich, and penguin, never learned to fly

Paragraph 4 is marked with an arrow (⇨).

➡ This debate has carried over to the evolution of bird flight. Many experts subscribe to the tree-down theory of bird flight. Early protobirds began their lives on the ground but gradually moved higher to acquire food and to avoid predators. Perhaps they moved upward to avoid predators at first and then returned to the ground each day when the time of danger had passed. In this way, some birds might have developed the ability to glide down to the ground, a faster method than climbing. Over time, they evolved to have flapping wings, permitting them more easily to escape from predators by flying to higher locations. Eventually, many bird species made high locations their homes, built nests in them, laid eggs, and raised their young there.

⇨ There are, of course, exceptions. They include flightless birds such as the heavy emu and ostrich and the water-loving penguin. A classic example of what can happen to birds that never evolved to fly is the dodo bird of Mauritius Island, which lived in isolation with no natural predators, never became capable of flight, and built nests on the ground. When humans arrived on the island and brought various predatory animals, the dodo became easy prey and rapidly went extinct.

*Glossary

protobird: an ancient extinct animal that is a link between reptiles and birds

26 According to paragraph 5, many biologists believe early birds initially failed to achieve flight from the ground because

Ⓐ the strength that would have been required for them to do that was too much

Ⓑ they have not been able to identify any birds in the fossil record which could do that

Ⓒ there is no evidence showing that early birds needed to achieve flight from the ground

Ⓓ the wings of early birds were not long enough to let them accomplish that

Paragraph 5 is marked with an arrow (➡).

27 The word "cardinal" in the passage is closest in meaning to

Ⓐ widespread

Ⓑ fundamental

Ⓒ initial

Ⓓ avian

28 In paragraph 6, all of the following questions are answered EXCEPT:

Ⓐ Which theory about how early birds learned to fly is considered the most likely?

Ⓑ What does the fossil record show regarding the abilities of early birds to take off from the ground?

Ⓒ What is something that animals need to do in order to be able to survive?

Ⓓ For how long did the force of gravity prevent early birds from taking off from the ground?

Paragraph 6 is marked with an arrow (⇨).

➡ Despite the popularity of the tree-down theory, some biologists argue that birds initially achieved flight from the ground by running and by flapping their wings to overcome the effects of gravity. They rightly point out that most birds today can achieve takeoff through these actions. However, their opponents argue that modern birds required millions of years to evolve to this stage and that early birds could not achieve ground takeoff. To do so, early birds would have required the ability to overcome the force of gravity by using all their strength to run and to flap their wings.

⇨ The fossil record, bereft as it is of many bird fossils, appears to indicate that early bird wings and bodies had not evolved enough to achieve ground takeoff. It also seems logical that by utilizing the power of gravity from a high position to attain flight rather than fighting against it, birds would have conserved energy, one of the cardinal rules of animal survival. In conclusion, the most likely scenario for the evolution of bird flight is that they began climbing to high places to avoid predators or to obtain food, became able to glide, and as their bodies transformed, learned the art of controlled and extended flight.

29 Look at the four squares [■] that indicate where the following sentence could be added to the passage.

The moa, a flightless bird from New Zealand, met a similar fate at the hands of the Maori.

Where would the sentence best fit?

Click on a square [■] to add the sentence to the passage.

There are, of course, exceptions. **1** They include flightless birds such as the heavy emu and ostrich and the water-loving penguin. **2** A classic example of what can happen to birds that never evolved to fly is the dodo bird of Mauritius Island, which lived in isolation with no natural predators, never became capable of flight, and built nests on the ground. **3** When humans arrived on the island and brought various predatory animals, the dodo became easy prey and rapidly went extinct. **4**

30 **Directions:** An introductory sentence for a brief summary of the passage is provided below. Complete the summary by selecting the THREE answer choices that express the most important ideas of the passage. Some sentences do not belong because they express ideas that are not presented in the passage or are minor ideas in the passage. **This question is worth 2 points.**

Drag your answer choices to the spaces where they belong. To remove an answer choice, click on it. To review the passage, click on **VIEW TEXT**.

There are many unanswered questions regarding animals achieving flight, among them being which animals first learned to fly and from where they first took off.

-
-
-

ANSWER CHOICES

1. Some birds, such as the dodo, never learned how to fly and eventually went extinct on account of that inability to fly.

2. Most biologists think that insects became the first animals to fly in the air several hundred million years ago.

3. Most animals feel safer in trees than on the ground since they can avoid large predators in that way.

4. A large number of biologists think that protobirds first learned to fly by climbing trees and then gliding down from them.

5. The fossil record lacks many examples of bird fossils whereas it has large numbers of dinosaur bones.

6. It would have been difficult for early birds to be able to take off from the ground because gravity was working against them.

Actual Test

09

Reading Section Directions

This section measures your ability to understand academic passages in English. You will have **54 minutes** to read and answer questions about **3 passages**. A clock at the top of the screen will show you how much time is remaining.

Most questions are worth 1 point but the last question for each passage is worth more than 1 point. The directions for the last question indicate how many points you may receive.

Some passages include a word or phrase that is underlined in blue. Click on the word or phrase to see a definition or an explanation.

When you want to move to the next question, click on **NEXT**. You may skip questions and go back to them later. If you want to return to previous questions, click on **BACK**. You can click on **REVIEW** at any time, and the review screen will show you which questions you have answered and which you have not answered. From this review screen, you may go directly to any question you have already seen in the Reading section.

Click on **CONTINUE** to go on.

Moonquakes

In the 1960s and 1970s, the American *Apollo* astronauts discovered seismic activity on the moon. They carried seismometers there and placed the items near their landing points, and the machines relayed data about the moon's seismic activity back to the Earth. They were in operation between 1969 and 1977, and during that time, scientists received data from approximately 12,000 lunar seismic events. They realized that moonquakes, as they called them, had some differences from earthquakes. They additionally categorized moonquakes into four types based upon their cause and location.

The major differences between earthquakes and moonquakes concern their intensity and duration. The most powerful earthquakes are of vastly greater intensity than moonquakes. While earthquakes can reach higher than 9.0 on the Richter scale, no moonquakes observed thus far have recorded a rating higher than 5.5. That is strong enough to cause earthbound buildings to shake and objects to fall and break but is unlikely to cause widespread death and destruction. The main reason for this difference in intensity is that the moon lacks tectonic plates, which slide and push against one another, like the Earth has. The strongest earthquakes normally occur where these plates meet in places called fault lines on account of the enormous amount of stress built up in those regions.

Another notable feature about moonquakes is that they last much longer than earthquakes. Earthquakes typically last for a few seconds—or minutes at most—and aftershocks may occur several hours or days later, but moonquakes can happen for hours. One recorded moonquake showed the lunar surface shaking without pause for ten minutes, and then there was intermittent shaking for several hours afterward. Geologists believe the lack of liquid water on the moon is the cause of the long-term shaking because on the Earth, water above and under the surface puts a damper on seismic activity.

As for the four types of moonquakes, there are those caused by meteorite impacts, those caused by the lunar surface heating when parts of the moon receive direct sunlight after being in shadow, those which take place deep beneath the surface, and those which occur shallower in depth. The first type is the result of the moon's surface being rattled by large meteorites striking it. While not an everyday occurrence, it happens often enough to be noted as a cause of seismic activity. The second type is called a thermal moonquake and happens because of the great differences in the moon's surface's temperature when it passes in and out of direct sunlight. When the surface begins reheating, it expands, causing ripples of movement in the upper crust. These can be intense enough to qualify as seismic activity, but they are relatively mild moonquakes low in intensity.

The third type of moonquake occurs far underneath the surface roughly 800 to 1,200 kilometers deep. These moonquakes are mild, rarely reaching above two on the Richter scale. Geologists suspect

these moonquakes are the results of tidal forces at work because observed ones usually occurred at regular intervals every twenty-seven days. That is the period of time required for the moon to complete one revolution around the Earth. Every twenty-seven days, the moon is at its closest point to the Earth and therefore tremendously influenced by its gravity. The pull of the moon's gravity causes the tides on the Earth, so it is possible that the Earth's gravity also influences the moon. Nevertheless, exactly how tidal forces cause these moonquakes is uncertain. It is known that the gravitational pull of the Earth causes some small-scale distortion of the moon as it approaches the Earth and then moves away from it. However, this has not been verified as being the direct cause of deep moonquakes. An additional mystery is that eighty percent of all known deep moonquakes have taken place in a single location.

The first three types of moonquakes produce mild seismic activity in comparison with the last, shallow moonquakes, which normally occur twenty to thirty kilometers beneath the moon's surface. Between 1969 and 1977, the seismometers detected twenty-eight shallow moonquakes, seven of which had intensity ratings above five on the Richter scale. Unfortunately, geologists lack enough data fully to understand these moonquakes, particularly why they are so intense.

*Glossary

seismometer: a device that collects information about earthquakes
aftershock: a small earthquake that follows a larger one

Moonquakes

➡ In the 1960s and 1970s, the American *Apollo* astronauts discovered seismic activity on the moon. They carried seismometers there and placed the items near their landing points, and the machines relayed data about the moon's seismic activity back to the Earth. They were in operation between 1969 and 1977, and during that time, scientists received data from approximately 12,000 lunar seismic events. They realized that moonquakes, as they called them, had some differences from earthquakes. They additionally categorized moonquakes into four types based upon their cause and location.

The major differences between earthquakes and moonquakes concern their intensity and duration. The most powerful earthquakes are of vastly greater intensity than moonquakes. While earthquakes can reach higher than 9.0 on the Richter scale, no moonquakes observed thus far have recorded a rating higher than 5.5. That is strong enough to cause earthbound buildings to shake and objects to fall and break but is unlikely to cause widespread death and destruction. The main reason for this difference in intensity is that the moon lacks tectonic plates, which slide and push against one another, like the Earth has. The strongest earthquakes normally occur where these plates meet in places called fault lines on account of the enormous amount of stress built up in those regions.

*Glossary

seismometer: a device that collects information about earthquakes

---

1   In paragraph 1, the author's description of seismometers mentions which of the following?

Ⓐ The rough number of events that they recorded taking place on the moon

Ⓑ The number of them that were placed on the moon by *Apollo* astronauts

Ⓒ The first time that they were ever used by scientists to detect earthquakes

Ⓓ The type of seismic data that they were used to collect on the moon

Paragraph 1 is marked with an arrow (➡).

2   The word "That" in the passage refers to

Ⓐ Vastly greater intensity

Ⓑ 9.0

Ⓒ The Richter scale

Ⓓ A rating higher than 5.5

3 The word "intermittent" in the passage is closest in meaning to

Ⓐ continual

Ⓑ violent

Ⓒ irregular

Ⓓ dangerous

4 In stating that water above and under the surface "puts a damper on seismic activity," the author means that water

Ⓐ makes earthquakes stronger

Ⓑ reduces the lengths of earthquakes

Ⓒ makes earthquakes less powerful

Ⓓ causes earthquakes to last longer

Another notable feature about moonquakes is that they last much longer than earthquakes. Earthquakes typically last for a few seconds—or minutes at most—and aftershocks may occur several hours or days later, but moonquakes can happen for hours. One recorded moonquake showed the lunar surface shaking without pause for ten minutes, and then there was intermittent shaking for several hours afterward. Geologists believe the lack of liquid water on the moon is the cause of the long-term shaking because on the Earth, water above and under the surface puts a damper on seismic activity.

*Glossary

aftershock: a small earthquake that follows a larger one

REVIEW

HELP

BACK

NEXT

HIDE TIME 00:54:00

More Available

5 Which of the following can be inferred from paragraphs 4 and 5 about thermal moonquakes?

Ⓐ They occur at a much more common rate than those deep beneath the moon's surface do.

Ⓑ Scientists believe that the Earth's tides may have some kind of an effect on them.

Ⓒ The ones that have been recorded had fairly low ratings on the Richter Scale.

Ⓓ Some of them have been violent enough to cause rather large amounts of damage.

Paragraphs 4 and 5 are marked with arrows (➡) and (⇨).

6 The author discusses "the tides on the Earth" in paragraph 5 in order to

Ⓐ refute some evidence that was collected by seismometers

Ⓑ discuss a theory that some individuals have speculated upon

Ⓒ argue for the need to collect more data regarding their effects on the moon

Ⓓ point out some important facts about how often they take place

Paragraph 5 is marked with an arrow (⇨).

7 In paragraph 5, the author's description of moonquakes occurring far underneath the moon's surface mentions all of the following EXCEPT:

Ⓐ The relationship that the Earth's tides may have with them

Ⓑ The precise area of the moon where they most commonly occurred

Ⓒ The level of intensity that they recorded on the Richter Scale

Ⓓ The frequency that they were observed happening

Paragraph 5 is marked with an arrow (⇨).

➡ As for the four types of moonquakes, there are those caused by meteorite impacts, those caused by the lunar surface heating when parts of the moon receive direct sunlight after being in shadow, those which take place deep beneath the surface, and those which occur shallower in depth. The first type is the result of the moon's surface being rattled by large meteorites striking it. While not an everyday occurrence, it happens often enough to be noted as a cause of seismic activity. The second type is called a thermal moonquake and happens because of the great differences in the moon's surface's temperature when it passes in and out of direct sunlight. When the surface begins reheating, it expands, causing ripples of movement in the upper crust. These can be intense enough to qualify as seismic activity, but they are relatively mild moonquakes low in intensity.

⇨ The third type of moonquake occurs far underneath the surface roughly 800 to 1,200 kilometers deep. These moonquakes are mild, rarely reaching above two on the Richter scale. Geologists suspect these moonquakes are the results of tidal forces at work because observed ones usually occurred at regular intervals every twenty-seven days. That is the period of time required for the moon to complete one revolution around the Earth. Every twenty-seven days, the moon is at its closest point to the Earth and therefore tremendously influenced by its gravity. The pull of the moon's gravity causes the tides on the Earth, so it is possible that the Earth's gravity also influences the moon. Nevertheless, exactly how tidal forces cause these moonquakes is uncertain. It is known that the gravitational pull of the Earth causes some small-scale distortion of the moon as it approaches the Earth and then moves away from it. However, this has not been verified as being the direct cause of deep moonquakes. An additional mystery is that eighty percent of all known deep moonquakes have taken place in a single location.

8   According to paragraph 6, what did the seismometers do?

  (A) They failed to record all of the shallow moonquakes occurring between 1969 and 1977.

  (B) They determined that shallow moonquakes were the most intense of all types of moonquakes.

  (C) They interpreted the data about moonquakes that they monitored for more than eight years.

  (D) They recorded a majority of shallow moonquakes rating more than 5.0 on the Richter Scale.

Paragraph 6 is marked with an arrow (➡).

➡ The first three types of moonquakes produce mild seismic activity in comparison with the last, shallow moonquakes, which normally occur twenty to thirty kilometers beneath the moon's surface. Between 1969 and 1977, the seismometers detected twenty-eight shallow moonquakes, seven of which had intensity ratings above five on the Richter scale. Unfortunately, geologists lack enough data fully to understand these moonquakes, particularly why they are so intense.

9   Look at the four squares [■] that indicate where the following sentence could be added to the passage.

Many of them are joined in a place called the Ring of Fire, where some of the Earth's most powerful earthquakes have happened.

Where would the sentence best fit?

Click on a square [■] to add the sentence to the passage.

The major differences between earthquakes and moonquakes concern their intensity and duration. The most powerful earthquakes are of vastly greater intensity than moonquakes. While earthquakes can reach higher than 9.0 on the Richter scale, no moonquakes observed thus far have recorded a rating higher than 5.5. **1** That is strong enough to cause earthbound buildings to shake and objects to fall and break but is unlikely to cause widespread death and destruction. **2** The main reason for this difference in intensity is that the moon lacks tectonic plates, which slide and push against one another, like the Earth has. **3** The strongest earthquakes normally occur where these plates meet in places called fault lines on account of the enormous amount of stress built up in those regions. **4**

10 **Directions:** An introductory sentence for a brief summary of the passage is provided below. Complete the summary by selecting the THREE answer choices that express the most important ideas of the passage. Some sentences do not belong because they express ideas that are not presented in the passage or are minor ideas in the passage. **This question is worth 2 points.**

Drag your answer choices to the spaces where they belong. To remove an answer choice, click on it. To review the passage, click on **VIEW TEXT.**

There are several types of moonquakes that take place, and they all have some differences from earthquakes.

-

-

-

ANSWER CHOICES

1. Three of the four types of moonquakes that were recorded happening were minor ones according to the Richter Scale.

2. There may be some kind of relationship between one type of moonquake and the Earth's tides on account of its periodic occurrence.

3. *Apollo* astronauts placed a large number of seismometers on the moon's surface to check whether or not moonquakes occur there.

4. Geologists need to have more access to data about moonquakes for them to learn more about these events.

5. Seismic events happening on the moon tend to be less intense than those which take place on the Earth.

6. Some of the moonquakes that were observed by the seismometers recorded them as being above 9.0 on the Richter Scale.

German Industrialization in the Nineteenth Century

Germany in the early nineteenth century was mostly an agrarian land lagging behind Britain, France, and other nations which had already begun industrializing. The primary reason for Germany's slowness in industrializing was resistance to change by the landowning families holding most of the power in the various German states prior to unification in 1871. This resistance, coupled with the conservative Protestant church, the monopolies of numerous craft guilds, and a complicated web of restrictions on trade and land reform, stifled any impetus to industrialize. This was truer of the northern German states than the southern ones, but overall, the norm was large farms and small-scale cottage industries with trade confined mainly to local areas.

The textile industry started in Germany in the 1780s, which was prior to the wars with France, but it was relatively small in scale compared to Britain and France. The same was true about the German iron industry and coal mining. It was not until many German states were conquered by the French under Napoleon Bonaparte that changes to the conservative nature of German industrial development got underway. The French promptly instituted reforms related to land ownership and diminished the powers of guilds, thereby opening the way for more interest in industrial enterprises. These helped the Germans industrialize after the final French defeat in 1815 with assistance from several other factors. Among them were the German emphasis on education, the German people's strong work ethic, and the region's vast natural resources, particularly coal, the primary fuel at the onset of the Industrial Revolution everywhere.

Despite these advantages, the pace of industrialization was initially sluggish. Then, in the 1830s and 1840s, several changes occurred. First, better agricultural yields resulted in food surpluses allowing more people to depart rural regions and to move to urban centers. This provided a large labor surplus for burgeoning industries.

More significantly, the web of various laws and taxes on trade between states was simplified by a trade union formed in 1834. This Zollverein, or German Customs Union, abolished the multitude of taxes imposed on goods moving across the numerous borders of the German states and replaced them with a single tax on goods no matter where they went. Prussia, a large German state, was the leader of this reform after having done the same with its internal trade after the French defeat. There was great resistance to tax reform because many rulers of small states depended heavily on taxes for income, but Prussia's power and growing influence brought most northern German states into the Zollverein.

Customs reform receives very much credit from historians for the modernization and eventual unification of Germany in 1871. Nevertheless, other factors played significant roles. Chief among them was the swift development of a large internal railway system. The first railway lines opened in 1836. By 1845, Germany had more than 2,000 kilometers of railways, and by the 1850s, the German states served

as a central hub of the growing European railway network. Much of this railway building was stimulated by foreign investment and bank loans, which financed the industrialization.

These railways opened new regions to development, especially the Ruhr River region of western Germany. The Ruhr had extensive deposits of coal, which fueled the developing iron and steel industries. Much of the early Ruhr development can be credited to the Krupp family of Essen, which started by making metal household goods in the eighteenth century and eventually became a global leader in iron, steel, and armament production. The railways transported surplus coal across Germany to power other industries. At the same time, Germany developed one of the world's preeminent textile dye industries, which was engineered by its leadership in industrial chemistry.

Despite these advances, with industrialization came problems, and social reforms for workers lagged behind the pace of economic development. Still, after German unification, Chancellor Otto von Bismarck introduced a series of welfare reforms to aid workers. Some were hospital insurance, accident insurance, a national pension plan, and a child labor act restricting the use of children in industry. These reforms protected workers and provided further stimulus for industrial growth. Ultimately, by the onset of the twentieth century, Germany was an industrial powerhouse behind only Britain and the United States.

*Glossary

Industrial Revolution: the period beginning in the 1700s when power-driven machines and the mass production of goods became prominent

armament: any kind of weapon or related equipment that is typically provided for the military

German Industrialization in the Nineteenth Century

Germany in the early nineteenth century was mostly an agrarian land lagging behind Britain, France, and other nations which had already begun industrializing. The primary reason for Germany's slowness in industrializing was resistance to change by the landowning families holding most of the power in the various German states prior to unification in 1871. This resistance, coupled with the conservative Protestant church, the monopolies of numerous craft guilds, and a complicated web of restrictions on trade and land reform, stifled any impetus to industrialize. This was truer of the northern German states than the southern ones, but overall, the norm was large farms and small-scale cottage industries with trade confined mainly to local areas.

➡ The textile industry started in Germany in the 1780s, which was prior to the wars with France, but it was relatively small in scale compared to Britain and France. The same was true about the German iron industry and coal mining. It was not until many German states were conquered by the French under Napoleon Bonaparte that changes to the conservative nature of German industrial development got underway. The French promptly instituted reforms related to land ownership and diminished the powers of guilds, thereby opening the way for more interest in industrial enterprises. These helped the Germans industrialize after the final French defeat in 1815 with assistance from several other factors. Among them were the German emphasis on education, the German people's strong work ethic, and the region's vast natural resources, particularly coal, the primary fuel at the onset of the Industrial Revolution everywhere.

*Glossary

Industrial Revolution: the period beginning in the 1700s when power-driven machines and the mass production of goods became prominent

---

11 The word "stifled" in the passage is closest in meaning to

(A) questioned

(B) abandoned

(C) banned

(D) suppressed

12 The word "diminished" in the passage is closest in meaning to

(A) lessened

(B) approved

(C) arranged

(D) emphasized

13 In paragraph 2, the author implies that guilds

(A) were forced to disband once Napoleon Bonaparte took over some German states

(B) were major factors in Germany's move to improve the status of its newest industries

(C) actively sought to prevent the German states from developing new industries

(D) stressed the importance of education and helped people develop a strong work ethic

Paragraph 2 is marked with an arrow (➡).

14 The author discusses the "Zollverein" in paragraph 4 in order to

- (A) give the names of some of the individuals who were responsible for its establishment
- (B) provide information on the tax rates for goods that were charged once it began operations
- (C) mention how profitable internal trade in Germany became once it was founded
- (D) explain how the process of the taxation of goods in Germany became more simplified

Paragraph 4 is marked with an arrow (➡).

15 Which of the sentences below best expresses the essential information in the highlighted sentence in the passage? Incorrect answer choices change the meaning in important ways or leave out essential information.

There was great resistance to tax reform because many rulers of small states depended heavily on taxes for income, but Prussia's power and growing influence brought most northern German states into the Zollverein.

- (A) Northern German states and Prussia joined the Zollverein, and that affected the rulers of small states, who wanted to increase their income from taxes.
- (B) Many leaders of small states opposed the Zollverein because they needed money from taxes, but Prussia was able to get many German states to enter it.
- (C) Because Prussia was so influential at getting German states into the Zollverein, many leaders of small states feared they would obtain fewer revenues from taxes.
- (D) Small German states resisted any kind of tax reforms because they believed the Zollverein, which Prussia supported, was sufficient for their needs.

Despite these advantages, the pace of industrialization was initially sluggish. Then, in the 1830s and 1840s, several changes occurred. First, better agricultural yields resulted in food surpluses allowing more people to depart rural regions and to move to urban centers. This provided a large labor surplus for burgeoning industries.

➡ More significantly, the web of various laws and taxes on trade between states was simplified by a trade union formed in 1834. This Zollverein, or German Customs Union, abolished the multitude of taxes imposed on goods moving across the numerous borders of the German states and replaced them with a single tax on goods no matter where they went. Prussia, a large German state, was the leader of this reform after having done the same with its internal trade after the French defeat. There was great resistance to tax reform because many rulers of small states depended heavily on taxes for income, but Prussia's power and growing influence brought most northern German states into the Zollverein.

REVIEW

HELP

BACK

NEXT

HIDE TIME 00:54:00

End

16 According to paragraph 5, which of the following is true about Germany's railway system?

    (A) Construction workers added more than 2,000 kilometers of railways each year in the 1850s.

    (B) Foreigners invested all of the money the Germans required to build up their railway system.

    (C) The railroads were considered crucial to the improvement of the German economy.

    (D) It developed at a rapid pace that let it become an important part of Europe's railroad network.

Paragraph 5 is marked with an arrow (➡).

17 According to paragraph 6, the Ruhr region developed because

    (A) most of Germany's factories were built there thanks to it being a transportation hub

    (B) a single family made considerable investments that allowed it to industrialize

    (C) it took advantage of the growing textile dye industry to become wealthy

    (D) the Krupp family convinced the German government to spend money on it

Paragraph 6 is marked with an arrow (⇨).

18 According to paragraph 7, which of the following is NOT true about Germany?

    (A) It instituted a number of reforms to help workers and children after it unified.

    (B) It became one of the world's top three economies by the end of the 1800s.

    (C) It industrialized so fast that it developed a number of social problems.

    (D) It looked to the United States and Britain for help with social welfare programs.

Paragraph 7 is marked with an arrow (➡).

➡ Customs reform receives very much credit from historians for the modernization and eventual unification of Germany in 1871. Nevertheless, other factors played significant roles. Chief among them was the swift development of a large internal railway system. The first railway lines opened in 1836. By 1845, Germany had more than 2,000 kilometers of railways, and by the 1850s, the German states served as a central hub of the growing European railway network. Much of this railway building was stimulated by foreign investment and bank loans, which financed the industrialization.

⇨ These railways opened new regions to development, especially the Ruhr River region of western Germany. The Ruhr had extensive deposits of coal, which fueled the developing iron and steel industries. Much of the early Ruhr development can be credited to the Krupp family of Essen, which started by making metal household goods in the eighteenth century and eventually became a global leader in iron, steel, and armament production. The railways transported surplus coal across Germany to power other industries. At the same time, Germany developed one of the world's preeminent textile dye industries, which was engineered by its leadership in industrial chemistry.

➡ Despite these advances, with industrialization came problems, and social reforms for workers lagged behind the pace of economic development. Still, after German unification, Chancellor Otto von Bismarck introduced a series of welfare reforms to aid workers. Some were hospital insurance, accident insurance, a national pension plan, and a child labor act restricting the use of children in industry. These reforms protected workers and provided further stimulus for industrial growth. Ultimately, by the onset of the twentieth century, Germany was an industrial powerhouse behind only Britain and the United States.

*Glossary

armament: any kind of weapon or related equipment that is typically provided for the military

19 Look at the four squares [■] that indicate where the following sentence could be added to the passage.

They were dwarfed by those that had been established by those two European Great Powers.

Where would the sentence best fit?

Click on a square [■] to add the sentence to the passage.

The textile industry started in Germany in the 1780s, which was prior to the wars with France, but it was relatively small in scale compared to Britain and France. **1** The same was true about the German iron industry and coal mining. **2** It was not until many German states were conquered by the French under Napoleon Bonaparte that changes to the conservative nature of German industrial development got underway. **3** The French promptly instituted reforms related to land ownership and restricted the powers of guilds, thereby opening the way for more interest in industrial enterprises. **4** These helped the Germans industrialize after the final French defeat in 1815 with assistance from several other factors. Among them were the German emphasis on education, the German people's strong work ethic, and the region's vast natural resources, particularly coal, the primary fuel at the onset of the Industrial Revolution everywhere.

*Glossary

Industrial Revolution: the period beginning in the 1700s when power-driven machines and the mass production of goods became prominent

20 **Directions:** An introductory sentence for a brief summary of the passage is provided below. Complete the summary by selecting the THREE answer choices that express the most important ideas of the passage. Some sentences do not belong because they express ideas that are not presented in the passage or are minor ideas in the passage. **This question is worth 2 points.**

Drag your answer choices to the spaces where they belong. To remove an answer choice, click on it. To review the passage, click on **VIEW TEXT**.

In the nineteenth century, Germany initially industrialized slowly but then increased its rate of development for various reasons.

-
-
-

ANSWER CHOICES

1 Once Germany became a wealthy country, its citizens encouraged their leaders to create some social welfare programs.

2 The German railway system expanded at a rapid rate, and it became crucial not only to German industrialization but also to Europe as a whole.

3 The Germans were forced to make changes by the French that would eventually help them develop industry.

4 The numerous German states were ultimately unified in 1871 thanks to the leadership of Otto von Bismarck.

5 Reforms, such as how taxes were levied internally, were instituted, and they helped increase trade in Germany.

6 At first, guilds, Protestant churches, and wealthy families tried to keep Germany agrarian as they were opposed to industrialization.

Roman International Trade

By 100 A.D., the Roman Empire controlled virtually the entire Mediterranean world in addition to extensive parts of Europe. Throughout the empire, a trade network delivered goods to and from the Italian peninsula, especially to Rome, the imperial capital. Trade was mostly localized, with goods being bought and sold between rural regions and nearby towns, but some took place across great distances and accordingly constituted one of the first real systems of international trade. Trade increased with the expansion of the empire, and growth was enhanced by agricultural surpluses, the advent of coinage, and the creation of a system of land and sea routes, most of which led to Rome. Further impetus for trade resulted from the necessity of feeding Rome's huge population and of supplying the empire's distant outposts.

The Romans had always engaged in trade in their own territory and in conquered lands, but it developed slowly. The wealthy families of Rome depended on land ownership and local sales of surplus farm produce for the majority of their wealth, so for many families, investing in international trade was a needless venture. There was an element of snobbery involved as wealthy landowning families considered trade beneath their status, too. There were also old laws restricting senators, who often belonged to rich families, from owning great numbers of large trading ships. To circumvent these social and legal restrictions, those wishing to engage in trade employed agents to do so. Some agents negotiated trade deals, others served as accountants, and others sold goods directly in open-air markets. As the Roman Republic and, later, the Roman Empire increased in size and power, these agents traveled far and wide to make new contracts and to develop new trade routes.

The principal Roman trade routes were to Gaul and Spain in the west, North Africa, especially Egypt, to the south, and Greece, Byzantium, and the Middle East to the east. Common goods imported to Rome were foodstuffs, salt, textiles, dyes, spices, precious metals, pottery, wood, marble, and glass. Most items were desired to maintain the lavish lifestyles wealthy Romans enjoyed. Included in this trade were enormous numbers of slaves, who frequently toiled on farms and in industries. From Gaul came large quantities of wine and glass whereas Spain had precious metals, including copious amounts of gold, silver, and tin. North Africa was the breadbasket of Rome as huge amounts of grain were shipped from there across the Mediterranean Sea to Rome's main port of Ostia. Egypt also produced fine wines while Libya was noted for its production of olive oil, and from the east came textiles, spices, and dyes. China and India supplied most of them as they slowly traveled by caravan along the Silk Road or went by ship across the Indian Ocean. From faraway lands in sub-Saharan Africa came exotic animals for the games and circuses that entertained the Roman masses.

Moving these goods was no simple matter, so the Romans employed three main methods: road,

river, and sea. Travel by road was the slowest and most expensive despite Rome having constructed a widespread network of roads wherever its armies went. River transportation was better, but routes were restricted according to the courses of the rivers. Sea transportation was by far the cheapest and most flexible. According to one estimate, the cost of road transportation was twenty-eight times that of sea transportation; however, sea transportation was fraught with danger, with ships at the mercy of the weather and, at times, pirates. Archaeologists have discovered many Roman shipwrecks and have determined the nature of Roman sea trade from the wreckage. Most trading ships could carry about seventy-five tons of cargo, but larger ones could transport between 300 and 600 tons. As for their cargoes, foodstuffs, especially grains, wines, and oils, carried in simple clay amphorae were foremost.

While the Roman Republic had embraced a free-market system, the Roman Empire gradually asserted state control over trade. It developed a state-controlled merchant fleet as opposed to depending on private shipowners for its transportation needs to ensure the constant supply of necessary goods, particularly food. Greater state control allowed more taxation on trade, bringing much-needed wealth to Rome's coffers while simultaneously improving the quality of goods and reducing fraud.

*Glossary

Gaul: an ancient area in Europe that was found in the land occupied by modern-day France, Belgium, and the Netherlands
amphora: a large jar used for storing liquids such as wine and oil

21 In paragraph 1, the author's description of Roman trade mentions all of the following EXCEPT:

Ⓐ Some of the reasons that trade during the time of the Roman Empire became greater in size

Ⓑ The provinces in the Roman Empire that provided most of the items that were traded

Ⓒ A reason why the trading of agricultural products was so important to Rome

Ⓓ The final destination for many of the trade routes that went throughout the Roman Empire

Paragraph 1 is marked with an arrow (➡).

Roman International Trade

➡ By 100 A.D., the Roman Empire controlled virtually the entire Mediterranean world in addition to extensive parts of Europe. Throughout the empire, a trade network delivered goods to and from the Italian peninsula, especially to Rome, the imperial capital. Trade was mostly localized, with goods being bought and sold between rural regions and nearby towns, but some took place across great distances and accordingly constituted one of the first real systems of international trade. Trade increased with the expansion of the empire, and growth was enhanced by agricultural surpluses, the advent of coinage, and the creation of a system of land and sea routes, most of which led to Rome. Further impetus for trade resulted from the necessity of feeding Rome's huge population and of supplying the empire's distant outposts.

22 The word "circumvent" in the passage is closest in meaning to

(A) show interest in

(B) repeal

(C) get around

(D) look after

23 The author discusses "agents" in paragraph 2 in order to

(A) explain the various types of work that they did while in the employ of wealthy families

(B) point out that they often became even richer than the families that hired them did

(C) state some of the difficulties they encountered in trying to develop new trade routes

(D) mention the low social status that they had to deal with while they were engaging in trade

Paragraph 2 is marked with an arrow (➡).

24 According to paragraph 2, what did many rich Roman families think about trade?

(A) They believed it was something that only the Roman government should be involved in.

(B) They considered it more efficient at creating wealth than merely farming the land.

(C) They felt that they should learn more about trade in order to dominate it.

(D) They thought it was something they should not do as it lowered their social status.

Paragraph 2 is marked with an arrow (➡).

➡ The Romans had always engaged in trade in their own territory and in conquered lands, but it developed slowly. The wealthy families of Rome depended on land ownership and local sales of surplus farm produce for the majority of their wealth, so for many families, investing in international trade was a needless venture. There was an element of snobbery involved as wealthy landowning families considered trade beneath their status, too. There were also old laws restricting senators, who often belonged to rich families, from owning great numbers of large trading ships. To circumvent these social and legal restrictions, those wishing to engage in trade employed agents to do so. Some agents negotiated trade deals, others served as accountants, and others sold goods directly in open-air markets. As the Roman Republic and, later, the Roman Empire increased in size and power, these agents traveled far and wide to make new contracts and to develop new trade routes.

PASSAGE 3

REVIEW

HELP

BACK

NEXT

HIDE TIME 00:54:00

More Available

25 The phrase "toiled on" in the passage is
closest in meaning to

Ⓐ resided on

Ⓑ labored on

Ⓒ visited

Ⓓ came from

26 According to paragraph 3, which of the
following is true about Roman trade?

Ⓐ The slaves that were traded mostly came
from western and southern regions.

Ⓑ Most of the grain that was used to feed
people in Rome came from southern
areas.

Ⓒ It was wholly contained within the Roman
Empire and the provinces that it ruled.

Ⓓ The precious metals which were imported
from Spain created the most wealth.

Paragraph 3 is marked with an arrow (➡).

➡ The principal Roman trade routes were to
Gaul and Spain in the west, North Africa, especially
Egypt, to the south, and Greece, Byzantium,
and the Middle East to the east. Common goods
imported to Rome were foodstuffs, salt, textiles,
dyes, spices, precious metals, pottery, wood,
marble, and glass. Most items were desired to
maintain the lavish lifestyles wealthy Romans
enjoyed. Included in this trade were enormous
numbers of slaves, who frequently toiled on farms
and in industries. From Gaul came large quantities
of wine and glass whereas Spain had precious
metals, including copious amounts of gold, silver,
and tin. North Africa was the breadbasket of Rome
as huge amounts of grain were shipped from there
across the Mediterranean Sea to Rome's main port
of Ostia. Egypt also produced fine wines while Libya
was noted for its production of olive oil, and from
the east came textiles, spices, and dyes. China
and India supplied most of them as they slowly
traveled by caravan along the Silk Road or went by
ship across the Indian Ocean. From faraway lands
in sub-Saharan Africa came exotic animals for the
games and circuses that entertained the Roman
masses.

*Glossary

Gaul: an ancient area in Europe that was found in the land
occupied by modern-day France, Belgium, and the Netherlands

27 Which of the sentences below best expresses the essential information in the highlighted sentence in the passage? Incorrect answer choices change the meaning in important ways or leave out essential information.

According to one estimate, the cost of road transportation was twenty-eight times that of sea transportation; however, sea transportation was fraught with danger, with ships at the mercy of the weather and, at times, pirates.

Ⓐ The Romans preferred to transport goods to different places by using water routes, but pirates and bad weather made using ships expensive and dangerous.

Ⓑ It was known that shipping by land was costlier than shipping by sea, but most Romans were not willing to risk the dangers of traveling on ships.

Ⓒ It is estimated that road transportation was much more expensive than sea transportation, but there were numerous difficulties involved in sea trade.

Ⓓ The Romans could move goods by ship both faster and cheaper than on land, but pirates often captured or sank ships carrying trade goods.

28 According to paragraph 5, the Roman Empire abandoned the free-market system of the Roman Republic because

Ⓐ doing so enabled the city of Rome to raise more of the funds that it required

Ⓑ the Roman emperors disliked private shipowners having so much control

Ⓒ a free-market system was considered inefficient by many Romans

Ⓓ state control was necessary because of the large numbers of wars Rome fought

Paragraph 5 is marked with an arrow (➡).

Moving these goods was no simple matter, so the Romans employed three main methods: road, river, and sea. Travel by road was the slowest and most expensive despite Rome having constructed a widespread network of roads wherever its armies went. River transportation was better, but routes were restricted according to the courses of the rivers. Sea transportation was by far the cheapest and most flexible. According to one estimate, the cost of road transportation was twenty-eight times that of sea transportation; however, sea transportation was fraught with danger, with ships at the mercy of the weather and, at times, pirates. Archaeologists have discovered many Roman shipwrecks and have determined the nature of Roman sea trade from the wreckage. Most trading ships could carry about seventy-five tons of cargo, but larger ones could transport between 300 and 600 tons. As for their cargoes, foodstuffs, especially grains, wines, and oils, carried in simple clay amphorae were foremost.

➡ While the Roman Republic had embraced a free-market system, the Roman Empire gradually asserted state control over trade. It developed a state-controlled merchant fleet as opposed to depending on private shipowners for its transportation needs to ensure the constant supply of necessary goods, particularly food. Greater state control allowed more taxation on trade, bringing much-needed wealth to Rome's coffers while simultaneously improving the quality of goods and reducing fraud.

*Glossary

amphora: a large jar used for storing liquids such as wine and oil

29 Look at the four squares [■] that indicate where the following sentence could be added to the passage.

Those items not purchased by the rich were promptly exported from Rome to various places that fell under its control.

Where would the sentence best fit?

Click on a square [■] to add the sentence to the passage.

The principal Roman trade routes were to Gaul and Spain in the west, North Africa, especially Egypt, to the south, and Greece, Byzantium, and the Middle East to the east. Common goods imported to Rome were foodstuffs, salt, textiles, dyes, spices, precious metals, pottery, wood, marble, and glass. **1** Most items were desired to maintain the lavish lifestyles wealthy Romans enjoyed. **2** Included in this trade were enormous numbers of slaves, who frequently toiled on farms and in industries. **3** From Gaul came large quantities of wine and glass whereas Spain had precious metals, including copious amounts of gold, silver, and tin. **4** North Africa was the breadbasket of Rome as huge amounts of grain were shipped from there across the Mediterranean Sea to Rome's main port of Ostia. Egypt also produced fine wines while Libya was noted for its production of olive oil, and from the east came textiles, spices, and dyes. China and India supplied most of them as they slowly traveled by caravan along the Silk Road or went by ship across the Indian Ocean. From faraway lands in sub-Saharan Africa came exotic animals for the games and circuses that entertained the Roman masses.

*Glossary

Gaul: an ancient area in Europe that was found in the land occupied by modern-day France, Belgium, and the Netherlands

30 **Directions:** An introductory sentence for a brief summary of the passage is provided below. Complete the summary by selecting the THREE answer choices that express the most important ideas of the passage. Some sentences do not belong because they express ideas that are not presented in the passage or are minor ideas in the passage. **This question is worth 2 points.**

Drag your answer choices to the spaces where they belong. To remove an answer choice, click on it. To review the passage, click on **VIEW TEXT**.

International trade was vital to the Roman Republic and the Roman Empire for a number of reasons.

-
-
-

ANSWER CHOICES

1. There were many dangers, especially pirates and the possibility of sinking, when transporting goods by sea.

2. The Romans used a variety of methods to transport goods, but sea trade was prominent, especially after the government took it over.

3. Because Rome had such a big population, the people living there comprised a large market for international trade.

4. Most Romans preferred the free-market economy of the Roman Republic to the economy dominated by the empire in later times.

5. Members of wealthy families employed agents to engage in trade, and these agents traveled throughout the empire to conduct business.

6. Important items such as foodstuffs and precious metals were transported to Rome and other places throughout the empire.

AUTHORS

Michael A. Putlack
- MA in History, Tufts University, Medford, MA, USA
- Expert test developer of TOEFL, TOEIC, and TEPS
- Main author of the Darakwon *How to Master Skills for the TOEFL® iBT* series and *TOEFL® MAP* series

Stephen Poirier
- Candidate for PhD in History, University of Western Ontario, Canada
- Certificate of Professional Technical Writing, Carleton University, Canada
- Co-author of the Darakwon *How to Master Skills for the TOEFL® iBT* series and *TOEFL® MAP* series

Allen C. Jacobs
- BS in Physics, Presbyterian College, Clinton, SC, USA
- BCE in Civil Engineering, Auburn University, Auburn, AL, USA
- MS in Civil Engineering, University of Alabama, Tuscaloosa, AL, USA

Decoding the TOEFL® iBT
Actual Test READING 1 NEW TOEFL® EDITION

Publisher Chung Kyudo
Editor Kim Minju
Authors Michael A. Putlack, Stephen Poirier, Allen C. Jacobs
Proofreader Michael A. Putlack
Designers Koo Soojung, Park Sunyoung

First published in December 2019
By Darakwon, Inc.
Darakwon Bldg., 211, Munbal-ro, Paju-si, Gyeonggi-do 10881
Republic of Korea
Tel: 82-2-736-2031 (Ext. 250)
Fax: 82-2-732-2037

ISBN 978-89-277-0863-6 14740
978-89-277-0862-9 14740 (set)

www.darakwon.co.kr

Photo Credits
ben bryant (p. 192) / Shutterstock.com

Components Test Book / Answer Book
10 9 8 7 6 5 4   23 24 25 26 27